# HANDBOOK ON CONTINUING HIGHER EDUCATION

# HANDBOOK ON CONTINUING HIGHER EDUCATION

edited by

## QUENTIN H. GESSNER

University of Nebraska-Lincoln

American Council on Education • Macmillan Publishing Company
NEW YORK

Collier Macmillan Publishers
LONDON

Macmillan Publishing Company
A Division of Macmillan, Inc.
866 Third Avenue, New York, N. Y. 10022

Collier Macmillan Canada, Inc.

Library of Congress Catalog Card Number: 86-16308

Printed in the United States of America

printing number
1   2   3   4   5   6   7   8   9   10


**Library of Congress Cataloging in Publication Data**

Handbook on continuing higher education.

(American Council on Education/Macmillan series
in higher education)
1. Continuing education—United States. 2. University
extension—United States. 3. Universities and colleges
—United States—Administration. 4. Universities and
colleges—United States—Curricula. I. Gessner,
Quentin H. II. Series.
LC5251.H33   1987        374'.973        86-16308
ISBN 0-02-911620-1

# CONTENTS

# FOREWORD

Among its other contributions, this book establishes a new meaning for the term "continuing education unit." In the present context, it does not signify, as it usually does, a form of measurement used in academic book-keeping and often abbreviated as a CEU. Instead, it signifies a college- or university-based organizational structure charged with specific responsibility for extending educational resources to reach clienteles other than traditional resident-on-campus students. Usually these clienteles are made up of adults engaged in the full stream of mature life; their learning is built upon the knowledge and competence they have already acquired by many means; and their education must be fitted within the activities required by lives that are often over-busy. The central theses that this book demonstrates are, first, that the programs presented in continuing education units must be designed and conducted in ways different from those customary on other parts of the campus and, second, that both experience and research provide a respectably large body of tested principles on which the administrators of such units may rely.

In an earlier era, a college or university was likely to have only one or two extension divisions that did the bulk of its continuing education work, with perhaps a few other people, often part-time, who discharged specific similar functions and who were scattered elsewhere in the total organizational chart. This concentration is no longer true. In the mid-1970s, one university was found to have no fewer than thirty-eight separate continuing education units. This institution is located in a small city near one corner of a populous state which has a large number of other institutions of higher learning, several of massive size, and all of them with their own constellations of continuing education units. When this count was first made, the chief issues it raised were whether such extreme diversification would, in time, help destroy the organic unity of the university and whether the people of the state would be well served by so many separate and often inadequately staffed forms of service competing for attention and resources. As later pages of this book will show, centralization and coordination are still major issues of continuing higher education, but the chief point of view expressed here is that many units will continue to exist in some present or altered form and that they need to be administered as educatively and efficiently as possible.

While nobody would deny this contention, the people who staff each unit are likely to consider their own tasks to be wholly unique. University-based continuing education is far from a new idea, but the great proliferation of units has occurred so rapidly and recently that those who control the operations of each one have little sense of being part of a tradition or of being one of a cluster of similar agencies. A book published several years ago, which dealt with the prospects for higher education, was entitled *Three Thousand Futures,* thus suggesting that each college and university in the United States has its distinctive destiny. If precedent were to be followed, this present book might well have been titled *Thirty Thousand Futures* to signify that the staff of each continuing education unit must follow its own unique pathway to the future.

While that conclusion is ultimately true, it ignores the fact that a great deal is known about why and how adults learn and the general principles that govern the designing and carrying out of continuing education programs. The field of adult education now has a respectable knowledge base. Many universities have graduate programs and degree sequences that have produced several thousand doctorates and a much larger number of master's degrees. Other university disciplines have contributed to an understanding of administration, finance, motivation, communications technologies, and other relevant topics. Reinforcing and uniting all this research is the wisdom distilled from experience. The authors of the chapters in this handbook have studied continuing education extensively, have considerable practical experience in the field, or both. Each of them is qualified to deal magisterially with the topics that they have been asked to write about. Some discuss very large and complex units (often university-wide in character) while others consider the needs of smaller and more narrowly defined ones. Some concentrate on the university itself, and others concentrate upon general aspects of program design. But in the total book, their work comes together as it fulfils their common purpose of providing a comprehensive handbook on continuing higher education.

Underlying the expertise, which will be helpful to general readers and to seekers after guidance on specific points, is a belief shared by all the authors that continuing education needs to achieve many new goals in creative ways. The teaching of adults was once far out on the periphery of college and university purposes. Now it pervades the structures and the programs of many institutions. Great satisfaction must be felt by those who (not very long ago) felt that they were crying in the wilderness when they said that learning should continue throughout life and who had to work hard to construct foundations beneath their castles in the air. Now our continuing education units must face the consequences of greater growth, which require broader frameworks of thought, enhanced services, and enlarged resources. Decisions at this point are dangerous; those who guide the destiny of every unit must move into new and unknown worlds of work where major new clienteles must often be served without the danger of losing too many of the old ones. In the episodic history of adult education, many institutions have passed through such periods of enlargement. Some have thrived; others died.

We must view this handbook, therefore, not as a final summative volume but as a report on the present beliefs of a group of leaders, all of whom expect that they and their colleagues must refine their expertise by both research and informed practice and that the future will be far better than the present because they have done so.

*Cyril O. Houle*
*Professor Emeritus, the University Chicago*
*Senior Program Consultant, W.K. Kellogg Foundation*

# PREFACE

This handbook is predicated on the concept that learning as a lifelong process is important to an increasing number of educators and that colleges and universities, particularly those in the public sector, have a basic responsibility for disseminating knowledge to the broader society from which they receive support.

The primary purpose of the handbook is to provide a practical, comprehensive overview of continuing education within postsecondary institutions. This publication has been prepared as a sourcebook for professional continuing educators who develop, administer, deliver, and evaluate continuing education programs offered by colleges and universities as part of their outreach effort. Particular attention has been given to providing concepts, ideas, and information for the relatively new or uninitiated person to the field of continuing higher education.

The handbook also will serve persons who are directly or indirectly involved in the conceptual and policy decisions regarding the future of continuing higher education. These individuals include college and university presidents, vice-presidents, deans, business officers, leading faculty members, governing board members, and legislators. Noncollegiate providers of continuing education who work on a cooperative basis with colleges and universities or have an interest in doing so should also benefit from the book.

Each contributor to the handbook has a rich and diverse background in continuing higher education. Collectively, the contributors represent substantial experience in managing continuing education programs as well as in teaching in the field of adult and continuing education and other disciplines at institutions of higher education in the United States and Canada. They represent institutions that are geographically located in different social, political, economic, state, and regional evnironments. In each chapter, they provide concepts and practical perspectives that should prove useful to the professional continuing educator and for those significant others who have a tangential relationship to the field and can assist in the expansion, enhancement, or emphasis on continuing higher education at postsecondary institutions.

In exploring the process of continuing higher education in the handbook, the reader will be aware that different language is used to describe some of the same concepts; terms are frequently used in juxtaposition to each other. One challenging, if not troublesome, issue in the development of a handbook for continuing higher education is the question of how to deal with the variety of terms used by continuing educators. In addition to *continuing higher education,* other terms used in the handbook are *continuing education, university extension, continuing education unit, evening college, cooperative extension, public service, community service, continuing professional education, adult learners, lifelong learners, adult education,* and *adult and continuing education.*

Since no single definition for any of the terms will suffice to satisfy all readers, we have chosen to use the terms within the specific context intended by the individual authors. This seems to be a rational approach when one considers the variety of circumstances under which the terms are used, that is, philosophically, conceptually, historically, organizationally, legally, and legislatively.

Some clarification, however, is useful. Therefore, the following descriptions are provided to enable the reader to understand better the general manner in which the terms are used throughout the book.

- *Continuing higher education* is used to describe the extension of knowledge through faculty and staff resources by colleges and universities.

- *Continuing education* is used to describe a process of continuous learning and to connote organized instruction for adult learners.

- *University extension,* sometimes called general extension, refers to an organizational unit at a college or university charged with responsibility for extending faculty and staff resources.

- *Continuing education unit* is used to describe a designated office, department, division, school, or college charged with specific responsibility for extending its faculty and staff resources. (The reader should not confuse the term with Continuing Education Unit (CEU), a unit of measurement used for recordkeeping purposes.)

- *Evening college* refers to an academic unit with responsibility for providing courses of study in the late afternoon and evening primarily for adults.

- *Cooperative Extension* refers to the traditional extension of faculty and staff resources from the colleges of agriculture and home economics. Today, Cooperative Extension functions on a much broader basis and, at some institutions, has merged with the general extension and continuing education unit.

- *Public service* is used by some institutions to refer to one aim of a continuing education unit and also to describe the institutions' overall outreach effort.

- *Community service* is a term incorporated into federal legislation. It is also used to describe the outreach efforts of community colleges.

- *Continuing professional education* refers to continuing education programs and activities designed for persons in professional fields and occupations.

- *Adult learners* refers to the primary clientele served by continuing education units.

- *Lifelong learning* refers to a process during a person's lifetime in which he or she continues to develop knowledge, skills, and attitudes.

- *Adult education* is used primarily in a historical perspective and in reference to the education of adults through both organized instruction and self-directed learning.

- *Adult and continuing education* generally refers to a field of study and related research.

The handbook begins with an introduction to continuing higher education. The need for continuing higher education in a learning society, the role of continuing educators, and their professional preparation are discussed. In Chapter 2 Adelle Robertson traces the historical background of continuing higher education from the early 1880s to the present. She points out that continuing learning was stressed in the early days of our country by such leaders as Thomas Jefferson and Benjamin Franklin and that the fundamental concepts of lifelong learning gained their modern interpretation from the history of education itself.

The major forces that presently affect continuing higher education and the related issues confronting colleges and universities provide the focus of Chapter 3. Kenneth Young describes the changes taking place in society, in the nation's educational system, and in the colleges and universities. He identifies crucial questions that must be addressed by institutions if they seriously intend to deal with the forces and issues affecting higher education.

In Chapter 4 John Snider describes six components of continuing higher education that are important in the management of a successful continuing education operation. He discusses the programmatic, political, and public relations dimensions involved in sustaining internal and external relationships that are vital to a continuing education enterprise.

Broad aspects of the overall management of continuing education within a college or university are discussed in the next six chapters. Dennis Prisk, in Chapter 5, identifies the advantages and disadvantages of various organizational patterns used in the administration of continuing higher education. He also discusses elements that are necessary for the creation of an effective organization and strategies that can be used in the management of a continuing education program.

In Chapter 6 Harold Miller focuses on external sources of funds for continuing higher education, such as federal and state dollars, corporate and private financing, and sources internal to an institution but external to continuing education. He also discusses using a combination of funding sources to finance a continuing education operation and individual program budgeting.

In Chapter 7 John Buskey describes the function of program planning and reviews a variety of planning models that have particular relevance for practitioners in postsecondary institutions. He proposes a generic planning model for the practitioner's use based on its overall applicability to continuing higher education. A step-by-step planning process is suggested.

Needs assessment, a part of the program planning process, is treated separately in Chapter 8 because of its critical importance to the practitioner in determining what kinds of programs should be developed to meet identified needs. Thomas Sork sharpens the definition of needs and needs assessment, identifies some of the common assessment approaches used, and provides a generic process of needs assessment with potential for wide application to continuing higher education.

In Chapter 9 Mary Walshok discusses a variety of methodological forms that can be used to deliver continuing education programs and considers some advantages and disadvantages of each. She also presents a set of decision criteria to be addressed in determining which delivery system will be most effective and appropriate in a given situation.

Richard Fischer provides a succinct, pragmatic approach to marketing in Chapter 10. He discusses the unique characteristics of the product called continuing education, the components of a marketing concept, the process for developing a marketing plan, and the basic approaches used in marketing continuing education.

In Chapter 11 Carl Lindsey and Leroy Marlow provide the reader with an overview of the purposes, context, and development of research and evaluation in the broad area of adult and continuing education. They offer a perspective on research and evaluation as related to continuing higher education and describe some of the approaches and processes used. Needed areas of research, issues that require attention, and future possibilities for research and evaluation in continuing education are discused.

Attention is given in Chapter 12 to continuing professional education in colleges and universities. Philip Nowlen focuses on the special characteristics of continuing education for professionals. He considers the relationship among professional schools, professional associations, and continuing education/extension units. He discusses the issues that need to be addressed by decision makers at postsecondary institutions in determining the role of their institution in providing advanced professional training.

Chapter 13 concludes the handbook with a look to the future of continuing higher education. Describing some of the trends that appear to be shaping continuing higher education in the future, the author identifies changes that are or should be taking place if colleges and universities are to play a dominant role in providing programs and services for adult learners and if they are to relate to the broader society in new and different ways.

The contributors hope the handbook will contribute to the effectiveness and efficiency with which colleges and universities manage continuing higher education to the benefit of society.

My deepest appreciation is offered to a number of people who made this book possible. To each of the contributors, a special thanks for their time and effort in preparing manuscripts. Diana King provided invaluable assistance with copy editing, as did Christy Dienstbier and Suzie Sybouts with typing the manuscripts. Lance Kramer, John Moe, Ken Young, John Buskey, Jim Bowman, and Sue Gessner all assisted by reading manuscripts, and Jim Murray of the American Council of Education provided advice and counsel during the developmental and editorial phases.

Quentin H. Gessner

# CONTRIBUTORS

**John H. Buskey** is associate provost for Conferences and Continuing Education at Miami University. Dr. Buskey has also served as an administrator at the University of Nebraska-Lincoln, the University of Chicago and at the University of Maryland.

**Richard B. Fischer** is associate director of Continuing Education at the University of Delaware. Dr. Fischer serves on the Finance Committee of the National University Continuing Education Association.

**Quentin H. Gessner** is professor of adult and continuing education and former dean of Continuing Studies at the University of Nebraska-Lincoln. Dr. Gessner has also served as an administrator at the University of Michigan and is a past-president of the National University Continuing Education Association.

**Carl A. Lindsey** is head of Planning Studies in Continuing Education at Pennsylvania State University. Dr. Lindsey is former associate director of Student Affairs Research at Pennsylvania State University and served as an assistant professor of psychology at the University of Houston.

**H. Leroy Marlow** is assistant director of Continuing Education at Pennsylvania State University. Dr. Marlow also serves as director of the Pennsylvania Technical Assistance Program and as a professor of management development at Pennsylvania State University.

**Harold A. Miller** is dean of Continuing Education and Extension at the University of Minnesota. Dr. Miller has served as an instructor in finance management at the Summer Institute for the Management of Lifelong Learning at Harvard University.

**Philip M. Nowlen** is executive director of Continuing Education at the University of Chicago. Dr. Nowlen has served as chairman of the Division of Continuing Professional Education and of the Editorial Board for Continuum for the National University Continuing Education Association.

**Dennis P. Prisk** is dean of Continuing Education at the University of Alabama. Dr. Prisk has also served as an administrator at Indiana University and at the University of Southern California.

**Adelle F. Robertson** served as dean of Continuing Education at the University of Virginia. Dr. Robertson also served as an administrator at the University of Delaware and as president of the National University Continuing Education Association.

**John C. Snider** is executive assistant to the chancellor for the Colorado State University System. Dr. Snider is a past-president of the National University Continuing Education Association.

**Thomas J. Sork** is assistant professor of Adult Education at the University of British Columbia. Dr. Sork has also served as an administrator at Colorado State University and Florida State University, and as a faculty member at the University of Nebraska-Lincoln.

**Mary L. Walshok** is associate vice chancellor for Extended Studies and Public Service and an associate professor of sociology at the University of California-San Diego. Dr. Walshok has been a recipient of a Kellogg Foundation National Fellowship award.

**Kenneth E. Young** is director of the Institute for Learning in Retirement at the American University. Dr. Young has also served as executive director of the National University Continuing Education Association and as president of the Council of Post-Secondary Accredition.

# HANDBOOK ON CONTINUING HIGHER EDUCATION

# -1-
# AN OVERVIEW OF CONTINUING HIGHER EDUCATION

## Quentin H. Gessner

*The aim of education is to enable*
*individuals to continue their education.*

*—John Dewey[1]*

Characterized by a common core of practice and purpose, innovation, growth, and an emerging maturity, continuing higher education is an exciting field of practice. It is considered to be the fastest-growing segment of higher education. Continuing higher education is a diverse, complex, and challenging enterprise that includes the development, delivery, marketing, and evaluation of programs and services from colleges and universities to audiences defined by individual institutions. Today's emphasis on continuing education in many colleges and universities attests to its importance and vitality in higher education's structure and future.

Higher education faces enormous challenges now and in the years ahead. America's need for improved skills and competencies based on new knowledge and technologies has never been greater.

We in higher education are challenged to provide increased educational opportunities for our citizens within the context of rapid technological change, unemployment, shifting market conditions, economic relocation, and human stress. Our country's economic and social problems are having a serious impact on higher education, making it difficult for colleges and universities to fulfill their primary mission of creating and disseminating knowledge at the level required to meet citizens' needs. Several problems confronting higher education include:

1

- *Changing demographics.* The average age of the nation's population is rising, while the number of traditional college-age students, eighteen to twenty-one years old, is declining. The new majority in higher education is constituted by older students interested in part-time educational opportunities. The concept of lifelong learning is an accepted reality for an ever-increasing number of adults. To accommodate these changes, many institutions of higher education will need to alter attitudes, services, and programs.

- *Limited resources.* Reductions in federal support make state support for higher education more difficult. Pressures for state funds place institutions of higher education in more competition for tax dollars. Universities have to cope with problems with limited resources. This suggests that universities must create and market new programs and activities through new and different relationships with external groups.

- *Competition from the private sector.* Colleges and universities are no longer the only major sources in the creation and dissemination of knowledge, as they were in the 1800s and early 1900s. Only one in four adults obtain their education through a college or university. Many organizations-for-profit in the private sector are competing with traditional postsecondary institutions by offering degree programs, continuing professional education, and noncredit programs. Frequently, these competitive offerings are limited to "high profit" programs for which there is a great demand. To ensure that the total scope of continuing education needs for adults is adequately met, many universities should seek new partnerships and relationships with the private sector for collaborative programming.

- *Legitimacy.* To regain and retain the prestige, leadership, reputation, and public support higher education has traditionally enjoyed, those in higher education must keep abreast of and adapt to the changing world. This means that the higher education community will need to change some of its traditional curricula and methods of program delivery to accommodate to the new era and at the same time maintain high quality education.

As colleges and universities attempt to resolve these problems, continuing higher education, both as a product and a process, can be used to move institutions toward excellence in providing educational opportunities for all citizens—old and young, full-time and part-time—in new and different ways. Ours is a learning society. Learning is basic to human progress. Education provides a better way of life for the individual, and university programs provide lifelong learning opportunities for our citizens.

Accordingly, an increasing number of educators are accepting that learning is a lifelong process and that colleges and universities have an opportunity and a responsibility to disseminate knowledge to adults through continuing education programs delivered in non-traditional ways. It is important to note that American colleges and universities, particularly land-grant institutions, have historically held a commitment to continuing education/extension-type programs. The rhetoric, however, has often exceeded the reality.

Traditionally, colleges and university programs have been de-signed for the young. The prevailing pattern has directed high school graduates to pursue a college degree to become educated and pre-pared to enter the workforce. Instruction was generally expected to occur in classrooms at times and locations convenient to the institution. Programs aimed at adults were viewed as optional for the learner and as a marginal activity for the institution. It is increasingly clear that with the explosion of knowledge and the accelerating rate of change in the world today, society cannot afford to place its edu-cational investment only in its youth. The need for colleges and universities to provide a system of education for young people and the value of that education are not questioned.

The question and a major issue in higher education is the extent to which colleges and universities should disseminate knowledge to citizens of all ages and at times and locations convenient to the learner. Related to this issue is the need for increased cooperation between higher education and the private sector. This is demonstrated by the number of degree programs now offered by corporations and professional associations.

Learning as a lifetime process must be considered a vital national goal. In *Adult Learners: Key to the Nation's Future,* a recently published position paper of the Commission on Higher Education and the Adult Learner, it was stated:

> For reasons of national interest embedded in the economic, political, and social determinants of the quality of life, the fostering of learning by adults is an immediate and compelling national need, a need requiring a lucid and forthright state-ment of national policy and immediate attention by the na-tion's colleges and universities.[2]

Higher education, as a social institution with a mission to dispense knowledge, must keep pace with the need for continued learning by adults.

In *A Nation at Risk: The Imperative for Educational Reform,* a report by the National Commission on Excellence in Education,[3] it was noted that the search for solutions to educational problems must include a commitment to lifelong learning. According to the report, educational reform should be focused on the goal of creating a learning society due to a "world of ever-accelerating competition in the conditions of the workplace, of ever-greater danger, and the ever-larger opportunities for those prepared to meet them." To achieve a learning society, colleges and universities have a special responsibility to expand and enhance the lives of adult learners through research, advanced professional development, and instruction.

In today's educational climate, the reevaluation and interest in adult learners are seen at many colleges and universities as means of survival. At these schools, there is a concerted effort to accommodate all learners, full-time and part-time, young and old, on the same basis. Other institutions, not threatened by a precipitous decline in enrollments, offer specially designed programs for adults through a continuing education/extension unit while continuing to serve the traditional-age student. At still other institutions, the potential of adult learners is virtually ignored.

To serve adults adequately, institutional commitments are needed to (1) adopt principles of lifelong education that include the assimilation of values and the development of competencies through continued learning for students and program participants, (2) improve access for adult learners by removing artificial and cumbersome barriers, and (3) extend faculty and staff resources to a broader segment of the population than the traditional eighteen to twenty-five year-old group.

Possible benefits to institutions implementing strong continuing education programs to serve adults could be new student markets, new sources of revenue, new forms of collaboration with other educational providers, new networks that strengthen the institution's support base, new research opportunities, improved public relations, and better relationships with legislators through service to their constituents. Unfortunately, the service mission at many colleges and universities has not been perceived as an important function of the institution's role and mission and has not received adequate support. Often emerging like a weed in a flower garden, continuing education/extension-type activities at many institutions have grown primarily due to the development and delivery of programs to meet client needs rather than through an orderly planning process. Consequently, in many instances continuing education programs have been held in low esteem by faculty, have received low priority among campus administrators, and have incurred high overhead costs. Where continuing education programs have been successful, attempts by departments and colleges to take over such programs have been consistently deferred.

At other colleges and universities, a high priority is placed on outreach functions. Programs and services are provided both on- and off-campus, using a variety of delivery systems. These institutions generally establish an organizational structure, including fiscal relationships, which enables them to maximize their continuing education potential. They provide the resources necessary for a successful continuing education program along with a reward system that encourages broad faculty and staff participation.

It would appear that the highest probability for success exists when the following elements are in place:

1. The governing board, the chief administrative officer, and the faculty and staff share a clear understanding of the need for and a commitment to vigorous and continuing support for continuing education programs.

2. There is a clear definition of the continuing education function, including its philosophy and objectives.

3. There is a clear understanding of how the development, delivery, and evaluation of continuing education programs and services are integrated into the institution's academic system.

4. There is a clearly identifiable administrative unit designated to coordinate the continuing education mission.

5. There is adequate budgetary support for the administrative unit responsible for the continuing education mission.

6. There is a strong statement that clearly establishes priorities for continuing education programs for each academic unit conducting outreach programs.

The extent to which colleges and universities place a high priority on continuing education can depend on a number of factors: role and mission, geographical location, cost, tradition, program emphasis, and resources. Also, differences in how continuing education is defined, how it is organized, and its leadership can affect its relative position on campus and its effectiveness in offering programs and services, both on- and off-campus.

To be effective, continuing education/extension/public service programs must be defined and legitimized by the institution serving as the sponsor. The decision to have continuing education as part of the integrated whole should come from the core of the institution and should be identified as part of the institutional mission. It should not be a program activity developed and conducted on the basis of an administrative rationale which results in continuing education operating as a marginal activity. Continuing education should become more central to the primary role and mission of institutions of higher education.

The diversity and complexity of continuing higher education undoubtedly contribute in part to the variety of circumstances in which it operates. This also serves to create policy and operational conflicts that can lead to differences of opinion over its centrality or marginality. Continuing higher education is where the idealism of academe interfaces with the reality of the private sector. The entrepreneurial nature of continuing education is self-evident. It operates in a climate of pragmatism, often promoted by people with a strong sense of idealism toward helping adults reach their personal and professional goals. Advocates of continuing higher education may find themselves at odds with faculty and campus administrators when they suggest change in an academic environment that often vigorously resists change. For example, placing an emphasis on continuing education programs and services can suggest a shift from a traditional approach of class scheduling to one that provides for greater flexibility in the time and location in which a class is held.

Unlike other campus units, continuing education programs are often expected to be financially self-supporting. The continuing education enterprise may have to function somewhat like a private business venture, so there is a strong reliance on marketing strategies. Thus, programs may only be offered in subject areas that attract sufficient numbers of participants able and willing to pay the costs. These are often people who have already achieved a high level of education and can afford to pay tuition and registration fees. Some institutions concentrate on college and professional school graduates to reduce tension between continuing education and the rest of the academic community; thus continuing education is philosophically aligned with the institution's perceived role and mission.

Decisions regarding which constituencies to serve and how they are to be served can be major issues affecting continuing higher education on many campuses and can lead to differences of the fundamental purpose of a college or university in relation to its service role. Colleges and universities have basically two functions: the creation and dissemination of knowledge; continuing higher education provides a delivery system that can assist an institution to align its central responsibility for service to society.

## ROLE OF CONTINUING EDUCATORS

There is considerable confusion in higher education as to what continuing education is, who should be responsible for programming, and how it should be organized, administered, financed, and evaluated. Definitions that clearly identify what constitutes continuing education/ extension/public service are often unclear. At some institutions, the emerging emphasis on continuing education as a strategy for increasing enrollments led to the demise of the continuing education/extension units. Continuing education functions were dispersed throughout the institution, and individual colleges were given responsibility to develop and conduct their own programs and services. Limited success followed, primarily because persons assigned to function as continuing educators had not been prepared to serve in that role.

Continuing educators are persons skilled in the development, management, and delivery of programs and services, and they see a special role for continuing education and for themselves. Their primary concern is with adults—students twenty-five years of age and older who are generally employed on a full- or part-time basis and who frequently have family responsibilities. Continuing educators specialize in the learning needs and desires of persons frequently referred to as "nontraditional students."

These students described as "nontraditional" may be matriculating toward a degree on a part-time basis, attending a weekend college, taking classes in the evening, or enrolling in courses through radio, television, computer, or independent study by correspondence. They may be adults participating in short-term, noncredit learning experiences designed to improve their professional and occupational skills and competencies, or they may be adults seeking new knowledge to cope with change. As reported in *Americans in Transition,* many adults are attracted to education during times of major life transitions, and the learning they seek is related to the change taking place in their lives.[4] For example, adults will return to college as a result of a period of trauma in their lives, such as divorce, death of a spouse, mid-life crisis, loss of a job, or general job dissatisfaction.

Accordingly, continuing educators believe continuing education enables adults to reevaluate their thoughts, concepts, and ideals. They believe that knowledge will assist a person to mature and to deal successfully with the changing social, political, and economic environment. As a result, they are committed to the proposition that adults should share in higher education's benefits and cannot accept the traditional delivery system as the only method for transmitting knowledge. While some adults over twenty-five years of age may be able to attend a mid-morning class on campus, many cannot. Consequently, continuing educators constantly seek to provide learning opportunities at times and places that are convenient to adult learners.

The expertise the person who is adequately prepared in adult and continuing education brings to the learning process is the knowledge of how to develop and deliver programs that enable adults to learn effectively and efficiently. Continuing educators serve as brokers or catalysts in creating the teaching-learning process. They serve also as change agents sensitive to the needs of adults. They know how and where to obtain appropriate instructional resources and assume responsibility for bringing providers and users together to participate in a program or activity that results in a learning experience.

Continuing educators view collegiate institutions as the means for helping people achieve goals and to solve problems in commerce, community, industry, and economic development. They live in a learner-oriented world where thought and action are interconnected. Consequently, to continuing educators the desirable end of knowledge is its utility. Their challenge is to provide appropriate continuing education programs and services to adult learners within their institution's geographical service area.

To meet this challenge, continuing educators should demonstrate that they understand the process of adult learning and can apply adult learning theories in the program planning process. They are expected to perform management functions that include, but are not limited to, setting goals and objectives, establishing priorities, and using evaluation techniques. They can also be expected to be competent in public relations, marketing, fund raising, research, and needs assessment.

Increasingly, continuing educators need to assume an important leadership role in planned change, resource management, organizational behavior, curriculum design, and the development of political relationships. They should, therefore, be conscious of change, both within their institution and in the larger society, so that planning strategies and programs can be modified and changed as appropriate. They should serve as strong advocates for continuing education and be centrally involved in the institution's political process and decision-making bodies. In doing so, they can serve as change agents within higher education.

In performing their role, continuing educators are often caught in a dilemma. They serve as part of an academic enterprise with all its traditions and processes, but at the same time they are expected to relate to the private sector which generally functions at a faster pace and with different goals and expectations. Consequently, continuing educators not only need to demonstrate diplomacy and tact, but they need to be action-oriented and, above all, have the capacity to dangle—to maintain a high tolerance for ambiguity.

Equally as important, professionals in continuing education should have a clear sense of mission, understand the importance of that mission, and have a personal philosophy about continuing education that identifies their professional objectives. This requires looking beyond the immediate daily tasks to sustain a sense of the whole and to define their role in helping people learn.

## HOW CONTINUING EDUCATORS ARE PREPARED

As a field of practice, continuing education draws heavily from the theoretical frameworks of many academic disciplines. Similarly, continuing educators begin their careers after previous experience in another academic area. This pattern can be viewed as both a strength and a weakness. Newcomers can introduce new ideas and help to strengthen a continuing education organization. Concurrently, it can be viewed as a weakness if newcomers lack formal academic training in such areas as the history and philosophy of adult and continuing education, adult learning theories, adult psychology, group dynamics, and program development.

Many new continuing educators have a background in education, but increasingly more come from business and other professional fields. They may have had previous experience as a professor, registrar, or administrator at an educational institution; as a marketing account executive, personnel director, or company president; as a practicing doctor, lawyer, or engineer; or from any of a number of licensed occupations.

The consistent, common element of persons entering the field from other careers is that they lack the professional preparation that aids a career in continuing education. The Kellogg Foundation, aware of this situation, has provided funds to the National University Continuing Education Association for the Continuing Higher Education Leadership Project (CHEL). Through this project, colleges and universities develop and provide programs designed to assist in the growth and development of newcomers as well as experienced practitioners in continuing higher education.[5]

On a more formal basis, graduate programs in higher education and adult education are offered to prepare professional continuing educators. Philosophically, it is desirable that all new entrants into a continuing education career at a college or university have knowledge from both fields.

Dr. Cyril O. Houle's statements in *Continuing Learning in the Professions* apply to all education, but are especially pertinent for the education of continuing educators. He writes:

> The conception of a profession as a fixed entity may cause its members to believe that their only need for learning is to maintain their individual careers and the collective status

they already possess. But the needs of society require that every professionalizing occupation becomes better than it is.[6]

As in any profession, continuing educators should continue to learn. To improve the performance of their responsibilities as professionals, continuing educators need to participate in various instructional programs, such as noncredit conferences, seminars, workshops, graduate courses, and individual and group efforts to discover new truths and answers to old problems. They should take advantage of opportunities to improve proficiencies through reading, visits to other institutions, consulting, research, practice of professional skills under the helpful guidance of expert colleagues, and through active participation in professional associations.

## SUMMARY

Education is essentially a continuing process of self-renewal. Therefore, opportunities for continuing education must be made available. The university, as an important source of knowledge and information in the educational process for adults, represents a powerful force, not only for providing continuing education opportunities, but for advancing the concept of an educated society.

One of the imperatives of our time is for universities to be committed to continuing higher education and to the process of lifelong learning. It is in the process of learning that colleges and universities can make a significant difference in the quality of life for people. It is also through the dedication and perseverance of those persons who serve in the role of professional continuing educators that continuing higher education will make a contribution to, and a significant difference in, the choices citizens make in a democratic society.

Democracy is dependent upon the wisdom of its people. Democracy depends on people making sound judgments and, therefore, should provide its citizens with opportunities to learn to make choices in a wise and prudent manner. For this, continued learning is essential. It is a crucial imperative not only for today, but for tomorrow.

Educated adults are needed now more than ever to ensure our collective growth and development as a society. Through continuing higher education, colleges and universities can assist adults in becoming all they can be and can thus make the world a better place in which to live. To this end, continuing educators must accept the challenge and responsibility to improve and expand continuing higher education as an integral and important part of American higher education. This handbook is dedicated to that mission.

## REFERENCES

1. Dewey, John, *Democracy and Education* (New York: Macmillan, 1961), p. 100.
2. Commission on Higher Education and the Adult Learner, *Adult Learners: Key to the Nation's Future* (Columbia, Md.: The Commission, 1984), p. 1.
3. National Commission on Excellence in Education, *A Nation at Risk: The Imperative for Educational Reform* (Washington, D.C.: The Commission, 1983), p. 17.
4. Aslanian, Carol B., and Bricknell, Henry M., *Americans in Transition* (New York: College Entrance Examination Board, 1980).
5. National University Continuing Education Association, "Successful Consultation Initiates NUCEA/Kellogg Leadership Project," *Continuing Higher Education Leadership* (Washington, D.C.: The Association, January 1985), p. 1.
6. Houle, Cyril O., *Continuing Learning in the Professions* (San Francisco: Jossey-Bass, 1980), p. 30.

# -2-
# A HISTORICAL PERSPECTIVE OF CONTINUING HIGHER EDUCATION

## Adelle F. Robertson

"The only use of a knowledge of the past is to equip us for the present," stated Alfred North Whitehead. That is one of the reasons for continuing educators to examine their professional roots. It is equally important to know that the concept of continuing education is entwined with the earliest history of the United States and was advocated by eighteenth-century leaders such as Thomas Jefferson and Benjamin Franklin. The legitimacy of continuing higher education can be measured partially by the stature of its advocates and partially by the length of time those ideas have endured.

If it is understood that the evolution of continuing higher education was the result of participation of the professoriate and administrators of colleges and universities as well as a response to the demands of various constituencies, practitioners gain a different perspective. In other words, as the development of continuing higher education is examined against the growth of colleges and universities, its relationship with other education processes emerges.

It is also important, as a practitioner, to consider continuing higher education as a continuum—to examine ideas that failed or succeeded and to evaluate the field by this approach.

For individuals who have chosen continuing higher education as their career, perhaps the most important reason for studying its history is to understand better what contribution they can make to the field.

In summary, practitioners of continuing higher education need to know the history of continuing higher education so they can build on it, articulate it to others, use it to refute criticism, and assess their own contributions.

The history of continuing higher education presented in this chapter will provide information organized topically rather than chronologically. The information is divided into the following topics: "Colonial Beginnings," "Professors and Presidents Take the Lead," "Evolution from College to University," "Professional Societies and Professionalization," "Critical Movements," and "Key Legislation." This telescoped history is not an attempt to show that continuing education is but a small part of the history of higher education but rather that the fundamental concepts making up lifelong learning gained their modern interpretation from the history of education itself.

## COLONIAL INITIATIVES

During the seventeenth and eighteenth centuries, the philosophical foundation was laid for continuing higher education. The early colonists were intent on founding a community committed to the development of piety, civility, and learning. Lawrence Cremin described the colonization:

> North America was colonized during the first phase of Europe's age of print, the initial two-hundred-year period after Gutenberg. . . . As a result, those who settled America were much less dependent on an oral tradition for the transmission of culture than they might have been even a hundred years earlier. And so along with everything else they forced into the crowded vessels that carried them to the New World— plants, animals, seed, ploughs and clothing—the colonists brought books.[1]

Although this emphasis on literacy was meant originally to spread reading and understanding of the Bible, it was soon observed that literacy could not be contained—its mastery also spread the knowledge of political, economic, social, and other secular concerns. "From the standpoint of . . . [the education of adults], the most significant development in colonial times was the establishment of the precedent of tax-supported common schools to insure the basic literacy of all."[2]

It is interesting to note that education of the adult or older student is not a phenomenon of the twentieth century. During the period of the American Revolution, nearly 40 percent of the students who entered college were at or above the age of twenty-one.[3]

> The high point for the proportion of older students came in the 1810's and 1820's when approximately 37 percent en-

tered at or above age twenty-one. Emphasis upon the mature students does indicate that the early colleges were fulfilling social functions much like the community and junior colleges of today. In contrast to claims in much of the previous historiography, they were not educating a youthful and irresponsible elite.[4]

## UTILITARIAN CURRICULA

Another distinctly American trend in eighteenth-century higher education was Jefferson's attempt to establish a more utilitarian emphasis in post-Revolution curricula. During his tenure on the Board of Visitors of the College of William and Mary and also as Governor of Virginia, he proposed the establishment of a professorship of law and police with the intent of preparing students for a life of public service.[5]

The close association between knowledge and its use that evolved with the development of the colonies was an important factor in the history and development of the concept of continuing higher education. This concept provided the foundation for technology transfer and state-of-the-art courses that would be offered through university continuing education units during the next century.

Events in the eighteenth century established a climate conducive to the later development of continuing higher education at the university level. "Easily identified instruments for the education of adults were the rising flood of letters of correspondence, pamphlets, editorials, books, speeches, poems, and plays which explored the issues and ideas of democracy."[6] The first newspaper, *Boston News Letter,* began in Massachusetts, and the first theater in Williamsburg. A playhouse was also added in New York in 1733. As these pamphlets, newspapers, speeches, and books devoted to topical issues were published and distributed, literacy became more important to citizens who had previously experienced no difficulty with their illiteracy.[7] The demand for schooling increased and the level of literacy improved in the colonies.

> At a time when the estimates of adult male literacy in England ran from 48 percent in the rural western midlands to 74 percent in the towns, on the basis of signatures on marriage registers, adult male literacy in the American colonies seems to have run from 70 percent to virtually 100 percent, on the basis of signatures on deeds and wills, militia rolls, and voting rosters.[8]

Benjamin Franklin is recognized as the Colonial Father of continuing education because of his own remarkable self-directed learning and his establishment of a discussion club called the Junto in 1727.

The importance of this effort is not in its originality but that it spawned so many other educational organizations and has survived in name until the present. Its pervasive influence was described by James Truslow Adams:

> We may count the American Philosophical Society, the Franklin Institute, the University of Pennsylvania, the first American Public Library, and the first Philadelphia Mutual Fire Insurance Company as offshoots of the talks at this club.[9]

Another offshoot of the Junto was the establishment of a subscription library for the use of Junto members and other Philadelphians.

## POLITICS AND EDUCATION

As American colonists moved into the nineteenth century, the most evident characteristics of education were its values as an essential factor in democratic governance and its potential to improve and change the day-to-day lives of all its citizens. The early belief that education was able to improve the quality of life supports the later development of lifelong learning. Quantitatively, the beginnings of higher education in the colonies were not impressive. The important achievement was that the European tradition of higher learning had been transplanted in the New World and survived through the eighteenth century.[10]

## PROFESSORS AND PRESIDENTS TAKE THE LEAD

One measure of the worth of a concept or the stature of a profession is the reputation of the people who espouse it and the recurrence of this acknowledgment over time. The concept of continuing education, because it lacked the structure of undergraduate and graduate education and because it had been pursued on a part-time basis, appears to have been introduced over and over throughout its history. Each time many of its proponents adopted its tenets with the evangelical zeal of original discovery.

The colonial fathers concentrated on establishing a basic educational system for the young that would ensure literacy, the transfer of the European heritage of Western civilization, and a widespread understanding of public administration and policy. With the exception perhaps of Benjamin Franklin, the early colonists did not address continuing higher education per se. Franklin, as the founder of the Junto and an example of perfected self-directed learning, provided the most direct model of continuing education. In his association with contemporaries such as Washington, Jefferson, and James Madison, he found support for his educational practices. Washington's belief in the diffusion of knowledge, Jefferson's support for the public libraries, and Madison's public service education obtained under John Witherspoon at the College of New Jersey formed an educational climate during the founding period of America that favored the later development of continuing higher education.

Support for the spread of knowledge was an important educational idea that was implemented later in the "extension" movement of the land-grant colleges and universities and in many of the experiments in continuing education, such as the Lyceum and Chautauqua.

## PROFESSORS

Benjamin Silliman, a professor at Yale at the turn of the century, was the prototype of today's continuing education instructor. Appointed a professor of chemistry and natural history at Yale in 1802, Silliman acquired an outstanding collection of minerals, which he used to give the first illustrated course in mineralogy and geology in an American college.[11] In addition to his teaching duties and in order to supplement his family income, he gave a course of popular lectures in natural science to a group of townspeople in New Haven. The response was so positive that he formalized his lectures in geology under the name of the Society for Promoting Useful Knowledge. "By 1859 his lectures had been extended south and west to Pittsburgh, Baltimore, New Orleans, Mobile, Natchez and St. Louis."[12]

It is possible that the success of the Silliman lectures impressed John Lowell, Jr., of Boston. When he made his will at age thirty-three, he included provision for a series of free public lectures on a variety of subjects for the benefit of the Boston community. The series was opened by Governor Edward Everett, who introduced Professor Benjamin Silliman of Yale University to keynote the series.[13]

The grandson of John Adams provided further support for the belief in lifelong learning in his well-known book, *The Education of Henry Adams*. Only 30 pages of the book addressed his formal schooling but over 400 pages were devoted to his education as an adult.[14]

Herbert Baxter Adams, a distinguished history professor at Johns Hopkins University, pioneered the idea of university extension in the United States at a meeting of the American Library Association. "What Adams saw in university extension was an escape from the fragmentariness and discontinuity of subject-matter inherent in any scheme of single lectures unaccompanied by any other discipline than voluntary attendance."[15]

James Earl Russell, dean of Teachers College at Columbia University, voiced additional support for extension in 1897. He endorsed the introduction of extension at Columbia University and later said:

> The aim of adult education is to inspire grown-ups to be something more than they are now and to do their work better than they now do it; at its best it leads to constantly increasing the richness of life, better appreciation of what life offers, greater satisfaction in the use of the mind and body and better understanding of the rights and duties of one's fellow man.[16]

Russell eventually chaired an advisory committee on adult education for the Carnegie Corporation.

John Erskine, a professor of English at Columbia University, initiated a General Honors course in which students read the classics of Western civilization—Homer, Herodotus and Thucydides, Darwin, Marx, and Freud—and attended a two-hour seminar once a week to discuss the assigned book. One of the interesting aspects of Erskine's conduct of the seminars was his confidence in leading discussions of books in theology, philosophy, literature, history, and biography, although his academic specialization was English literature of the Elizabethan period.[17] His holistic view of the educated man had relevance for continuing education and its tenets and was influential with other professors who chose to work with adults.

Mortimer Adler, a student in one of Erskine's seminars, was so enthusiastic about this style of questioning and learning that he later refined the process and modified the book list, in collaboration with Robert Hutchins, president of the University of Chicago, in order to establish a Great Books seminar at that university. The Great Books movement at St. John's College and Annapolis and adult seminars all over the country developed from this seminar.

In 1928 Edward L. Thorndike, an eminent psychologist at Columbia University, wrote *Adult Learning*, in which he applied his psychological theories to older students. He also served as president of the American Association for Adult Education in 1934–1935.

This brief synopsis serves to illustrate that a variety of professors and others have written and theorized about continuing education over the years with a cumulative effect on its validity. Many college and university presidents, too, have used continuing education for many of their educational initiatives in higher education.

## COLLEGE AND UNIVERSITY PRESIDENTS

Although not a college president, Stephen Van Rensselaer, a Hudson River patroon, founded one of the first technical schools in the United

States. His belief in "the diffusion of a very useful kind of knowledge with its application to the business of living," led to the rationale for land-grant colleges and universities.[18] Students at the Rensselaer Polytechnic Institute learned by experimenting, collecting specimens, visiting manufacturing plants, and taking field trips off-campus. The Rensselaer Polytechnic Institute awarded the first engineering degree in 1835; however, more importantly for continuing higher education, the Institute established the first organized field work program in an American institution of higher education. Van Rensselaer later became the first president of the National Lyceum.

As mentioned earlier, John Lowell, Jr., provided money for free public lectures for members of the Boston community. This led to the founding of the Lowell Institute in 1839 and the support of a variety of public educational programs. "In 1910, A. Lawrence Lowell, as Trustee of the Lowell Institute and as the newly appointed President of Harvard University, formed the Commission on Extension Courses in greater Boston and the program of University Extension at Harvard."[19]

Francis Wayland, president of Brown University in 1842, felt a need to modify the classical curriculum in order to maintain student enrollment at the university. He stated, "In no other country is the whole plan for the instruction of the young so entirely dissevered from connection with the business of subsequent life."[20] Wayland was familiar with the concept of continuing education and felt knowledge should not be separated from the use of continuing education.

Johns Hopkins University was patterned after the German research universities with an emphasis on the accumulation and discovery of knowledge. President Daniel Coit Gilman supported this mission; however, he also held a strong belief in the diffusion of knowledge. "In 1876 President Gilman made planned lecture series for the 'educated public,' including specifically arts students, teachers, lawyers, physicians, clergymen, bankers, and businessmen, an integral part of the system of instruction at Johns Hopkins."[21] He also established the Workingman's Institute at Canton, Maryland, in 1879, where lecture series, a library, and vocational instruction were provided.

During his presidency at the University of Minnesota, George Vincent was associated with the Chautauqua movement, a summer assembly for summer school teachers on the shores of Lake Chautauqua in New York. He also provided in his writings a clear rationale for the development of university extension.

William Rainey Harper, who was later president of the University of Chicago, joined Chautauqua in 1883 as professor of Greek and Latin in the School of Languages. During this time he became involved in the evaluation of correspondence instruction as a learning option. Harper granted full recognition of university extension while president of the University of Chicago in 1892. "In his basic plan for the institution, he gave extension equal status with the four other university divisions he envisaged."[22]

In his presidential inaugural address at the University of Wisconsin in 1903, Charles R. Van Hise, who had formerly been an extension instructor, said that service to the state was an important function for a university. During Van Hise's tenure, Lincoln Steffens, a journalist and political philosopher, wrote an article, "Sending a State to College," in which he cited the University of Wisconsin's offer to teach "anybody-anything-anywhere."[23] The "Wisconsin Idea" was received with enthusiasm throughout the state and its basic philosophy was supported by Van Hise.

Two articulate contemporary advocates of continuing education are Derek Bok at Harvard University and Steven Muller at Johns Hopkins University. Muller's philosophy concerning the future includes the need for a strong relationship between the university and its outreach mission:

> The new American university may emerge as an institution liberated significantly from earlier constraints of space and human age. The outreach of the University will become vast. Members of its faculty will be able to interact personally by means of new communications technology with colleagues across barriers of language as well as space. One implication is that the relationship between matriculant and university will become lifelong, regardless of geography.[24]

## EVOLUTION FROM COLLEGE TO UNIVERSITY

With the Morrill Land-Grant legislation of 1862 in effect and the number of state institutions increasing, the stage was set for the emergence of the university in contrast to the college. From 1865 to 1890, three concepts of academic reform for institutions of higher education developed: practical public service, abstract research after the German model, and dissemination of cultural standards.[25] American educators may claim the introduction of practical public service, but the other two concepts were derived from the country's European, particularly British, roots.

The populace was anything but friendly to the foreign, the abstract, or the esoteric.[26] Individuals such as Andrew Carnegie contributed to these sentiments with such comments as:

While the college student has been learning a little about the barbarous and petty squabbles of a far-distant past, or trying to master languages which are dead, the future captain of industry is hotly engaged in the school of experience, obtaining the very knowledge required for his future triumps [sic]. . . . College education as its exists is fatal to success in that domain.[27]

Anti-intellectualism was not limited to industrialists. "In the South, 'Pitchfork Ben' Tillman promised to abolish the University of South Carolina during his gubernatorial campaign of 1891."[28] Officials at the University of Wisconsin refused to print one student's grades in comparison to another's because a student who attained a gentleman's "C" was presumed to be equal to one who achieved all "A's." Phi Beta Kappa was banned at the University of Michigan for similar beliefs.[29]

Despite a sometimes negative climate, the reform movement progressed. Cornell University opened in 1865. It was the first new educational institution to advocate public service and also the first institution to showcase the potential of the Morrill Land-Grant Act of 1862. Ezra Cornell's goal was to establish an institution where any person could find instruction in any subject.

The reform movement goal supporting abstract research received strong impetus with the funding of Johns Hopkins University in 1876. The school was modeled on the German ideal of detailed observation and meticulous investigation. Later, the founding of Stanford University (1889) and the University of Chicago (1892) helped solidify support for the concept of research in the reform movement.

The liberal culture goal of the reform movement was not as easily accomplished because it required an environment built upon tradition and an audience that would accept "culture" in preference to utility and research. Woodrow Wilson, president of Princeton University, was perhaps one of the most able supporters of the liberal cultural movement. He believed in humanities as the essential component of education and thought Princeton should be a place where a student found himself, not his profession.[30]

During the development of the university as an institution of higher learning granting undergraduate, graduate, and professional school degrees from 1865 to World War I, land-grant colleges emerged as powerful state institutions. Johns Hopkins University, Clark University, and the University of Chicago were founded as primary research institutions; Yale University offered the first Ph.D. degree in 1861, and technical institutions such as the Massachusetts Institute of Technology were established. A more dramatic change, however, occurred in the relationship between administrators and faculty.

In the early colonial period of the college, the image of a professor as an independent expert whose discipline transcended the mission of the institution was rarely found.[31] Instead, in institutional entities such as Harvard, Yale, and Princeton, the faculty and the president and staff generally reflected a harmonious organization with one perspective. With the advent of graduate education, specialized faculties, and the emphasis placed on research at many universities, faculty members began giving allegiance to their disciplines. Institutional loyalty had been replaced by loyalty to the advancement of knowledge.

## PROFESSIONAL SOCIETIES AND PROFESSIONALIZATION

An offshoot of this allegiance to a discipline was the proliferation of professional societies and journals, such as the American Institute of Architects (1859), the American Dental Association and the National Education Association (1857), the American Library Association (1876), and the American Bar Association (1878). These associations helped create the cult of professionalism that provided support for the concept of graduate education, thereby directly influencing the contemporary university.

The appearance of research universities with specific professional interests, such as Johns Hopkins in medicine, Harvard in law, and the University of Pennsylvania and the University of Virginia in business, provided the setting and faculty for the increase in professional schools. Professionalization is one of the distinctive characteristics of higher education during the past hundred years and has been especially pronounced since 1941.

There are several possible explanations for the rise in professionalization. The first was the rapid advancement of science and related disciplines for reasons of national defense. The development of the atom bomb through the Manhattan project at the University of Chicago, experimentation with radar, the introduction of operations research, work on the hydrogen bomb in the 1950s, and the reaction to the launching of Sputnik in 1957 focused the minds of many university faculty members on scientific investigation. Subsequent government interest and federal dollars were not limited to space exploration and atomic energy but were expanded to the humanities, arts, energy, health, and poverty programs. This interest forged a new relationship between the federal government and institutions of higher education.

A second reason was the acceleration of "professionalism" in a variety of occupations. Early claims on the "professional" designation were established by the fields of medicine, law, and theology. Following World War I, engineers, social workers, architects, pharmacists, business managers, teachers, and continuing educators sought to legitimize their work as professionals. Since one of the elements in most professional strategies is an extended period of preparation with a university degree upon completion, this goal greatly affected enrollment in undergraduate and graduate schools and created demand for more faculty and facilities. In addition, the advent of increasing professionalism resulting from social need and the individual's vested interest created tremendous potential for continuing education.

Although it is difficult to establish causal relationships between the present intensive professionalization and its origins, the increasing complexity of society, the explosion of knowledge, the interest of the federal government in research, and the commitment of the professoriate to discipline rather than to university have indeed contributed to this development.

## CRITICAL MOVEMENTS

There was a series of concentrated activities, beginning with the Lyceum movement in 1826 through the establishment of community colleges in the 1960s, through which a framework for the concept of continuing higher education was developed. Each activity built on the thought and commitment from the previous activity, and a philosophy of lifelong learning began to emerge.

The Lyceum has special relevance for continuing higher education. Josiah Holbrook, while a student at Yale, chose Benjamin Silliman as his mentor. They shared an interest in science, and Holbrook may have been influenced by Silliman's enthusiasm and skill in translating theory into application for mass audiences. Holbrook followed the lecture circuit after his graduation, speaking to a variety of New England audiences on mineralogy and geology. He later wrote an article in the *American Journal of Education,* where he described a

> plan which called for each town to form an adult learning center, or lyceum, where townspeople would come to discuss topics of mutual interest, hear speakers from among their own membership, and witness scientific demonstration. . . .
> By 1835 the country boasted 3,000 town gatherings, 100 county organizations, and 15 state-level clearinghouses, according to Holbrook's generous estimates. . . . The inception, growth, and decline of the American lyceum parallels the model of all adult education enterprises as it develops in response to some perceived need, catches on as a result

of certain favorable forces, flourishes so long as needs are met, and dies out or is absorbed by other programs meeting yet newer needs.[32]

Fifteen years after the Cooper Union, which provided applied arts and science courses free of charge in New York City, was founded, John Heyl Vincent organized the first summer assembly for Sunday School teachers on the shores of Lake Chautauqua, New York. The teachers spent a fortnight on the lake and listened to lecturers on entertaining topics as well as moral and religious subjects. A correspondence program called the Chautauqua Literary and Scientific Circle developed from the assembly and was so successful that a diploma program was added. "During the middle 1880s it was said approximately 100,000 people were reading the *Chautauqua*."[33] William Rainey Harper was an associate of Vincent. When he became president of the University of Chicago, he introduced the concept of correspondence courses in the liberal arts for undergraduate credit. In later years many state universities adopted the practice of offering correspondence study, and Columbia University offered a variety of courses keyed to leisure pursuits.

## UNIVERSITY EXTENSION

University extension developed naturally as a program of the land-grant institutions. There was an opportunity for university extension to achieve more independence when federal funding for cooperative extension was provided by the Smith-Lever Act in 1914. At some institutions, summer, evening, and off-campus credit courses, as well as noncredit programs, were under the university extension umbrella. Despite initial acceptance of this type of instruction by adults, enrollments leveled off in the early 1900s and declined in some areas of the country. During this time changes were occurring at the University of Wisconsin that influenced extension activity throughout the country. University of Wisconsin President Charles R. Van Hise and Governor Robert M. La Follette had been fellow students at the University of Wisconsin. They pooled their ideas about the relationship between state government and the university, and their discussions resulted in the creation of the "Wisconsin Idea."

By the implementation of the Wisconsin Idea, university faculty members were used to advise state and municipal governments in order to improve their efficacy, and faculty members were sent to all parts of the state to act as resource persons to community members.[34] One person observed, "The University of Wisconsin has become a kind of 'consulting engineer' in the public life of the state."[35] An extensive correspondence program was also initiated by officials of the Wisconsin Idea. Faculty members approved credit for the academic correspondence courses; however, only a limited number of correspondence courses could be applied toward a degree. The most successful effort of the Wisconsin Idea resulted in a vocational course program for apprentices and artisans. Industrial training, a municipal reference bureau, and a package library from which books were sent in response to citizen requests were also introduced by Van Hise. A critical factor in the success of the program was the choice of respected faculty members, such as Louis Reber, former dean of Engineering at Pennsylvania State University. Although many universities did not set up advisory services for local and state governments or initiate correspondence programs, the spirit of the Wisconsin Idea was contagious.

Van Hise's leadership and the success of the Wisconsin model led extension directors to select Wisconsin for their national conference site in 1915. This conference marked the founding of the National University Extension Association. Twenty-two institutions became charter members of the organization and all but four (University of Chicago, Pittsburgh, Harvard, and Columbia) were state colleges or universities. Louis Reber, who was serving as director of Wisconsin's extension division, was elected president of the new association.

The expansion of credit and noncredit programs to meet the needs of employed persons or housewives who could not leave home in the daytime came with the increase in the number of urban colleges and universities. There were obvious advantages for private as well as public urban institutions to schedule courses and programs for part-time students. The location was convenient, the courses were frequently ones taught in the day sessions, and existing facilities could be used. However, it was soon realized that courses and methodology developed for younger daytime undergraduates were not always appropriate for the older evening student, and although classrooms were available, laboratories, libraries, and student services such as advising and testing were also necessary. Despite these problems, by the 1920s, the evening division or college was well-entrenched and in many cases rivaled the vigorous extension operation.

The idea of a residential conference center, which would provide a self-contained environment for seminars, institutes, workshops, executive programs, and conferences, began at the University of Minnesota in 1936 with funding from the Public Works Administration. The Minnesota Center contained dining rooms, lobbies, a lounge, conference rooms, offices, a chapel, and bedrooms for 120 adults. Beginning in 1951, the Kellogg Foundation made sizable donations for the construction of Kellogg Centers of Continuing Education. Today there are Kellogg Centers at California State Polytechnic University, Columbia University, Michigan State University, University of Georgia, University of Nebraska, University of New Hampshire, University of Notre Dame, University of Oxford, England, and Utah State University. A Kellogg-supported conference center, built in 1963, at the University of Chicago, was converted to a graduate dormitory in 1984.

Another type of conference center emerged on many campuses when mansions or estates were willed to educational institutions. Syracuse University and the Universities of Illinois, Delaware, and North Carolina all have such centers. The existence of an accompanying endowment or other funding support frequently determines whether residential conference centers remain fiscally sound operations.

## COMMUNITY COLLEGES

The 1960s brought a rapid proliferation of community colleges and legislation in support of education. Malcolm Knowles, Professor Emeritus of Adult Education at North Carolina State University, identified six factors that contributed to the dramatic increase in community colleges.

1. Larger demand for skilled technicians and paraprofessionals, particularly in allied health.
2. Faith in social and economic mobility through education.
3. Impact of the "Great Society" programs in providing federal aid for the community college to provide opportunities for minorities.
4. Convenient part-time study at low cost.
5. Elimination of past scholastic problems by open door admission.
6. Increased competition for admission to a four-year college.[36]

Prior to the expansion of community colleges in the 1960s, evening colleges and/or continuing education units provided many of the programs and services that are currently offered at community colleges. This has meant an adjustment in the mission of some of the continuing education units at four-year institutions. Upper-level and graduate offerings are less economical than undergraduate courses because of smaller enrollments and the need for greater diversity. Also, the qualifications of the graduate faculty are more stringent than for faculty members teaching undergraduates. These changes have triggered, in many cases, a shift to noncredit programming developed around the unique resources of the institution. Philosophically, the institutionalization of many continuing education courses through the community college was a progressive step forward in continuing higher education. It will require more innovation, better needs assessment, and greater flexibility in programming if continuing education units at colleges and universities are to retain their share of the old market or stake out a claim for new clientele.

## LEGISLATION

Two pieces of legislation were passed in the eighteenth and nineteenth centuries that were to have a major impact on the evolution of higher education in the United States—the land ordinances of 1785 and 1787 and the Morrill Land-Grant Act of 1862.

The land ordinances of 1785 and 1787 provided that land be set aside for universities in each new state as Congress organized the lands west of the Alleghenies and north of the Ohio River into the Northwest Territory. The insistence on educational opportunity as the West was developed is illustrated in the Ordinance of 1781. It stated, "Religion, morality, and education being necessary to good government and the happiness of mankind, schools and the means of education shall forever be encouraged."[37]

Justin Morrill, a Vermont legislator, initiated the Morrill Land-Grant Act of 1862. It has influenced the direction of American higher education, as well as continuing education, more than any other federal legislation to date. Funding for at least one college in every state to provide instruction in agricultural and the mechanical arts was ensured by the Act. Each senator and representative entitled a state to thirty thousand acres of federal land that could be sold to obtain funds for the support of the new institution. "In some states (Michigan, Maryland, and Pennsylvania) existing state schools of agriculture were awarded benefits. . . . In fifteen states, where the state university had become well developed, the land-grant institution became a part of the existing unit."[38]

In 1890 the federal government required that states admit blacks to their land-grant colleges or provide "separate but equal" colleges to accommodate them. "Every state with a significant Negro population chose the latter alternative, often converting a normal school into an 'A' and 'I' or 'A' and 'T' [arts and industry or agricultural and technical] college which, while never equal, was at least separate."[39]

Although the foundation legislation was provided by the Morrill Land-Grant Act of 1862, it was the Hatch Act of 1887 that ensured government support for university experimental farms and led to the establishment of the demonstration technique as a major instructional method. The Smith-Lever Act of 1914 connected cooperative extension to the land-grant concept and strengthened the role of continuing education in the university. General university extension, which included all off-campus work outside of agriculture and home economics such as correspondence courses, credit and noncredit programs, lecture series, conferences, and workshops, developed from the land-grant concept of extending institutional resources to the citizens of a state.

## VETERANS AND MILITARY PROGRAMS

Public Law 346 of the Servicemen's Readjustment Act of 1944, more commonly known as the G.I. Bill, also had a major impact on higher education. This legislation provided a "program of education and training which [made] it possible for an eligible veteran to pursue a course of his own choice in any approved school or job-training establishment which [would] accept him."[40] In his book *Adult Learning,* Edward L. Thorndike suggested that adults' ability to learn had very little correlation with age. Sixteen years later this finding was reinforced as hundreds of thousands of returning veterans invaded campuses across the country. Previous myths about the harmful effects of mixing adults with college-aged students were tested. The veterans, for the most part, did achieve well academically, and their presence on campus introduced flexibility in many university procedures. Credit by examination for military education and experience and correspondence courses were accepted.

The military education programs of the University of California and Louisiana State University had many elements in common with the G.I. Bill. These programs were developed in response to Army and Air Force directives to encourage active military personnel to raise their educational levels. Students were allowed credit for military experience and military education and were permitted to obtain credit by examination. A program was offered by the University of California in Japan, and the Louisiana State program operated through centers in the Caribbean with records maintained on the Baton Rouge campus.

The "New Frontier" of John F. Kennedy and the "Great Society" programs of Lyndon B. Johnson generated unprecedented federal funds for research and facilities and for students' access to higher education during the 1960s. Following the 1957 launching of Sputnik, the National Defense Education Act was funded in 1958 to promote better teaching methods in science, mathematics, and modern languages. Congress extended the National Defense Act in 1965 to provide for student loans, fellowships, and guidance services. Under the Higher Educational Facilities Act, enacted in 1963, public and private institutions of higher education were eligible for federal grants and loans to construct and improve their facilities. The Economic Opportunity Act, passed in 1965, helped higher education institutions provide part-time work for students from low-income families. During the same year, the Higher Education Act was funded to provide educational opportunity grants for promising needy students. Community service was an important part of this act, and seed money was provided for innovative programming through continuing education units at universities in many states. The establishment of the Basic Education Opportunity Grant program in 1972 changed the pattern of funding, and funds were sent directly to the student instead of the institution.

In 1975 Senator Walter Mondale authored and introduced the Lifelong Learning Act as an amendment to Title I of the Higher Education Act. The Act was designed to provide better facilities for adult learners, better counseling services, and to support research and teacher training. However, the bill became a casualty of higher priorities in the new administration. Although it was passed, Congress failed to fund it in the fiscal year 1979 budget or request funding for fiscal year 1980.

## SUMMARY

As the history of continuing education at the college and university levels is examined, it can be seen it is clearly interwoven with the history of higher education. Throughout the history of higher education, continuing education concepts have been an integral part of most traditional institutions, and innovative practices in continuing education frequently have been introduced or supported by the presidents and professors of these leading institutions. History shows that anything is possible in academia if the timing and support are right. During wartime and its aftermath, there was great flexibility in the acceptance and awarding of credit, and the most prestigious association in higher education, the American Council on Education, developed and published the standards. One fact is evident. To the extent that continuing higher educators recognize the mission and goals of their parent universities and to the extent that continuing higher educators can articulate their relationship to them, they will be vital members of the academic community and will most probably prosper.

# REFERENCES

1. Cremin, Lawrence A., *American Education* (New York: Harper and Row, 1970), p. 28.
2. Grattan, C. Hartley, *In Quest of Knowledge* (New York: Association Press, 1955), p. 139.
3. Burke, Colin B., *American Collegiate Populations: A Test of the Traditional View* (New York: New York University Press, 1982), p. 103.
4. Ibid.
5. Rudolph, Frederick, *The American College and University* (New York: Knopf, 1962), p. 41.
6. Knowles, Malcolm S., *A History of the Adult Education Movement in the United States* (New York: Krieger, 1977), p. 13.
7. Cremin, op. cit., p. 545.
8. Ibid., p. 546.
9. Adams, James Truslow, *Frontiers of American Culture* (New York: Scribner, 1944), pp. 157–158.
10. Brubacher, John S., and Rudy, Willis, *Higher Education in Transition* (New York: Harper and Row, 1976), pp. 22–23.
11. Rudolph, op. cit., p. 223.
12. Knowles, op. cit., p. 15.
13. Portman, David N., *The Universities and the Public* (Chicago: Nelson-Hall, 1978), pp. 22–23.
14. Grattan, op. cit., p. 306.
15. Ibid., p. 185.
16. Ibid., p. 278.
17. Adler, Mortimer J., *Philosopher at Large* (New York: Macmillan, 1977), p. 30.
18. Rudolph, op. cit., p. 230.
19. *University Extension Course Catalogue 1984–85* (Cambridge: Harvard University, 1984), p. 201.
20. Bledstein, Burton J. *The Culture of Professionalism* (New York: Norton, 1976), p. 242.
21. Grattan, op. cit., p. 185.
22. Ibid., p. 190.
23. Portman, op. cit., pp. 24–25.
24. Muller, Steven, "A New American University," in *A New America?*, ed. S. R. Graubard (New York: Norton, 1978), p. 42.
25. Veysey, Laurence R., *The Emergence of the American University* (Chicago: University of Chicago Press, 1965), p. 9.
26. Ibid., p. 13.
27. Ibid., p. 13–14.

28. Ibid., p. 15.

29. Ibid., p. 13.

30. "Alumni Dinner, Orange, 10 November 1904," *Woodrow Wilson Papers* (Washington, D.C.: Library of Congress, 1904).

31. Jencks, Christopher, and Reisman, David, *The Academic Revolution* (Garden City, N.Y.: Doubleday, 1969), p. 1.

32. Shawn, Neil M., "The American Lyceum and Adult Education," *Lifelong Learning: The Adult Years,* Vol. 11, No. 7 (Washington, D.C.: Government Printing Office, March 1979), pp. 8–27.

33. Portman, op. cit., pp. 83–89.

34. Ibid.

35. Hard, William, "A University in Public Life," *Outlook 86* (July 1907), p. 667.

36. Knowles, op. cit., p. 302.

37. Kane, William T., and O'Brien, John J., *History of Education* (Chicago: Loyola University Press, 1954), p. 377.

38. Portman, op. cit., p. 24.

39. Jencks and Riesman, op. cit., p. 422.

40. Hutchins, Clayton D., and Munse, Albert R., *Federal Funds for Education, 1950–51 and 1951–52* (Washington, D.C.: Government Printing Office, 1952), p. 69.

# -3-
# FORCES AND QUESTIONS IN CONTINUING HIGHER EDUCATION

## Kenneth E. Young

Almost constant change has been experienced in American higher education since its modest beginnings in 1636. The Harvard University of today is a much different institution than the Harvard College of colonial times. Present-day higher education has radically changed from the handful of small, residential colleges that existed in 1776. These changes have been the most rapid and extensive during times when the nation itself was undergoing great transformation. For example, at the close of the nineteenth century, the United States was in the process of moving from an agricultural society to an industrial society. This profound reorientation was reflected in the demise of many colleges offering "classical" education and the establishment of state universities and land-grant institutions. A number of other significant alterations in curricula, teaching methods, and student clienteles also took place during that time.

Today the United States is evolving into a "post-industrial society." Futurist Alvin Toffler suggested:

> Today, behind the confusion of change, there is a growing coherence of pattern; the future is taking shape . . . what is happening is not just a technological revolution but the coming of a whole new civilization in the fullest sense of the term.[1]

Note: Some material in this chapter has been drawn from the Epilogue of the text *Understanding Accreditation* (San Francisco: Jossey-Bass, 1983.

Such a significant shift holds important implications for colleges and universities—particularly as they relate to adult students and continuing education. More recently, Toffler stated in his book *The Adaptive Corporation:*

> 1955–70 were years of almost uninterrupted straight-line growth in an equilibrial environment. In such a period, the formula for adaptation is relatively simple. Managers look smart—indeed, they very often *are* smart—if they simply do "more of the same."
>
> Since then this straight-line strategy has become a blueprint for corporate disaster. The reason is simple: instead of being routine and predictable, the corporate environment has grown increasingly unstable, accelerative, and revolutionary. Under such conditions, all organizations become extremely vulnerable to outside forces or pressures. And managers must learn to cope with non-linear forces—i.e., situations in which small inputs can trigger vast results and *vice versa.*[2]

The above generalization clearly applies to higher education as well. The steady growth years—in enrollments and in funding—have ended. Competition, for students and for dollars, has greatly increased. The computer and other new technologies provide new opportunities but also create new challenges for colleges and universities. Public attitudes and expectations are changing. As a result, the roles played by higher education are changing.

## MAJOR FORCES AFFECTING CONTINUING HIGHER EDUCATION

When fundamental changes are experienced in a society, those changes show themselves in many different ways and affect different parts of the society at the same time. This chapter examines major societal forces that are affecting continuing higher education. It also examines changes in educational institutions that affect the education of adults.

### SOCIAL CHANGES

OUR SHRINKING WORLD.    Marshall McLuhan has written of the "global village" and R. Buckminster Fuller talked about "spaceship earth." These colorful terms recognize that: "The major issues of our time are no longer national—but global. Peace—economic progress—

resources—pollution—disease—world tourism—global communication—global transportation—weather modification—space . . ."[3]

Two important inventions, the jet airplane and the communication
satellite, have transformed our planet. Consider that the Concorde
now flies from the United States and Europe in three-and-one-half
hours, and satellite communication permits an almost instantaneous
transmittal of information. Conflicts in the Middle East can suddenly
reduce United States oil supplies and throw the economy into disarray,
and conflicts across the globe send refugees to our shores. Fast,
profound changes are occurring in the "global village."

How can colleges and universities best prepare people to live
effectively in this kind of world? What kinds of changes must our
educational institutions make to adapt to a new order?[4]

AN INFORMATION SOCIETY. In 1973 Daniel Bell forecast "the coming
of the post-industrial society," and wrote of the changing shape of
the economy from goods to services.[5] Nine years later John Naisbitt
pointed out that the overwhelming majority of service workers are
actually engaged in the creation, processing, and distribution of information.[6] He wrote, "The information society is an economic reality,
not an intellectual abstraction."[7] Naisbitt observed we are drowning
in information but starved for knowledge. To complicate matters, the
U.S. Department of Education and the National Science Foundation,
in a 1980 report, stated that most Americans are moving toward
"virtual scientific and technological illiteracy."[8]

College and university personnel must find better ways of ab-
sorbing, ordering, and disseminating new knowledge. Departments
and disciplines must be reorganized as research findings blur old
lines. For example, the new fields of genetic engineering and bio-
physics cross old boundaries. Most importantly, college and university
personnel must face the obligations and opportunities of an important
new role—the constant re-education and updating of the American
workforce to accommodate to the structural shifts resulting from the
information revolution.

NEW VALUES. In one of the important books written in the last decade,
Daniel Yankelovich described the "shifting plates of American culture."[9] As the American economy enters a new, more stringent phase,
he saw Americans leaving behind the excesses of the "me-decade"
for what he called a new "ethic of commitment"—new rules of living
that support self-fulfillment through deeper personal relationships and
more enduring commitments to the world of work and the business
of common survival.

Colleges and universities are now found to be the home of many generations that represent different forms or stages of these "shifting plates" of culture—from 18-year-old freshmen to the rapidly growing group of older part-time students to faculty members who are variously products of the Depression, World War II, the booming 1950s, and the turbulent 1960s. Personnel in institutions of higher education have a large responsibility for preparing society to understand and deal with such significant cultural changes.

POPULATION SHIFTS.    Profound demographic changes are being experienced in the United States. The tremendous baby boom that occurred after World War II was followed by a decline in birthrates during the 1960s and 1970s that, in turn, has been succeeded by a second "slower" baby boom. Meanwhile, the over-65 age group is growing rapidly; this group now outnumbers teenagers for the first time in history and will continue to rise dramatically to 32 million by the turn of the century.

At the same time, the second largest wave of immigrants in United States history must be absorbed—13.9 million in all, many of them from Asia and the Pacific islands. Minorities already constitute the majority of school enrollment in twenty-three of the nation's twenty-five largest cities; by the year 2000, fifty-three major cities will have a majority population of minorities. The growth of the Hispanic population is the highest of all groups; 60 percent of the Hispanics are located in three states—California, Texas, and New York. In addition, populations are continuing to shift from the Frost Belt (the Northeast) to the Sun Belt (the Southwest).

These demographic changes pose what may be "life-and-death" questions for many colleges and universities. For example, the future of an institution located in a rural area in the Northeast that serves only 18- to 24-year-olds will be quite different from that of an urban institution in the Southwest with a diversified student clientele. National policy in education must become diverse and flexible to serve the needs of varied regions and groups.[10]

ECONOMIC AND FINANCIAL CHANGES.    The period of almost constant growth in enrollments related to the traditional full-time student and increases in federal financial support for higher education appears to have come to an end. There have been cutbacks in traditional financial aid programs and less money for research and special projects, with the exception of national defense, at colleges and universities. Personnel in some states are stepping in to raise their levels of support, but in many others they are not. Also, with the exception of a few states, such as New York and Pennsylvania, state aid is going primarily to public institutions. Efforts have been doubled in virtually all colleges and universities to obtain funds through gifts and contracts. However, there is increasing conflict between public and private institutions; personnel in public institutions are aggressively seeking support from donors and those in private institutions pushing for more aid from federal and state sources.

At the national level, the push for a modified flat tax on incomes, if successful, may eliminate or limit more severely tax-deduction opportunities that have benefited higher education. Gifts to colleges and universities and employee education could be adversely affected.

There is now more competition between higher education and the marketplace, particularly business and industry. New technological tools and software for the purposes of employee training are being developed and marketed by corporations. Research arms, on the model of the Bell Laboratories, have also been created by personnel in large corporations. A host of separate "think tanks," such as the Brookings Institution, the Heritage Foundation, and the Hudson Institute, are actively engaged in research. In addition, other social institutions— government agencies, trade and professional associations, labor unions, libraries, museums, churches, etc.—are building their own educational programs, some of them quite elaborate.

Personnel in many universities and other complex institutions are beginning to adopt an "every tub must sit on its own bottom" philosophy. This means that colleges, schools, and divisions within the institution must be self-supporting, bringing in enough income to cover all costs (including overhead). This financial test poses special problems for the more traditional arts and sciences programs. But it also may force personnel to think more flexibly and creatively about institutional roles.

GOVERNMENTAL REDIRECTION.  During recent years the federal government has shifted from what amounted to a "hands-off" approach toward higher education to an activist, regulatory role in the late 1960s and 1970s. The federal government is now less involved in funding and oversight but more concerned with special issues, for example, genetic research, intercollegiate athletics, and profitmaking activities. Government also is becoming one of higher education's biggest "customers" as various agencies increasingly contract with colleges and universities for education and training programs.

At the state level, attitudes and practices are also shifting. K. C. Green observed that the state role in higher education has changed considerably during the past fifteen years—from passive provider to concerned underwriter.[11] Louis W. Bender hypothesized that "history some day may record that, during the last quarter of the twentieth century, state government evolved into the role of controller of the postsecondary enterprise."[12]

## EDUCATIONAL CHANGES

REFORM MOVEMENTS. The 1983 report of the National Commission on Excellence in Education, *A Nation at Risk,* was the first of a series of critical documents that stimulated debate and triggered educational reform programs in more than twenty states.

Writers of various reports and persons who encourage reform efforts assume that schools are the primary, if not exclusive, source of learning, ignoring the important roles of other social institutions.[13] These reports and reform efforts also fail to deal with such factors as the increasing movement of students into private schools; conflicts between unionized teachers and disaffected taxpayers (particularly the growing number of childless adults); the declining quality of college students majoring in education; a decrease in the number of teachers entering the field and an increase in the number leaving the field because of low salaries and poor working conditions; the impact of the computer and television on learning modes; the unique socioeconomic problems of cities and suburbs; and pervasive financial difficulties.

UNCLEAR ROLES. The traditional lines between secondary and postsecondary education, already blurred, are becoming increasingly meaningless as high technology opens up new worlds of learning to everyone. Further, the borders between traditional academic disciplines have begun to be erased by new areas of research. Colleges and universities will be forced to engage in what may be a never-ending process of self-evaluation and redefinition.

POSTSECONDARY EDUCATION. The term "higher education" (those degree-granting colleges and universities offering traditional academic programs and mainly serving full-time students recently graduated from high school) has been gradually giving way to the term "postsecondary education" (an ever-expanding variety of institutions, programs, and delivery settings and under various forms of sponsorship serving an increasingly diverse population of learners of all ages with widely differing educational objectives). Many "traditional" colleges and universities are engaging in a growing number of educational activities not directly related to producing graduates with degrees. At the same time, a variety of "nontraditional" institutions are beginning to award credits and degrees as well as offering a great range of noncredit educational programs.

In the early 1900s, the heads of the great railroads persisted in thinking that their business was running trains rather than moving people and goods. And within the last twenty years, the decision makers in the automobile industry have continued to respond to the public's previous desire for speed, power, and social status rather than meeting the current need for economical and dependable transportation. Will higher education leaders cling to the notion that a college or university only offers degree programs in on-campus learning for young full-time students, or will they see their institutions as part of a much larger educational enterprise?

CONTINUING PROFESSIONAL EDUCATION. Professions are constantly changing and evolving as new specializations appear and take over specific practices previously performed by others. Rapidly increasing knowledge and new technologies are leading to near constant change in the professions. The "half-life" in many professions is rapidly declining. Now, within five years or so of graduation, half of what a person learned in professional school is obsolete and half of what that person needs to know was not taught in the curriculum.

Probably the most rapidly growing activity in higher education is continuing professional education, and most of this is noncredit education. Harvard University, for example, each year serves 45,000 part-time adult students—most of them doctors, lawyers, business executives, and educators learning the latest developments in their fields.

## INSTITUTIONAL CHANGES

PART-TIME STUDENTS. This group already has become dominant in all but a small number of colleges and universities. Part-time students accounted for 41.7 percent of the 1983 enrollments, according to the National Center for Education Statistics. The average rate of increase over the past seven years for part-time students has been 4.9 percent, while the average increase for full-time students has been 2.3 percent. These figures reflect for-credit enrollments; they do not include noncredit programs.

OLDER STUDENTS. Adults between the ages of 35 and 44 comprise the fastest growing age group in the United States. This adult age group will increase by 30 percent between 1980 and 1990, while the number of 18- to 24-year-olds will decline by 16 percent in the same period. In 1983, according to the National Center for Education Statistics, most college students were over 21 years of age, and 36 percent were 25 or over. The average age of college students has been increasing steadily over the past ten years and will continue to rise.

NONCREDIT LEARNING.    There is no way of knowing the size or growth rate of noncredit learning in colleges and universities. Personnel at the National Center for Education Statistics are attempting to gather figures on noncredit learning but have run into problems of definition and comparability. Data on noncredit programs are customarily not collected and reported by colleges and universities. What evidence is available, however, suggests there is an enormous and rapidly growing amount of activity in this area. It includes (1) technology transfer (the interpretation, transmission, and application of research findings to potential users); (2) continuing professional education; (3) contract training; and (4) activities such as conferences, institutes, workshops, alumni colleges, summer programs, and study-travel tours.

CHANGES IN CREDIT EDUCATION.    For better or worse, academic credit is a basic element in a college degree. In most public institutions, state funding is provided on a formula basis related to full-time equivalent enrollments in credit courses. However, credits may be earned in a number of nontraditional ways: (1) through the assessment of experiential learning; (2) by examination, such as the College Level Examination Program; (3) on the basis of recommendations of the American Council on Education made after evaluating noncredit courses offered by the military or business and industry; and (4) as a result of transfer from one institution to another.

Credit for courses offered jointly by the educational institution and a noncollege sponsor—a business, a labor union, or a professional association—is being granted by an increasing number of colleges and universities. Also, personnel in institutions with declining enrollments can be strongly tempted to convert noncredit courses into credit courses. Finally, credit courses now can be delivered in many modes—by computer, television, or a combination of methods—as well as by correspondence study.

NEW TECHNOLOGIES.    There has been experimentation with a variety of new approaches to learning in a few colleges and universities, but limited funds and perspectives have prevented a broad-gauged approach to the use of technology in higher education. Few leaders seem to have recognized the potential for truly individualized instruction made possible by combining the telephone, the copier, the computer, and the television set and its many aids into a single, integrated electronic system, to be used along with group learning and independent study. Only now is the potential of satellites for linking up professors, students, libraries, and data bases beginning to be seriously explored by some institutions.

COLLABORATION AND CONSORTIA. Over the years, there has been a number of efforts to achieve collaboration among various colleges and universities. Many such efforts, such as the University of Mid-America, died when special funding disappeared. Other efforts, such as the Washington, D.C., Consortium of Universities, continue to function but at a very modest level. The national organization, Council for Interinstitutional Leadership, maintains only a part-time office housed in the American Council on Education. Not only colleges and universities but libraries, museums, and businesses were brought together by more ambitious efforts, such as the Compact for Lifelong Educational Opportunities (CLEO) in Philadelphia. CLEO, which was originally supported by a large grant from the W. K. Kellogg Foundation, ceased to function when grant funds were discontinued.

Why have opportunities for collaboration and cooperation, when the advantages appear to strongly outweigh the disadvantages, met with resistance from colleges and universities? There are probably many factors at work, including institutional inertia, strong feelings of turf protection, differences in students and programs, pervasive academic autonomy, and the complicated demands of collaborative efforts. Where consortia have been developed, an identity and focus of their own tend to develop over time, effectively separating them from their sponsoring institutions.

Colleges and universities are confronted with difficult new problems or unsettling new dimensions are added to old problems when major forces affecting education are considered. Following are some of the most important questions with which universities and colleges must deal in the coming decade.

## MAJOR QUESTIONS FACING CONTINUING HIGHER EDUCATION

### PURPOSE

Will institutions of higher education reexamine their objectives, change their focus if necessary, and re-order their priorities in the light of changing conditions? As previously stated, the general society has changed and is continuing to change in dramatic ways. Most colleges and universities have changed, too, although many have not recognized or acknowledged the significance of these developments, and others have resisted change. Many college and university leaders cling to outmoded mental pictures of their institutions, images that are no longer accurate. These leaders make speeches and write articles that describe these nonexistent institutions, and they make policy and develop plans based on these unrealistic notions, which is even more dangerous.[14] Alvin Toffler, in his most recent book, *The Adaptive Corporation,* stated:

> A corporation without a strategy is like an airplane weaving through stormy skies, hurled up and down, slammed by the wind, lost in the thunderheads. If lightning or crushing winds don't destroy it, it will simply run out of gas. Without some explicit assumptions about the long-range future, and strategic guidelines for dealing with them, without a vision of its own future form, even the largest and seemingly most secure organizations face disaster in a period of revolutionary, technological and economic turbulence.[15]

This warning applies as well to educational institutions.

## ORGANIZATION

How will colleges and universities organize themselves in the future to cope with changing roles? Edmund F. Ackel, president of Virginia Commonwealth University, observed that only a very small number of colleges and universities has, in the last five to ten years, failed to develop some kind of adaptation to the needs of adult students, and some institutions have made substantial modifications in their structure and functioning. He described three stages of adaptation: the *laissez-faire* stage in which there is no special recognition of adult students; the *separatist* stage which provides segregated programs for adult students; and the *equity* stage which acknowledges that the institution serves adult students.[16] Ackel's paper neatly capsulized many of the organizational issues facing colleges and universities in the 1980s.

There appears to be growing confusion, however, about the role of the college or university and continuing education and the place of continuing education within the college or university.

Personnel in some major universities, however, have rationalized they have no acknowledged responsibility for continuing education, arguing that their primary functions, in order of importance, are: research, graduate and professional education, and undergraduate education for a small, select group of pre-professional students. Such institutional personnel have not come to terms with certain realities. First, financial support for research will come, particularly from business and industry, in large part only if university personnel can translate and transmit research findings into information that can be used by others (which calls for continuing education). Second, many established professions (e.g., law and medicine) are receiving more new practitioners than they can readily absorb, whereas there is a growing need for continuing professional education (see later section). Third, among the major challenges for undergraduate education are the selection of students who have capacities to learn and the provision of tools with which to continue their learning.

In other institutions of higher education, attempts have been made to "integrate" continuing education activities by moving credit courses from a separate college, school, or division of continuing education into appropriate academic departments. This approach makes good sense on paper but rarely proves successful in actual practice. Some traditional faculty members will teach "continuing education courses" for extra pay on an overload basis, but few willingly take on such assignments as part of their regular teaching load, especially if it means teaching in the evening, on weekends, or off-campus. They are even more resistant if, as usually is the case, they have to redesign their courses for special clienteles and adapt to new delivery systems. Furthermore, the academic reward system, supported by most institutions and virtually all professional associations, does not encourage faculty involvement in continuing education.

Faculty members in still other colleges and universities are clinging to the notion that "continuing education" is somehow different, in quality or kind, from "regular education." They not only assign it to a special unit within the institution but hold to policies that require special notations on transcripts and limit the number of continuing education credits that can be applied toward a degree. They also ignore the existence elsewhere in their organization of many continuing education-like activities—for example, continuing professional education.

## FINANCE

How will colleges and universities cover costs in the future? To state the case in business terms, most colleges and universities have been selling a service (education) and a product (degrees) to a market (18- to 24-year-olds) that is now declining. Furthermore, colleges and universities have not been able to cover costs of production by sales (tuition) but have had to depend upon subsidies from the government and gifts, encouraged by tax policy. They are weighed down by a heavy investment in facilities and equipment, most of it outmoded and suffering from deferred maintenance. They may also carry a burden in the form of an aging, tenured faculty whose productivity declined with post-World War II reductions in teaching loads, who do not necessarily have the kinds of expertise currently needed, and who may resist the use of new technologies. "We have a pre-Gutenberg faculty in a post-Gutenberg university," said Steven Muller, president of Johns Hopkins University.[17]

The costs of acquiring a college degree have now risen so high (and likely will continue to climb) that increasing questions are being asked about cost effectiveness.[18] For example, how many persons will want to invest four years of time and $50,000 in order to get a baccalaureate degree and an elementary school teaching credential in order to qualify for a job with a starting salary of $15,000?

The military is aggressively recruiting the same group of young people from which higher education traditionally draws its students. And if the armed forces are unable to get their share any other way, they will push for required national service. Meanwhile, officials in business and industry increasingly are competing with colleges and universities, offering education and training programs, both credit and noncredit, through thousands of proprietary schools and by means of correspondence, computers, and other new programs. In addition, accredited, degree-granting institutions include the General Motors Institute, the Rand Graduate Institute for Policy Studies, the Arthur D. Little Management Education Institute, and the Wang Institute.

## DELIVERY SYSTEMS

Will colleges and universities lead or follow in the development and use of new technologies? It has been commonly said that the military services are twenty years ahead and business and industry ten years ahead of education in making effective use of new technology for learning. It is now possible to deliver education from an institution to the student by means of correspondence courses, telephone, computer, radio, television (one-way or two-way), videotapes, and videodiscs. The technology is in place; good software is lacking. Over a ten-year period, $150 million is being spent by the Corporation for Public Broadcasting Annenberg Projects in an effort to produce necessary learning materials. The Department of Defense and many large corporations also are eager to provide funding for the development of software for their purposes. College and university faculties, however, have been amazingly resistant to these opportunities.

## COMPETITION

Will colleges and universities be able to compete effectively with business and industry and other sponsors of education and training? Colleges and universities, as has already been pointed out, face increasing competition with business and industry, particularly in the area of noncredit education for adults. Ironically, a significant amount of that competition involves certain faculty members who are contracting with corporations to develop and teach education and training programs and to design software. More competition in the research area is also being experienced by institutions of higher education—from think tanks and from for-profit companies, often established by current or former faculty members.

## QUALITY ASSURANCE

Will colleges and universities continue to regulate themselves effectively in a rapidly changing world, or will there be more governmental regulation? Higher education has had, on balance, a creditable history of self-regulation—"a wide range of collective actions to maintain responsible practice in all areas of operation."[19] This record has been epitomized by accreditation—"a process by which an institution of postsecondary education evaluates its educational activities, in whole or in part, and seeks an independent judgment to confirm that it substantially achieves its objectives and is generally equal in quality to comparable institutions or specialized units."[20]

The ability of institutions to engage effectively in self-regulation has been challenged by recent changes in higher education and by changes now occurring in the larger society. Higher education personnel now must face anew such questions as: What is an educational institution? What is the meaning of a degree? What are the differences between credit and noncredit courses?[21] For example, how is quality assured and who is responsible for assuring it when an "institution" in one part of the country or the world sends "courses" by satellite to a student 3,000 miles away? Officials of the Assessment of Long Distance Learning via Telecommunications Project (ALLTEL), sponsored by the Council on Postsecondary Accreditation and the State Higher Education Executive Officers, have been wrestling with this question.

Continuing education, serving nontraditional students with nontraditional programs and utilizing nontraditional delivery systems, has always posed special problems for state governments that authorize educational activities, voluntary accrediting agencies that engage in quality assurance, and federal agencies that determine eligibility for certain funds (such as student aid programs). These problems are now becoming increasingly complex as more colleges and universities become heavily involved in continuing education, business and industry step up their educational activities, and computers and satellites reduce the need for classroom instruction.

Such developments raise questions about how continuing education should be regulated and accredited and who should have the primary authority and responsibility for oversight. Even with state governments, there are struggles for control between state institutional governing boards, coordinating boards, and various state agencies.

## CONTINUING PROFESSIONAL EDUCATION

Will colleges and universities play a meaningful role in the updating of practitioners and specialists, or will professional associations and for-profit organizations dominate? University officials have long accepted the role of providing preprofessional and professional education, and programs for paraprofessionals in various areas of specialization are being increasingly offered by four-year colleges and community colleges. In recent years, personnel in institutions of higher education have been offering more continuing professional education, frequently in collaboration with professional associations. For example, a pilot project was funded by the Kellogg Foundation, under which Pennsylvania State University personnel have been working with selected professions to identify proficiencies and design educational experiences to achieve them.

For the most part, however, continuing professional education, particularly in most of the senior professions, is offered primarily by national and state professional organizations, with few if any ties to colleges and universities. The professions also make only limited use of professional school faculty, because much of continuing professional education deals with new practices, new laws, and new equipment, which university personnel may be slow to pick up. For-profit organizations (e.g., pharmaceutical companies) also sponsor many seminars and workshops, which may be continuing professional education, product promotion, goodwill development, or all three combined.

College and university personnel must evaluate their role in continuing professional education and decide whether it is to be performed alone or in conjunction with professional associations and/ or proprietary organizations. Further, the internal organization of institutions of higher education needs to be analyzed: is each professional school to function autonomously in this growing area, or is there an appropriate role for a college, school, or division of continuing education?

## BUSINESS AND INDUSTRY

How will colleges and universities relate to corporations in such areas as research, contract training, and financial support? With declining government funding, institutions of higher education are turning to the world of business for support, but money comes with strings. Officials in business and industry want: (1) an opportunity to determine the kind of research and first access to research findings; (2) tailor-made education and training programs delivered in the most convenient and useful ways; and (3) the right to designate the use of gifts. These new relationships then raise new ethical and administrative questions.

An estimated $30 to $60 billion a year is poured into education and training by corporations. Untold dollars are also spent on this activity by nonprofit organizations. Education has been listed by most trade and professional associations as their first priority. Billions of dollars are spent every year on education and training by federal agencies (no one knows exactly how much). Even more is spent by state and local governments. Although much of this learning is conducted in-house, officials of these organizations also contract out and would do more contracting if their educational needs could be satisfactorily met at the right price. In recent years, an entirely new group of for-profit companies has appeared to respond to this demand. Many of these learning needs can be appropriately met by personnel at colleges and universities. They consist of such programs as executive management development, personnel training, and intensive foreign language offerings. These opportunities, however, have been either ignored or acknowledged in highly inappropriate ways by most colleges and universities.

## FACULTY

As many colleges and universities increasingly serve adult and part-time students and become more involved in noncredit education and contract training, will the role of the faculty change?

> The fact is that the real authority in the university is not hierarchical, as in business or in the military; it is not even "separate" as it is in principle in the United States Government. It is not a system of checks and balances so much as a diffusion of authority.[22]

Although this description does not apply to persons in most community colleges or public four-year colleges, it does accurately describe many universities and highly regarded independent colleges.

Faculty members in these institutions are for the most part "professional entrepreneurs." They will ignore as long as possible the implications of the changes identified here and will resist efforts made to have them adapt their behaviors to new conditions. Many institutions now suffer from a "tenure bulge"—a large number of faculty members who were appointed during the high growth years of post-World War II. As these faculty members retire over the next five to ten years, many colleges and universities will move toward the appointment of more part-time adjunct faculty members. Also, as enrollment declines and financial crises are faced by a growing number of institutions, governing board officials will enact exigency programs eliminating less productive departments, programs, and faculty members. Finally, as Todd Furniss, formerly with the American Council on Education, suggested, a number of faculty members may move in the direction of other professions, creating their own "corporations," and contracting with colleges and universities to provide services.[23]

## SUMMARY

Many colleges and universities are going to resist change or will not change enough or in the right ways to adapt to new conditions. Some institutions (e.g., certain fundamentalist church colleges) will continue to thrive because their specific clientele and a special set of circumstances will enable them to serve the particular limited market. Others will survive but lose strength and appeal. Still others—perhaps several hundred—will die or suffer grave wounds. These will be the Penn Centrals and the Braniffs of higher education. Those institutions that realistically come to terms with the forces and issues affecting higher education will not only survive but prosper. It is important to note that the continuing education function in colleges and universities can be the key to adopting to the changes identified. The successful college or university will be one that:

> puts the student first and the institution second, concentrates more on the former's needs than the latter's convenience, encourages diversity of individual opportunity rather than uniform prescription, and de-emphasizes time, space, and even course requirements in favor of competence. It has concern for the learner of any age and circumstances, for the degree aspirant as well as the person who finds sufficient reward in enriching life through constant, periodic, or occasional study.[24]

## REFERENCES

1.  Toffler, Alvin, *The Third Wave* (New York: Bantam, 1981), p. 349.

2. Toffler, Alvin, *The Adaptive Corporation* (New York: McGraw-Hill, 1985), pp. 1–2.
3. Estandiary, F. M., *Up-Wingers* (New York: Popular Library, 1977), pp. 120–121.
4. Botkin, Mahdi and Mircea, *No Limits to Learning: Bridging the Human Gap* (London: Pergamon, 1979).
5. Bell, Daniel, *The Coming of the Post-Industrial Society* (New York: Basic Books, 1973).
6. Naisbitt, John, *Megatrends* (New York: Warner Books, 1982), p. 14.
7. Ibid., p. 19.
8. *New York Times,* October 23, 1981.
9. Yankelovich, Daniel, *New Rules* (New York: Random House, 1981).
10. McNett, Ian, ed. *Demographic Imperatives: Implications for Educational Policy* (Washington, D.C.: American Council on Education, 1983).
11. Green, K. C., "Program Review and the State Responsibility for Higher Education," *Journal of Higher Education,* 51 (1) (1981), pp. 76–80.
12. Bender, Louis W., "States and Accreditation," in *Understanding Accreditation,* ed. Young, Chambers, Kells, and Associates (San Francisco: Jossey-Bass, 1983), p. 271.
13. Niebuhr, Jr., Herman, *Revitalizing American Learning* (Belmont, Calif.: Wadsworth, 1984).
14. Young, Kenneth E., "Good-Bye Security Blanket," *Currents,* Vol. 9, No. 10 (Washington, D.C.: Council for Advancement and Support of Education, 1983), pp. 48–52.
15. Toffler, Alvin, *The Adaptive Corporation* (New York: McGraw-Hill, 1985), pp. 171–172.
16. Ackel, Edmund F., *Adapting the University to Adult Students: A Developmental Perspective* (Washington, D.C.: American Council on Education, Commission on Higher Education and the Adult Learner, 1981).
17. Muller, Steven, speech presented at the AANE Annual Convention, April 1983.
18. Bird, Caroline, *The Case Against College* (New York: McKay, 1975).
19. El-Khawas, Elaine, "Accreditation: Self-Regulation," in *Understanding Accreditation,* ed. Young, Chambers, Kells, and Associates (San Francisco: Jossey-Bass, 1983), p. 55.
20. Young, Kenneth E., "Accreditation: Complex Evaluative Tool," in *Understanding Accreditation,* ed. Young, Chambers, Kells, and Associates (San Francisco: Jossey-Bass, 1983), p. 21.
21. Young, Kenneth E., "The Future of Accreditation," in *Understanding Accreditation,* ed. Young, Chambers, Kells, and Associates (San Francisco: Jossey-Bass, 1983), pp. 390–406.
22. Pandarus, "One's Own Primer of Academic Politics," *American Scholar,* 42 (4) (Autumn 1973), pp. 569–592.
23. Furniss, Todd, *The Self-Reliant Academic* (Washington, D.C.: American Council on Education, 1984).
24. Carnegie Commission on Non-Traditional Studies, *Diversity of Design* (San Francisco: Jossey-Bass, 1973), p. xv.

# -4-
# COMPONENTS OF SUCCESSFUL CONTINUING HIGHER EDUCATION PROGRAMS

## John C. Snider

Many continuing higher education operations on large and small campuses have achieved great success and credibility through excellence in on- and off-campus programming. But what about the others—institutions in which continuing education operations are nearly nonfunctional and lack support from both campus academicians and potential clientele? What factors determine success or failure?

Administrators, programmers, client groups, institutional mission, and the external environment can all affect the success of an operation. For example, an effective continuing education unit is generally characterized by institutional leaders that appreciate and understand the complexity and comprehensiveness of continuing education as an integral part of the total institution. This suggests there are elements that appear to be essential to understanding and managing a successful outreach program. This chapter focuses on six major components of successful continuing education programs: academic environment; student services; communications and technology; facilities and support services; diplomatic relationships; and leadership and advocacy.

## ACADEMIC ENVIRONMENT

The academic environment represents the single most important component of continuing higher education programs. The principal responsibility for program quality, development, and renewal in institutions of higher education lies with the academic units on campus. The continuing education profession complements the academic unit by using its members as principal actors in the creation of new programming for outreach purposes. One of the most common mistakes continuing educators make is to design and implement programs without involving academic units that have a vested interest in the substance of the program. For example, a workshop entitled "Stress Management in the Office" may appear to be the prerogative of any of several academic units: psychology, business management, human development, or education. One department or a combination of several of these departments could potentially become the academic sponsors of the program.

Each college and university has specific approval procedures for courses and programs so that no department chair, dean, or academic vice-president should be bypassed. Yet, the communications process can be short-circuited in the programming of academic courses and workshops with disastrous results. For example, a private business corporation may request a continuing education unit to provide its employees with a customized course in computer graphics for academic credit. In his or her enthusiasm to respond, the continuing educator designs the course to the company's specifications and finds the necessary hardware, a convenient location, and a qualified adjunct faculty member to teach the course. Then, and only then, does the continuing educator go to the computer science department to share what has been accomplished and to request academic credit for the course. The department head, the computer graphics faculty member, and the departmental secretary who normally handles continuing education paperwork for the department have not been involved in the process of program development. The response is predictable.

The program development process for both credit and noncredit courses and programs must include basic guidelines to avoid serious administrative and protocol problems. First, personnel in the continuing education office must establish good working relationships with all academic units and departments on the campus. The most frequent communications will be with departments and individual instructors; however, the continuing educator must not forget that the dean's office exercises considerable control over programming through its budgetary power.

Second, the signature course approval process must be strictly followed. In many instances, four or five signatures are necessary— the department chair, the college dean, the faculty member, the continuing educator who plans the course or program, and the dean or director of the continuing education unit. Obviously, there are programs where this step is unnecessary, such as a brief program for a special group such as Boys State or a high school cheerleader camp, where only physical facilities are required. In such cases, formal academic approval is usually not necessary or desirable; a special contract approved by the institution's business office and legal counsel is more appropriate.

Third, it is necessary to define, formally and in writing, the basic instructional conditions and financial arrangements for courses and programs. This is not only good academic practice but also good business and is critical to the long-range success of any continuing education program.

Even when the guidelines for good programming are followed, conflicts may still arise. Usually, problems can be handled by the primary parties involved. However, at times, the dean of continuing education and other upper-level administrators may need to resolve a conflict if an agreement cannot be reached at the faculty level.

## STUDENT SERVICES

The typical continuing education student, as shown in most enrollment studies, is an adult who has family and/or job responsibilities, has experienced a prolonged absence from formal education, and is attending school part-time. Like their full-time counterparts, continuing education students need advising and counseling, financial assistance, career services, help with study skills, and registration information.

Student services for the adult, part-time student require the use of techniques and operational strategies different from those provided for traditional students. Advising and counseling for adult students must be available at times convenient to students who have work and family responsibilities. Advising may need to take place at a work site rather than on campus. Moreover, adult, part-time students often experience considerable anxiety when returning to formal educational programs; their advising process must include help with anxiety reduction and study skills and test-taking techniques. Finally, good advising of adult students includes information about appropriate on- and off-campus services.

Developing a basic financial aid program for the adult, part-time student is one of the major challenges facing today's professional continuing educator. To date, federal, state, and local governments have been slow to recognize the need and importance of providing financial assistance for adult, part-time students. Some public officials feel that adults have already been provided with a high school education and perhaps even a college education, so what more do they need? The reasons for more education are too numerous to mention; one only needs to refer to Cyril Houle's recent book, *Patterns of Learning*, in which he suggested that "the central conception of education in the future is likely to be that of lifelong learning."[1] Or, one could turn to Milton Stern's *Power and Conflict in Continuing Professional Education*[2] to learn of the global need for persons to continue to learn throughout their lifetime. The professional continuing educator must be well-informed and ready to convince federal, state, and local governments to fund financial assistance programs to serve the adult, part-time student.

The continuing educator must also work closely with campus financial officers. Some financial aid officers perceive the adult, part-time student as draining away valuable financial aid resources. Good planning and communication are necessary to prevent this attitude from taking hold if adult, part-time students are to participate in the institution's financial aid program.

Career planning services are also an important part of the continuing higher education program. Although many adults enroll in continuing education classes for job-related reasons, an equally large number of the adult client population are exploring career opportunities or considering career changes. For these students, good career information is invaluable; its availability may be critical to the success of the operation. Students are most likely to enroll in and pursue an educational program through an institution providing the career counseling services they need.

Assistance with study skills is also an integral part of the student services process. Because many adult students have high anxiety levels about their academic performance, they need assistance and assurance in developing study skills. The continuing educator must be prepared to offer assistance on time management, reading methods, note taking, and preparation for test taking.

Good student registration methods are critical because of the conditions under which the adult student usually returns to school. If the adult student is treated like a computer number or an eighteen-year-old student and is expected to spend hours in line or rushing from office to office, he or she is likely to give up and go home or find another institution with a better registration process. There are many registration requirements that all institutions necessarily impose on both traditional and nontraditional students, such as obtaining selected demographic information and information pertaining to prerequisites taken and courses desired. However, the continuing educator can develop alternative processes and procedures at various locations to facilitate registration for the forty-year-old homemaker with children at home or the unemployed carpenter in search of work who comes to register for evening classes after a busy day. Such procedures might include special evening registration periods, registration at shopping centers and work sites, phone-in and mail-in registration, and computerized registration systems. The attitudes of staff members who register adult students also affect the success of the process. If students are treated courteously and professionally, enrollments are likely to flourish and grow.

The student services component is extremely important to the success of the continuing education program. Student services should be provided by personnel specially trained and willing to work with the needs of the adult, part-time student.

## COMMUNICATIONS AND TECHNOLOGY

New technologies to meet the needs of students living in an information-oriented society are being developed at most institutions of higher education. A campus radio station and an audiovisual center are no longer sufficient to keep up with the technological demands of society. Computers; television services, from satellite broadcasting to closed circuit and cable; simulators; telephonics using educational telephone networks; and laser technology have become part of the campus scene.

But what does this mean to the continuing educator? It's a golden opportunity! If we live in an information society, as John Naisbitt,[3] Alvin Toffler,[4] and others have suggested, continuing educators who serve the adult, part-time student must design programming using new technologies.

To do this, the continuing educator must learn what technologies are available on campus and their potential uses. A campus-based cable television system is of no value to the adult, part-time student unless the continuing education programmer is aware of the system's uses. Several criteria will help the continuing educator select the right technology or process: (1) acceptability and convenience to the adult, part-time population; (2) potential for faculty acceptance; (3) costs to the continuing education unit; (4) complexity of the course or program content; and (5) availability of technology to the continuing education operation.[5]

Convenience to the adult student is critical. A majority of part-time, adult students have full-time responsibilities in the home, workplace, or both. Their time for viewing courses on television is limited by other activities. The use of computer labs or educational telephone networks has similar constraints. For example, if the campus television system can only be used for continuing education programs on Sunday between midnight and 5:00 A.M., or if the computer lab is only open to the adult, part-time student at 9:00 A.M. on Monday morning, problems arise. The solution is to approach administrators in the appropriate departments and request they develop more convenient schedules for the adult population.

Faculty members must also be considered. High-tech equipment and support systems are worthless if faculty members do not have a positive attitude toward the use of technology in the teaching process. Although most faculty members who instruct in continuing education programs accept new teaching techniques, they must have opportunities to learn how to incorporate new technologies into their classes. The responsibility for providing information to faculty members concerning the effectiveness of various types of technology in the educational process may fall on the professional continuing educator.

A classification of telecommunications technologies and their potential for instructional use may be derived by answering four questions:

1. *Function.* Is the technology used to transmit information, to stimulate student response, to motivate learning through other media, or to provide learners with feedback?

2. *Accessibility.* Is the technology available in most homes, like broadcast television and radio, or is it similar to point-to-point microwave television, only available at specially equipped facilities and, therefore, accessible only to those learners for whom the location is convenient?

3. *Intervention.* Is the technology like radio, which does not allow students to stop or repeat the presentation at their convenience, or is it like audiotape or correspondence, which does offer students such control?

4. *Interaction.* Can the students make comments or ask questions during the instructor's presentation, only at some later time, or not at all? Can faculty and students interact freely?

A classification of media on the basis of interrelated criteria is described in Table 4.1.

Once the decision to use electronic media to deliver instruction has been made, the continuing educator needs to organize an instructional "team." Each team consists of technical experts from the telecommunications/media center, academic experts—the faculty members—and continuing educators. The role and importance of each member of the team are clearly understood and valued. The faculty member is in charge of content. The media center is in charge of the technology. The continuing educator is in charge of student

TABLE 4.1. Classification of Media on the Basis of Interrelated Criteria.

| TECHNOLOGY | Function 1 | Student Accessibility 2 | Intervention 3 | Intervention Student Control 4 | Availability Difficulty COST |
|---|---|---|---|---|---|
| AUDIO<br>Radio<br>Radio (SCA)<br>Audiotape | Transmit information<br>Motivate | Home<br>Designated equipped sites<br>Cassette recorder | Immediate: NONE<br>Written correspondence student/faculty | OFF/ON (may tape for later use if equipped)<br>Able to replay if taped | Highly available<br>Easily produced<br>Low Cost |
| VIDEO<br>Broadcast TV<br>Cable TV (1-way)<br>Videotape<br>ITFS<br>Satellite (1-way)<br>Slow-scan | Transmit complex ideas, information<br>Illustrate<br>Demonstrate | Home<br>Home w/cable access<br>Specially equipped room<br>Specially equipped site | Immediate: NONE<br>Written correspondence student/faculty | OFF/ON (tape for later use if equipped)<br>Replay<br>Real Time (may tape for later use if equipped) | 98% of American homes<br>Expanding availability<br>High production costs |
| AUDIO<br>Telephone<br>Teleconference | Transmit information<br>Provide feedback<br>Stimulate discussion | Home and/or special rooms<br>Special rooms | Immediate student/faculty faculty/student student/student | Discussion/Interaction<br>Ask questions | Readily available<br>Easily implemented<br>Comparative low cost |
| VIDEO<br>Microwave<br>2-way Cable TV<br>2-way slow scan<br>Electronic blackboard<br>Video teleconference | | Specially equipped rooms | | OFF/ON<br>Ask questions<br>Tape for later use<br>Provide feedback<br>Discussion with illustration | Rarely available<br>Difficult to implement<br>Extremely high cost |

Source: "Innovation in Outreach: A Plan for Distance Education at the University of Wyoming" by Marcia Bankirer. Unpublished doctoral thesis, Feb. 1982. University of Wyoming—Laramie. Reprinted by permission.

services, marketing and advertising, registration print materials, and other matters pertaining to the nontechnical delivery of the program.

The academic freedom of the faculty member is extremely important, whether the team is designing a totally new course or adapting a package created by another institution or agency. Today, there is a proliferation of courses packaged for television and computer delivery, partially due to programming provided by the Annenberg Corporation for Public Broadcasting grants and the Adult Learning Service of the Public Broadcasting System. However, the continuing educator may face a "not invented here" attitude when trying to introduce such courses to the faculty. The instructional team can overcome these problems by comparing the cost of purchasing or leasing a program with the cost of producing the same program. In addition, the continuing educator can discuss ways to personalize the program to fit the needs of the faculty member, the curriculum, and the student.

When using existing programs or producing new ones, the media center provides expertise and creativity in the scheduling and delivery of instruction. Mutual understanding and communication between the faculty member, the media center, and the continuing educator is essential for success.

The delivery of instruction via electronic media poses special opportunities for the continuing educator. Because it is the job of the continuing educator to recruit students, methods of registration, advising, textbook procurement, and other services must be designed. It is not desirable to design instruction for individual home delivery if the only source for the text is on-campus or if registration can only be accomplished in the registrar's or continuing education office between 9:00 A.M. and 5:00 P.M. on weekdays.

The use of technology provides opportunities for reaching new populations of students or more effective and economical ways of reaching all students. However, to do this, the continuing educator must know what is available and how it works in the teaching-learning process and must communicate effectively with faculty members and administrators to secure needed delivery systems at appropriate times and under the right conditions. The capability of an institution to provide a system of technological communication throughout its service area should be integrated with the continuing education mission of the institution.

## FACILITIES AND SUPPORT SERVICES

Serving nontraditional students in nonconventional ways requires the availability and management of a variety of special facilities and services. The primary need for facilities includes classroom and laboratory space on- and off-campus during evening and weekend hours. Conference facilities may also require planning and coordination through the continuing education unit; regional offices or branch campuses may be the continuing educator's responsibility as well.

On-campus classrooms and laboratories are usually relatively easy to schedule through the registrar's office or facilities management office, but good communication is critical. Conflicts over the use of facilities generally focus on the cost of utilities and custodial services. However, if the institution personnel have expressed basic support for the mission of continuing education, the conflict can usually be resolved by effective articulation of the goals and outreach mission to the appropriate administrators involved in the utilization of facilities.

Scheduling off-campus space is often more of a challenge. First, the continuing educator must address the question of the best location, geographically and in terms of security. The adult, part-time student often cannot or may not wish to travel great distances to attend continuing education programs, so a convenient location is essential. Second, the condition of the facility is important. Good security, parking, lighting, accessibility, climate control, and classroom atmosphere are key ingredients for successful off-campus programs. Corporation executives will not want to attend a "tax institute" that offers spartan dormitory accommodations, meeting rooms that lack good acoustics and climate control, or where street traffic can be heard over the keynote speaker. The homemaker who wishes to attend an evening art course will not register if the class is scheduled at an elementary school that offers child-size desks or a parking area that is not well lighted. Continuing educators must also handle off-campus facility rental costs and contract negotiations. Public and private schools, military bases, religious institutions, community centers, business and industry meeting rooms, shopping centers, hospitals, county extension centers, federal government meeting rooms, and public libraries are all potentially good locations for off-campus programs.

Regional learning centers and branch campuses involve more complex planning and management. The continuing educator planning such a facility should analyze the demographics of its geographic service area over the short- and long-term. The central administration and governing board of the institution may need to be involved in the planning process. There seems to be a trend in continuing education to locate off-campus centers in "hot" areas of high enrollment before any formal planning takes place. When problems then develop, the question is invariably asked, "Why was this regional office established?" Spontaneous development of off-campus facilities may have positive short-term benefits such as large enrollments when the facility is first opened. However, the continuing educator should be aware of potential administrative and political problems that may arise, even when initial program needs are met, because the new off-campus center is located in a geographical area with minimum growth potential.

Continuing higher education, by its very nature, is an outreach program that provides lifelong educational opportunities to people who live and/or work in the geographic area served by the institution. For some institutions, the geographic area is defined by the city limits, while for other institutions, it includes a region or the entire state. Other colleges and universities serve students on a national or worldwide basis. Regardless of the area served, serious attention must be given by each institution to the business of facilities management. The facilities for large, expensive conferences and institutes, small noncredit courses, and graduate-level laboratory courses all need careful scrutiny from the continuing educator. Experience shows that continuing educators who underestimate or disregard the importance of facilities management soon notice loss of enrollments. Adult students will not tolerate poor facilities.

Support services, such as meeting room arrangements, coffee and food service, audiovisual equipment, and recreational activities, are all necessary elements in the facilities management process.

## DIPLOMATIC RELATIONSHIPS

The effective continuing education enterprise that survives the economic, academic, and political exigencies of the 1980s is one whose leadership is well-endowed with the diplomatic skills necessary to develop and maintain an intricate network of professional relationships. These relationships represent one of the most important aspects of the role of a continuing educator. The network generally consists of linkages among universities, state colleges, community colleges, professional associations, local, state, and federal agencies, and the private sector. Effective communication techniques are the key to developing a successful network.

For continuing educators associated with a major research university, the challenge may be to establish positive relationships with state and community colleges within the geographic territory served by all the institutions. Some continuing educators make a strategic mistake in thinking that the university is superior to all other institutions in their area and that communication with smaller institutions is unnecessary. Quite the contrary! The better the relationships between institutions, the more likely their continuing education programs are to succeed. Naturally, competition will exist between programs. However, where good professional relationships and networks exist, continuing educators refer programs and clients to one another.

Professional associations fall into two general categories for the continuing educator—those associated directly with continuing education and those associated with other disciplines or professions. The former category includes such organizations as the National University Continuing Education Association (NUCEA), the Association for Continuing Higher Education (ACHE), and the American Association for Adult and Continuing Education (AAACE).

In discussing professional associations outside the field of continuing education, Milton Stern[6] speaks of the "disorderly market" where many different professional associations compete for the right to provide continuing education programs for their members. Stern suggested that the marketplace is in a state of rapid flux that demands careful study and the development of a diplomatic network with such organizations on the part of professional continuing educators. Many collaborative continuing education programs result from this type of effort.

Federal, state, and local agencies are becoming increasingly important to the professional continuing educator. Whether the relationship involves in-service training for agency employees, conferences on campus to which agency employees are sent, or tuition and loan guarantees provided to continuing education operations by agencies, the connection is a natural one. Government agencies in every state offer a significant opportunity for continuing education programming. The military, U.S. Forest Service, Social Security Administration, and other federal, state, and local government agencies provide continuing education for employees and/or clients on an ongoing basis. However, these agencies will not always seek out the nearest college or university continuing education program. It is up to continuing educators in the area to develop the professional relationships that will lead to contracts for the provision of continuing education programs.

## LEADERSHIP AND ADVOCACY

It is necessary and important for continuing educators to provide the necessary leadership and to serve as the advocate for continuing education on the campus. A complex and somewhat unusual set of operations is involved in continuing education, and the implications provide a major challenge both internally and externally for colleges and universities. The growth and development of a continuing education program on a campus will depend upon the willing contributions of faculty and staff from the colleges and academic departments and the many service units of the institution. The continuing educator must therefore develop a network of policy and practical working arrangements to coordinate and facilitate contributions by the variety of resources available in the campuswide structure.

The continuing educator in the process of developing a successful program must first ascertain what values and mission are appropriate to continuing education at his or her institution. The statement of mission and values of the continuing education operation should include an articulated set of statements that provides direction and value-driven goals for the organization. The following mission and values statement was developed by the continuing education staff at a major university and can serve as an example of the type of goals statement that is the foundation of a continuing education program.

### "Forward University": Mission and Values

The mission of the Division of Continuing Education at "Forward University" is to serve the educational needs of citizens of the state, the region, and the nation. Our goal is to provide quality lifelong learning opportunities to adults of all ages. Success at achieving our goal depends upon a clear understanding of our professional and organizational values. We have identified a framework of beliefs that reflect what is desirable for the Division of Continuing Education from the standpoint of our mandate from the Legislature and our values as a staff. Our values include:

*Service.* We strive to give prompt, courteous, and professional assistance, to disseminate complete and accurate information, to exceed normal expectations in our advocacy role, and to research/respond to the educational needs of our clientele.

*Quality.* Quality is an important concept in all our undertakings. We evaluate our programs, procedures, and resources with an appreciation of, and a striving for, academic excellence.

*Action Orientation.* High expectations and timely response characterize our action orientation. Risk-taking is a recognized feature of a highly responsive organization, and the Division of Continuing Education balances the benefits of timely response and professional accountability when defining projects and goals.

*Integrity.* When representing our organization, we strive to be honest. We take pride in our educational advocacy role, our achievements in furthering the academic excellence of "Forward University," and our spirit of cooperation with other state universities.

*Leadership.* We take pride in providing educational leadership on many fronts. As a premiere continuing education provider in the state, we feel it is necessary to deliver exemplary services and programs for the University to the community, the state, the region, and the nation.

*Innovation.* We value personal, professional, and operational flexibility for providing a climate conducive to innovation.

*Self-Supporting.* Sound fiscal management is the basis for self-supporting financial health. We seek to maintain a record of high productivity and effective cost controls.

*Professional Growth.* Through analysis, projection, and planning, we provide resources for our staff to continue learning for the sake of personal enrichment, skills development, and career enhancement.[7]

To provide the leadership and to serve as the advocate for the continuing education organization, as described in the above example, continuing educators need to articulate their role, function, and values to the institution's central administration, academic colleges and departments, support services units, and significant other groups, both on- and off-campus.

Central administration linkages are critical to the success of an effective continuing education program, whether at a comprehensive land-grant university or a rural community college. Because most continuing education units are considered academic divisions of the institution, the continuing educator should develop and maintain close professional rapport with the chief academic officer and staff. The advantages from such a liaison are many. The chief academic officer can open doors to other vice-presidents and deans on campus, and the positive public image generated by continuing education programs can in turn benefit the entire institution. On the other hand, when this relationship is neglected, the continuing education unit can be reduced to second-class status. The continuing educator should attempt to establish an ongoing relationship with the president or chancellor of the institution only through the office of the chief academic officer.

Good articulation with academic departments on campus is essential to the survival of a continuing education operation because the principal responsibility for program quality lies with the academic unit. The continuing educator must develop and maintain good communication with collegiate deans, department heads, and key staff members. It is not only important to establish these relationships but also to work within the institutional policy framework for continuing education as it relates to academic deans who oversee the academic departments. There are situations where academic departments may wish to develop an outreach program with some degree of autonomy for academic and economic reasons and to keep the continuing education dean's office informed but not intricately involved. This type of arrangement may be permissible based on policy, or the lack thereof, for continuing education on a particular campus. If this is the case, the continuing educator must be sensitive and accommodate the situation as necessary.

Service units on campus support the continuing education programs. The registrar's office, financial aid office, counseling and advising, security police, food services, and physical plant are all necessary to the success of the program. Some continuing educators have learned the significance of support and service units the hard way, that is, when classrooms are locked at night, grades are not back from the registrar's office on time, or when the coffee service does not arrive at the conference facility by 10:00 A.M.! To avoid such unfortunate occurrences, the continuing educator must take time to develop and maintain good working relationships with these offices or delegate this responsibility to other professional staff members. It is also incumbent upon the continuing educator to inform support service staff of the importance of providing the appropriate services to participants in continuing education programs and the differences between the older adult, part-time student and the traditional-age, full-time student.

Campus groups associated with an institution can also play significant roles relative to the continuing education mission. These groups include student organizations, the institution's foundation (which may be separately chartered), research centers, the governing board, and the alumni association. Finally, legislative bodies, particularly education committees, are of genuine importance to all continuing educators. The continuing educator must take the initiative in searching out these groups and developing the necessary relationships to ensure that successful programs are created.

Continuing education includes a number of operations requiring cooperation from many units within the institution. Proactive leadership and good communication lead to positive relationships on campus that can make the continuing educator's job much easier. The bottom line: the professional continuing educator must be a zealous leader and advocate for continuing education not only off-campus but also right at home, on-campus.

## SUMMARY

Successful continuing education units are generally characterized by leaders who appreciate and understand the complexity and comprehensiveness of continuing education as an enterprise integral to the total institution. Such understanding includes a functional knowledge of the six major components of successful continuing higher education programs described throughout the chapter. An understanding of these components can assist the continuing educator to function more effectively in carrying out his or her responsibilities.

## REFERENCES

1. Houle, Cyril O., *Patterns of Learning* (San Francisco: Jossey-Bass, 1984), p. 223.
2. Stern, Milton R., ed., *Power and Conflict in Continuing Professional Education* (2nd ed.; Belmont, Calif.: Wadsworth, 1983).
3. Naisbitt, John, *Megatrends* (New York: Warner Books, 1982).
4. Toffler, Alvin. *The Third Wave* (New York: William Morrow, 1980).
5. Strother, George B., and Klus, John P., *Administration of Continuing Education* (Belmont, Calif.: Wadsworth, 1982), p. 95.
6. Stern, op. cit., p. 5.
7. Colorado State University, Division of Continuing Education, *Annual Report* (Fort Collins: Colorado State University, 1983–1984), p. 2.

# -5-

# ORGANIZATIONAL MODELS AND ELEMENTS OF AN EFFECTIVE ORGANIZATION

## Dennis P. Prisk

There are few right or wrong options in organizing continuing education at a college or university. Each institution is unique, and its character is generally reflected in the organizational pattern of its continuing education unit. However, some general guidelines may be helpful in organizing a continuing education unit.

The first issue to consider is the intrainstitutional matter of defining areas of jurisdiction between the continuing education unit and other collegiate units. There has been a great deal of discussion regarding the question of "centralization versus decentralization" during the last several years. In a centralized model, the major responsibility for continuing education is contained in one office; in a decentralized model, individual academic units on campus are responsible for the delivery of continuing education programs in their area of interest. The size of the institution (FTE), type (public or private), and geographical location (rural, urban, or suburban) are some of the factors that influence the degree to which a continuing education unit is centralized or decentralized. Most continuing educators, however, could probably agree that the question is not whether their continuing education unit is at one extreme or the other. Rather, the issue is where between these two points on a continuum a continuing education unit is located and on what basis continuing education programs and services are developed, administered, and delivered.

The relative advantages and disadvantages of centralized and decentralized models of continuing education programs and services can be summarized as follows:

### Relative Advantages of Centralization

- Broad service to an institution's constituencies
- Broad use of delivery systems
- Provision of fiscal support for wide range of programs and services
- Consolidation of support services
- Cost-effective
- Consistent application of institutional policies and procedures
- Broad resource utilization
- Wide use of interdisciplinary programs
- Provision of leadership and advocacy for the adult learner and continuing education
- Standardized institutional goals/objectives for continuing education
- Greater response flexibility
- Nonduplication of client contracts
- Provision for consistent public relations
- Broad implementation of the institution's public service mission

### Relative Disadvantages of Centralization

- Separation of continuing education from collegiate units
- Less inclination of faculty to participate
- Overdependence on few individuals
- Less likelihood of collegiate administrators to participate
- Collegiate units may not perceive continuing education as part of their mission

### Relative Advantages of Decentralization

- Continuing education philosophy more fully embraced by collegiate unit
- Greater willingness of faculty to participate
- Individual finances handled by college units
- Continuing education an integral part of collegiate unit

- Greater interest shown by collegiate administrators in continuing education
- Greater flexibility at department level
- Responsibility for results placed on collegiate unit
- Collegiate resources focused on programs in their disciplines

### Relative Disadvantages of Decentralization
- Educational needs of some segments of society not met
- Range of programs offered limited
- Total institution may not benefit financially
- Duplication of support services, staff, equipment
- Limited use of regular and adjunct faculty
- More difficult to determine institutional direction for continuing education
- Inconsistent policy planning and application
- Greater difficulty in maintaining institutional resource allocations

Differences in the two models exist in the decision-making process as it relates to the application of basic philosophy in program delivery, financial accountability, utilization of support services, and development of interdisciplinary programs.

It is important to note that there are few pure centralized or decentralized models. It should also be noted that exceptions to the relative advantages and disadvantages of each item can be found depending upon the specific organizational structure, philosophy, and goals and objectives of continuing education at individual institutions.

The important question when addressing the issue of how to organize continuing education is not centralization versus decentralization per se. The critical question should be how to provide an organizational structure in which continuing education, both conceptually and operationally, can function most successfully, consistent with the institution's role and mission and its goals and objectives. The intent should be to avoid a highly centralized continuing education unit that functions marginally to the rest of the institution, or a highly decentralized continuing education program that allows for an inconsistent and ineffective institutional outreach effort.

Perhaps the best approach is to utilize advantages from both models by having the administrative function for continuing education assigned to a clearly identified continuing education unit and at the same time integrate responsibility for program development, quality control, evaluation, and faculty participation within the academic system. This approach to organizing continuing education has the effect of centralizing the administrative function while decentralizing the academic function. Irrespective of the organizational structure established, it is imperative that the role and mission of a continuing education unit and its relationship to other collegiate units be clearly identified.

A study conducted by the Association of Continuing Higher Education (ACHE) revealed a near equal number of centralized and decentralized continuing education units. However, the data indicated that the larger the institution, the more likely it was to be decentralized.[1] Interestingly, in the National University Continuing Education's (NUCEA) 1982–1983 survey, personnel at 71 percent of the participating institutions indicated that responsibility for continuing education had not shifted significantly during the last three to four years. Moreover, almost 87 percent of the institutions indicated that in the next five years there will be no significant shifts in continuing education responsibility to academic colleges and schools.[2]

A review of more than 100 organizational charts and a discussion of organizational patterns with other continuing educators did not yield any ideal organization for continuing education management. It appears the continuing education administrative structures at many colleges and universities had no particular rationale and were simply determined by the chief academic officer. Studies conducted during the past twelve years have consistently revealed the following most common characteristics in a continuing education organization: (1) the most frequent name of a unit is the Division of Continuing Education; (2) the chief continuing education administrator reports to an academic vice-president; (3) the title of the continuing education administrator is dean; (4) the unit is financially self-supporting; (5) administrative functions include registration services, marketing, and budgeting; and (6) program activities almost always include noncredit courses and other activities. The responsibility for summer sessions, evening credit courses, extension courses (off-campus credit), and telecommunications is distributed in a variety of ways from school to school.

There are a variety of organizational models within continuing education units that may include departments based on delivery system type or subject area. For example, delivery system subunits may include: conferences and institutes, short courses, workshops and seminars, off-campus (extension) credit courses, television, and independent study by correspondence. In other models, the subunits may be organized on the basis of subject areas, such as: business and management, professional development, engineering, education, and health sciences.

Some institutions have adopted other models. For example, an office of business and industry within the continuing education unit may have responsibility for all credit and noncredit programs related to that discipline. This is different than utilizing a separate office of conferences and institutes to manage noncredit courses and an extension office to coordinate all credit courses offered on a nontraditional basis. In this model, it is assumed the staff of the office of business and industry can discuss with faculty members various program options. These options include format (conferences or evening noncredit short courses), time, location, and whether offerings should be credit, noncredit, or optional. This model also mitigates the need for a separate summer school office, since the programs can presumably be held any time during the calendar or fiscal year. The same model could work for engineering, allied health sciences, and other professions. This structure has the advantage of more efficiently utilizing resources and minimizes confusion over what is a conference as opposed to a workshop. It also provides the academic college or school one office in continuing education with which to work. Specialized delivery systems, such as independent study by correspondence or telecommunications, can still exist within these hybrid models. Moreover, support services such as marketing and promotion, registration, recordkeeping, and budgeting will, to a large extent, remain as separate offices within the continuing education unit. A continual reshaping of the program units will achieve a higher level of efficiency and effectiveness.

## ELEMENTS OF AN EFFECTIVE ORGANIZATION

### HUMAN RELATIONS

Administrators in continuing education are in the "people business." As a result they need to consider the human dimension within their administrative units and spend time nurturing those with whom they work.

In *The 100 Best Companies to Work for in America*, it was suggested that making the employee feel his or her contribution to the company is important is essential to good personnel relations and performance. For these companies, the traditional, manipulative employer-employee (we-they) relationship is replaced by a "we are all in it together" spirit. It was further suggested by the authors that "this unwritten pact among employees often begins with one or more key individuals who genuinely care about the quality of the experience of everyone in the company."[3] This type of management philosophy can be used successfully in public institutions, for example, in continuing education units. Developing and maintaining favorable working conditions is increasingly important in the management of an effective continuing education organization.

## POLITICS

Continuing education administrators have had to develop a refined sense of political savvy as a matter of survival. There is a voluntary relationship between many continuing education units and the schools and colleges within their institution. The role of politician does not come easily to many in continuing education; however, because continuing education administrators often negotiate this relationship with other campus administrators on a daily basis, their political skills need to be finely tuned.

The political control of continuing education on campuses is likely to remain a problem in the foreseeable future. In 1976, when the issue of centralization versus decentralization seemed to reach national epidemic proportions, Milton Stern, dean of Continuing Education at the University of California in Berkeley, suggested that administrators review their own programs to see what they "can use to serendipitous political effect institutionally."[4] Peter Drucker, professor of social science at Claremont (California) Graduate School, writing in *Managing in Turbulent Times,* agreed that it is sensible to know and understand politicians and to be known by them. However, he also suggested that a manager must be active, not reactive. "The new manager . . . will be effective only if he ceases to see himself—and to be seen—as representing a 'special interest.' "[5] Out of necessity, continuing education administrators have lobbied for their own cause. Continuing education administrators in the future will need to represent the good of the institution and aid their own unit in the process.

Judith Diamondstone, of the Philadelphia College of Textiles and Science, wrote, "Skillful political behavior in many situations can influence and change the organizational structure as well as create pressure to define the mission better."[6] The more consummate their skills as politicians, the more successful continuing education administrators will be in solidifying and maintaining continuing education's base, as well as bringing about change when appropriate.

## DECISION MAKING

Other elements found in effective organizations are identified in *In Search of Excellence,* by Thomas J. Peters and Robert H. Waterman.

These elements include a decision-making process that requires a minimum amount of time to analyze the issue before action can be taken and the willingness to take risks. Colleges and universities are often bogged down in bureaucracy. Continuing education units, while sometimes trapped in this milieu, have often been able to move more quickly, particularly in the noncredit area. Effective continuing education programs should operate on what Peters and Waterman called a "Do it, fix it, try it" philosophy.[7]

It will be increasingly important in the future for continuing educators to reward creativity which involves risk taking. Inevitably there will be false starts, but continuing educators must be willing to take risks—to offer "loss leaders" to test the market. The willingness to fund such risks, which is referred to later in the chapter, is equally important.

## LEADERSHIP

None of the previously discussed elements mean much without leadership, especially a type of leadership appropriate to the times. Stanley Davis of Boston University's School of Management suggested that leaders in our society are using the wrong models for managing most corporations and organizations. While we have a postindustrial, service-based economy, all the managing models in use were developed in, by, and for industrial organizations. As corporate managers seek to change patterns of management, continuing educators will need to consider these new models.

Consonant with the new models will be a new style of management. Industrial organizations were defined by their structure—discrete boxes on an organizational chart. However, Peters and Waterman suggested that too much structure can be a liability in today's fluid and changing environment. One characteristic, then, of tomorrow's leader is the ability to manage *change*. Those who resist change are stagnating because they risk growth. It has been suggested that growth, and by implication change, consists of three steps:

1. Ending—an ending is not always recognized when it occurs. It can be a period of "disidentification," of becoming unglued, disoriented, and even disenchanted.

2. A neutral time—neither yesterday nor tomorrow, a time of transition. A bit empty in tone and feeling, a time to perceive a new reality.

3. Beginning—a time when there is an emerging glimmer or image of the new reality which is strong enough to become a goal.[8]

The future administrator will need to understand and manage the process of growth and change. Because they are more involved with strategy than their predecessors, future administrators will find decision making on matters of daily operation to be less critical. Thus, the leadership role is a searching one. Continuing education administrators often discover that nothing is more valuable than possessing the capacity to back away and gain a fresh perspective—to recognize that beginnings follow endings.

While experts may differ as to which leadership style is most effective, one that is receiving much attention is the *situational* approach. Administrators who use this approach have a keen grasp of their employees' needs and abilities, a strong sense of the organization's direction, and are secure in their abilities. Tomorrow's administrator may not be highly skilled in the assumed traditional areas of competency, such as, marketing, budgeting, and program development. Rather, the new continuing education administrator will serve as a facilitator and consultant to the staff. Increasingly, the continuing education administrator of the future will be expected to articulately and coherently represent his or her organization to critics and supporters alike; he or she will be more sensitive to public opinion and respectful of the public or private organization of which he or she is a part.

## NETWORKING

The leader will need to make use of new structures when using a situational management approach. One such structure is the *network*. Networks are organizations that share information informally through such communication channels as telephone calls, letters, newsletters, and computers. Networks often arise out of a specific situation or event; they may be formed and dissolved spontaneously.

Essentially, networks cut against the grain of the bureaucratic structure. The bureaucracy is hierarchical, monopolistic, and competitive; it is based on an assumption that the world is atomistic and can be separated into mutually exclusive categories. The network is nonhierarchical, mutualistic, and cooperative; the premise is that the world is holistic and there are no parts, only a whole. Walls are built in bureaucracies while gates are constructed in networks.[9]

The leader of a continuing education program may be involved in several networks at several levels simultaneously. These networks may be external or internal, but both can help the administrator take advantage of new markets and improved communications. Externally, for example, administrators in Florida and Oregon (who are not in direct competition with each other) can share the successes and failures they have had with new conferences or seminars. This allows both programs to be creative and innovative while eliminating unnecessary risk. Similarly, a continuing education administrator in Michigan can share information with an administrator in the College of Arts and Sciences at the same institution, enabling both to become more aware of advantageous potential program areas or political situations.

Networking can offer both solutions and problems to the administrator internally. A network that allows the administrator to respond flexibly and rapidly to change can be seen in a matrix that brings together individuals from separate subunits to solve a particular problem. At the same time, the leader of a hierarchy can be frustrated by networks. Knowledge is power and sometimes the authority of the leader can be dissipated by networks through the proliferation of information. This dilution can often prevent those in the continuing education program from speaking with one voice or can cause friction among different departments. Even considering the drawbacks, networks should, on the whole, be viewed positively by leaders of continuing education programs. Leaders are required to be creative, flexible, political, and swift in their approach to problems; these possibilities are offered the leader through networks.

## THE CONTINUING EDUCATION "CULTURE"

Since 1982 there have been a number of articles written on the subject of corporate "culture." One such article appeared in *Fortune* magazine entitled "Wanted: Corporate Leaders." The subtitle read, "Must have vision and ability to build corporate culture. Mere managers need not apply."[10] It is important for continuing education administrators to consider the culture of their organization; they should not be "mere managers." The way an organization is perceived by administrators and staff members in a continuing education unit is its culture. If the image of the culture is supportive of future growth, the results can be overwhelming. If, on the other hand, the culture's image is out-of-date due to lack of creativity, a belief that the past was best, or ignorance, the results can be highly unsatisfactory and the effect on planning can be disastrous. Recognition of the continuing education culture and its pervasiveness is a critical first step in the development of long-range strategies. Failure to do so can result in staff resistance to change. The continuing education administrator must have a vision of the future and be able to motivate his or her staff. If employees are proud of their employer and feel appreciated, they will perform their jobs more effectively. Alan Glou, a management consultant, indicated that the primary reason why good people leave organizations is that they do not feel valued or useful.[11]

## ENCOURAGING CREATIVITY

The virtue of *creativity* must not be underestimated. Conflict resolution, staff supervision, policy development, and team building are all important skills. However, they mean little if creativity is lacking in the organization.

Creativity does not always mean coming up with the newest, most innovative idea. It can mean applying an old idea to a new environment; it can mean challenging previously held assumptions. Creative thinking involves considering alternatives to a proposed solution and not rigidly demanding a "right" way of operating. To go outside the rules and link dissimilar ideas may result in totally new options. The management of ideas and the conscious effort to encourage thinking contribute to a creative, dynamic organization.

Like any effective leader, a continuing education administrator must find a way to generate ideas from his or her staff. It takes courage on the part of the employer and employee, since creativity can incur failure and rejection. Roger Von Oech, president of Creative Think in Palo Alto, said, "No doubt about it, new ideas are a risky business. If things didn't change, we wouldn't need ideas. But things do change, and without new ideas, the only alternatives are stagnation and mental rigidity." Administrators will find it imperative to create the type of environment where the growth of ideas will be nurtured.

## STRATEGIC PLANNING

Though many continuing educators plan their unit's activities, few can claim to engage in strategic planning. Strategic planning serves organizational needs in several ways: "Strategic planning includes all of the activities which lead to a development of a clear organizational mission, organizational objectives, and appropriate strategies to achieve the objectives for the entire organization."[12] The strategic planning process is illustrated in Figure 5.1.

The successful continuing education unit obtains information, develops a strategic plan, and allocates resources accordingly. Such a conceptual framework allows the plan to adapt to changing circumstances, and allows for more rational operational planning among the continuing education subunits—subunits that, by their essential human constitution, periodically produce the friction that impedes smooth implementation of the conceived "modus operandi."

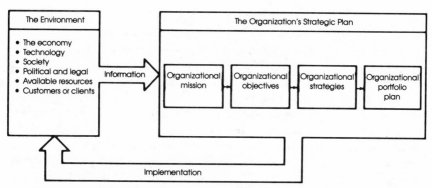

FIGURE 5.1. The Strategic Planning Process. From *Fundamentals of Management* by J. H. Donnelly, Jr., et al. Copyright 1981 by Business Publications, Inc. Reprinted by permission.

## IMPLEMENTING AN ORGANIZATIONAL PLAN

There are a number of strategies that can be used to implement an organizational plan for continuing education. The following plan makes some assumptions that, while generally true, will not apply to every institution. Adaptations of this plan can be made by considering the special circumstances found at each institution.

The first generalization is that continuing education operations have grown like randomly sown flowers rather than from a thoughtful basis. Until recently, there was a marked increase in the number of bureaus, centers, and institutes on college and university campuses. Many began as research or teaching projects; some were funded by contracts and grants. A large number were supported by general revenues. Eventually many began to offer conferences, workshops, and seminars, which compounded the difficulty of defining the role of continuing education. Public service, which is often assumed to be the responsibility of continuing education units, has not been clearly defined at many institutions. While some continuing education administrators discuss the disorderly market among external providers of continuing education, the market is no more coherent on campus.

Given this state of affairs, the second assumption is that there is a desire on the part of the college or university to change the form in which it offers continuing education programs. Without firm support from the administration, no strategy for change will succeed . In most cases the administration will be called upon to underscore its commitment to change with additional resources, including, but not limited to, new positions, additional equipment monies (some of which may be one-time allocations), and increases in operating funds.

Gaining *institutional support* for the reorganization of a continuing education unit is crucial. However, understanding the role of continuing education at an institution and proposing an organizational plan for its support is no assurance of success; there is no patented formula for gaining the organization's support. In a study conducted in 1978 by the Carnegie Council on Policy Studies in Higher Education, college and university presidents were asked, "In your judgment what are likely to be the most important issues facing American higher education between 1980 and the year 2000?" Continuing education programming was listed by only 7 percent of the respondents. Further, no president of the fifty leading universities sponsoring federally funded research for academic programs listed continuing education programs as a goal. While more comprehensive colleges and universities appeared to be more committed than other types of institutions, the total 7 percent response rate ($N$=163) was not encouraging.[13]

Nonetheless, once a determination is made by an institution to support its continuing education unit, the first step should be a clear and comprehensive definition of its *mission*. If such a mission statement exists, it should be updated. Whether the statement is updated or drafted, repositioning the continuing education division in its marketplace is of paramount importance.

Several steps are involved in mission definition or redefinition. Although it is difficult to say which is most important, perhaps the assessment of the *institution's image* should come first. This may mean addressing such questions as, "Is the institution known for research?" If so, is there an area of speciality? Is classroom teaching its major emphasis? Has the institution established a reputation for public service? Next, there should be an inventory of the continuing education unit's *liabilities and assets*. What are the unit's strongest program areas? What types of facilities are available? What is the level of quality at which the unit's services are delivered? What data base does the unit maintain to conduct market surveys? What is its funding base?

As important as it is to define the mission of the continuing education unit, it is equally important to state what it is not. For example, recognition of *program obsolescence* is often overlooked in continuing education. Further, continuing education administrators need to say no to campus administrators, faculty, and community leaders who expect the continuing education unit to be all things to all people and yet are unwilling to provide adequate resources. If the institution is attempting to manage limited resources more efficiently, so, too, must the continuing education unit. Administrators must determine how to make the most effective use of all continuing education resources—money, people, equipment, and facilities.

In the quest for faculty support of continuing education, the rhetoric regarding the quality of academic programs and values clarification has sometimes caused *auxiliary support services,* such as financial aids, admissions, and counseling, to be overlooked by the continuing education unit. To what extent are these services needed for the success of the continuing education unit's mission? Finally, the zeal that supporters of continuing education often feel and express will need to be minimized so the most rational, logical thinking can be devoted to mission definition.

Since form follows function, the next step in planning for change involves the *organizational structure.* To some extent, structural design will depend on the philosophy of the continuing education administrator; however, a number of fundamental questions remain. Will the support functions of the continuing education unit—budgeting, registration services, marketing—be centralized? That is, will there be an office for each of these functions that will provide services for the entire division? Will they be partially decentralized? Should the program units be given broad policy guidelines within which to operate and then be permitted to function somewhat autonomously? Will all new programs require the approval of the administrator or a program review board? In the course of reorganization, how will priorities be determined? For example, if a program position becomes vacant, will it be reassigned to another program office or administrative support area, such as registration? Rather than having separate program units controlling such areas as conferences and institutes, management development, and short courses, should they be merged to achieve a higher level of efficiency and effectiveness? Can the same program staff manage both credit and noncredit courses? Who will be involved in the process of reviewing organizational alternatives? The answers to these questions and others will assist the continuing education administrator in determining the most appropriate and effective organizational structure.

Then, once the organizational structure has been determined, an *appropriate staffing pattern* must be identified. Initially, a difficult task in any structural reorganization is assessing whether or not current continuing education unit staff members have the right skills for the new organization. Most likely, some staff members will need to be reassigned to other responsibilities within the unit. Job descriptions may need to be rewritten and new ones created. Some staff members may need to be relocated elsewhere within the institution. Such relocations, which affect careers and egos, will provide a test of the organization's support for change.

Undergirding all planning are the *policies and procedures* that are intrinsic to the organization, that is, how the tasks are accomplished and how they will be accomplished given a new organization and staffing pattern. Since this is the tangible bureaucratic part of the organization, the processes and forms should be kept simple and straightforward. Decisions in this area involve determination of the level at which continuing education policy can be changed, enforced, and interpreted. For example, if the registration procedures are performed manually and if automation is to occur, who will be responsible for converting the systems? Finally, whose responsibility is it to review periodically policies and procedures?

An example of institutional support in providing resources to accompany organizational change is the acquisition of microcomputers. Will the administration make available for example, one-time monies to purchase a sufficient amount of hardware to automate the administrative procedures?

Whatever choices the continuing education administrator makes in organization, staff alteration, and clarification of policies and procedures, the focus should be on fulfilling the mission of the continuing education unit and the institution it represents. Patricia Cross stated: "The planning for adult learners means thinking about new roles, new missions, and new relationships for higher education, as well as the needs and interests of the adult learners."[14]

A key to the continued success of continuing education is the development, implementation, and evaluation of a long-range planning process. It is one thing to articulate a set of five-year goals; it is quite another to update these plans annually, determine the degree to which they are achieved each year, and evaluate the effectiveness of the planning process.

Continuing education administrators in the future will need to be concerned with such terms as profit and cost centers, program mergers, per capita costs, advertising, management science models, information systems, market share, and strategic planning. They will need to be committed to professional development. Equally important, they will require training in sophisticated planning methods, resource allocation, decision making, and administrative and instructional uses of computers. They should also be expected to assume a pivotal role in linking their institutions of higher education to state agencies and corporations for assistance in economic development.

In short, continuing education will not escape the influence of profound societal, economic, and political pressures and changes that will affect higher education in the foreseeable future. As a result, continuing education administrators who are able to read the pressures and adapt to change will be able to serve their institutions with confidence and success.

## SUMMARY

The mission of the continuing education unit must be consistent with that of the institution of which it is a part. Due to a number of external and internal forces, institutions of higher education may have trouble defining their mission.

Although the issue of centralization versus decentralization is still valid, it is more important that a determination be made by a continuing education unit of its location on the continuum between these two points.

There are elements that contribute to a more effective organization, regardless of institutional philosophy. Strategic planning, an increased appreciation of the human dimension, a more astute understanding of policies, timely decision making, a willingness to take risks, and strong leadership will be required to develop a stronger continuing education unit.

Strategies for change can take several directions. One such process requires securing institutional commitment, defining (or redefining) the mission of continuing education, organizing to deliver that mission, determining an appropriate staffing pattern, reviewing policies and procedures, and initiating a long-range planning process.

## REFERENCES

1.  Prisk, Dennis P., "Organization of Continuing Higher Education," in *A Summary of Policies and Practices in Continuing Higher Education,* ed. Dennis P. Prisk (Knoxville, Tenn.: Association for Continuing Higher Education, 1982), p. 5.
2.  "1982–83, National University Continuing Education Association Survey of Member Institutions" (Photocopy).
3.  Levering, Robert, et al., *The 100 Best Companies to Work for in America* (Reading, Mass.: Addison-Wesley, 1984), p. x.
4.  Stern, Milton R., "The Politics of Continuing Professional Education," *Adult Leadership,* 25 (April 1977), p. 251.
5.  Drucker, Peter F., *Managing in Turbulent Times* (Cambridge, Mass.: Harper and Row, 1980), p. 217.
6.  Diamondstone, Judith M., "Organizational Structure and Mission Effectiveness: A Place for Continuing Education," *Continuing Higher Education,* 30 (Fall 1982), p. 8.

7. Peters, Thomas J., and Waterman, Robert H., *In Search of Excellence* (New York: Warner Books, 1982), p. 134.

8. *Future Scan,* Security Pacific National Bank—Futures Research Division, No. 257 (December 21, 1981), p. 1.

9. *Future Scan,* Security Pacific National Bank—Futures Research Division, No. 281 (June 14, 1982), p. 1.

10. Kiechel III, Walter, "Wanted: Corporate Leaders," *Fortune,* May 20, 1983, p. 135.

11. Glou, Alan, "Eight Reasons Why Good Employees Leave Jobs," *Resource Newsletter of the American Society for Personnel Administration,* November 1982, p. 6.

12. Donnelly, Jr., James H., et al., *Fundamentals of Management* (Plano, Tex.: Business Publications, 1981), p. 89.

13. Stadtman, Verne A., *Academic Adaptations* (San Francisco: Jossey-Bass, 1980), p. 175.

14. Cross, K. Patricia, "Continuing Higher Education in the 1980's," *Continuing Higher Education,* 31 (Winter 1983), p. 4.

# -6-

# ESTABLISHING A FINANCIAL STRUCTURE WITH EXTERNAL AND INTERNAL FUNDING SOURCES

## Harold A. Miller

The business of planning and presenting educational programs for adults in the 1980s is a complicated and challenging task. Such programs are high risk with severe competition from many sources. The management of a continuing education program in an institution of higher education is a peculiar hybrid: part education, part business, part politics, part financial counseling, and part fund-raising. Financial resources and techniques that can be used to gain support for continuing higher education are the focus of this chapter.

A variety of funding sources available for continuing higher education are discussed in the chapter. Sources external to colleges and universities, such as federal dollars available from many government departments and bureaus, state funding, grants from corporations and foundations, and donations from individuals, are discussed. Some of the potential contributions to continuing education that can be gained by having faculty members teach as part of load are outlined in the section on internal funding. In addition, tuition income and registration fees from credit courses and noncredit programs which serve as the basic financial resource for programming in continuing higher education are examined. Finally, a sample program budget, demonstrating how various funding sources can be combined, is presented.

# EXTERNAL FUNDING SOURCES

## FEDERAL FUNDING

There is a long history of federal funding for continuing education. The first incident of federal funding for continuing education occurred when the Continental Congress provided money for training soldiers in 1779.

Throughout the years there have been other occasions when the federal government has provided money for the education of adults when it has been in the national interest; defense, agriculture, vocational rehabilitation and education, citizenship, equal educational opportunity, literacy, and libraries are examples.

The modern basis for federal aid to postsecondary education took a new turn in 1862, when President Abraham Lincoln signed the first Morrill Act. With this legislation, the states were allowed by the federal government to sell certain federal lands and to invest the money in safe stocks ("yields not less than five per centum"). The income from these stocks would then "constitute a perpetual fund . . . to the endowment, support, and maintenance . . . of at least one college where the leading object shall be . . . to teach such branches of learning as are related to agriculture and the mechanic arts."[1]

In 1890 a second Morrill Act extended the provision of the first act to institutions "which did not thrive under the original Morrill Act endowment."[2] For the most part, these were public institutions, serving black students.

The Morrill Act had a major impact on the development of public higher education in the United States. The right of the state to educate its citizens was recognized by the Act. This was a particularly important concession from the federal government during the struggle between the Union and the Confederate states. But, the Morrill Act also began an important funding trend because it allowed the federal government to influence educational policy in the states through monetary grants.

After passage of the Hatch Act, which established agriculture research in 1887, and after expansion of the Morrill Act funding in 1890, Congress passed and Woodrow Wilson signed the Smith-Lever Act in 1914. A mechanism for funding an extension service to advance the findings of land-grant colleges and their agricultural research programs was created by the Smith-Lever Act. Under the terms of the Smith-Lever Act, each land-grant college would receive $10,000 (to be matched by the state), plus a supplement based on its rural population, for home economics and other extension work such as local agricultural demonstrations by county agents.[3] Because the dissemination of agricultural research findings was focused on the country's farmers, the Smith-Lever Act was the first and most extensive attempt by the federal government to fund college and university programs to educate adults. No other aid program provided to institutions for the continuing education of adults has been initiated on such a broad scale or sustained as long in the history of the United States.

In later years other efforts were made to convince the United States government to extend the provisions of the Smith-Lever Act to other fields. The short-lived State Technical Services Act of the 1960s was an effort to use universities for technology transfer. The strong efforts of general extension and continuing education deans and directors at colleges and universities to establish a parallel to the Smith-Lever Act for disciplines other than agriculture produced, in 1965, Title I for Community Service of the Higher Education Act.

Title I for Community Service of the Higher Education Act was a faint shadow of the Smith-Lever Act. Congress was unwilling to vest the responsibility for general extension in the land-grant colleges, or any other specific group of institutions, so it placed the responsibility for allocating Title I funds on state governments. This resulted in a competitive struggle for funds between postsecondary institutions. Although the authorization for Title I was established at $50 million, the appropriation in any year of its history never reached that amount. Nevertheless, Title I is an example of a recent commitment by the federal government to the education of adults through direct support to institutions.

In 1973 Congress passed the Comprehensive Employment Training Act (CETA) to fund the continuing education of some adults. CETA was funded at a relatively modest level to provide education and job training for unemployed or underemployed adults. It was replaced in 1983 by the Job Training Partnership Act, which provided for job training and employment opportunities for economically disadvantaged, unemployed, and underemployed people.

It seems clear that, with the exception of agricultural education, the federal government has not been inclined to assist the states in the education of their adult citizens.

VOUCHERS FOR INDIVIDUALS. A more interesting and lively history of federal aid to continuing higher education is seen in the way the federal government has provided funds to individuals. Perhaps the most significant individual aid program was the Serviceman's Readjustment Act of 1944 (the G.I. Bill).

Under the G.I. Bill, the veteran received money for education at approved institutions (public, private, and proprietary). After the veteran selected a school, the funds were sent to the individual who then paid for his or her education at the institution of choice. After World War II, thousands of older adults were educated through the G.I. Bill, and it changed, unalterably, the way the federal government approached funding for continuing education. Veteran's education programs have changed through the years. Currently a voucher system allows matching of personal funds with federal funds accumulated during service.

Another example of the shift toward individual aid is evident in the way the Internal Revenue Code allows adults who are improving their job skills to deduct education expenses from their net income.

These examples suggest that the federal government has changed its strategy for funding the continuing education of adults. Whereas it was once thought best to fund continuing education for adults by endowing colleges and universities, the wide array of postsecondary institutions now leads the federal government to encourage the education of adults by sending funds directly to the student who then buys the education he or she desires.

There is, however, still a great diversity in the way the federal government provides aid to adult students. For example, in 1973 the National Advisory Council on Extension and Continuing Education reviewed the federal government's domestic programs to determine the number and amounts of funding devoted to continuing education. According to the Advisory Committee report, $2.6 billion was spent in 208 programs for the continuing education of adults in a variety of ways—from individual grants to subcontracts and categorized aid grants to institutions.[4] A later review, conducted by the College Board in 1976, showed 270 such programs.[5] These reports illustrate the variation that exists in federal funding for continuing higher education.

It was further noted by the Advisory Council that the federal government did not have a coherent approach for funding continuing higher education. Authors of the report charged that the federal government had complicated the higher education picture by creating "categorized programs of narrow and specialized purpose,"[6] which led to the establishment of "miniextension units" in higher education institutions rather than using the network available through the continuing education extension units already in existence on many campuses.

CONTINUING HIGHER EDUCATION ON THE WASHINGTON SCENE. There are a number of national associations that support continuing higher education. Several of these associations maintain Washington offices to enhance their relationship and impact on other educational associations and on government agencies. Most of these associations are housed in or near the national Center for Higher Education at One Dupont Circle. Many cooperative efforts are encouraged by the proximity of these offices. For example, personnel in the governmental relations office of the American Council on Education frequently join with their counterparts in other higher education associations to discuss upcoming legislation and devise strategy. Issues pertaining to continuing higher education are discussed and staff members of the National University Continuing Education Association (NUCEA) and others are given an opportunity to take the leadership in setting goals and coordinating action on the Hill.

There are many, sometimes competing, forces in the higher education community. One illustration is the effort by NUCEA to stimulate a lobbying initiative for aid to part-time students that faces opposition from those who fear such an effort would diminish aid to full-time students. Thus, it is sometimes difficult to achieve a consensus among the higher education lobby in Washington.

How valuable is consensus among the various higher education associations? Repeatedly, members of Congress have advised representatives of higher education that consensus is important for the passage of legislation and appropriations to support legislation. While the combined efforts of the higher education associations have improved efforts to achieve consensus, it is, however, possible that the higher education community will focus its political efforts on gaining consensus to the detriment of some of its own constituents.

As one reviews the history of funding of the continuing education of adults, it is evident that the Congress has responded to many education constituencies, including farmers, veterans, organized labor, low-income groups, small businesses, and state and local governments. While members of Congress call for consensus, they authorize and appropriate bills that serve their constituent groups. As an example, education is one of a number of needs of farmers in the United States. As farmers represent votes—certainly more votes than deans of agriculture—bills that provide education for the farmer are passed and funded.

It is a peculiar paradox that so many constituencies are served by continuing higher education but the political support of so few is gained. Within the higher education community, continuing education is frequently identified as a marginal activity in relation to its traditional constituency, which has proven to be a notoriously weak voting bloc—namely, 18- to 22-year-old students. Therefore, it seems reasonable to suggest that continuing educators in higher education should seek to align themselves with the national constituent groups they serve, since many such groups have lobbyists in Washington who could be helpful in urging Congress to act on behalf of their constituents.

Another source of federal funds is suggested in the 1973 report of the National Advisory Council on Extension and Continuing Education. Because federal funds spent on continuing education are spread over 200 federal agencies, there are many opportunities to apply for funds. It takes some creative thought to design programs to use these funds while maintaining the institution's integrity and special focus. Furthermore, not every federal education program will fit the institution. But the continuing education unit within a college or university can often devise innovative and imaginative programs that meet federal program guidelines and that enhance the institution's educational impact in the community.

## STATE FUNDING

There is wide variation from state to state in the level of support given to continuing higher education. In many states credit instruction offered to adults in degree programs is funded at state-supported institutions at the same or similar levels as that given to younger students. In a few states, credit courses offered through continuing education units receive less than equivalent state funding. Generally, noncredit instruction, other than in agriculture, does not receive state support. A comprehensive survey of what funding is available to support continuing higher education in the various states would be useful. To that end, a study of the status of the state role in lifelong learning was conducted in 1982, under the auspices of the Education Commission of the States (ECS). Funded by the Kellogg Foundation, the status of adult education is six pilot states was carefully examined by the Lifelong Learning Project. Twenty-seven other "associate states" also participated in the study; in all, thirty-three states were examined in the comprehensive study. The Lifelong Learning Project was more than a survey, however. The preface to the study stated it was designed to be an action project to stimulate states in the planning for and development of public policies that favored the extension of adult learning services, including an analysis of funding alternatives.

APPROACHES TO STATE FINANCING FOR CONTINUING HIGHER EDUCATION. In a paper prepared for the ECS Lifelong Learning Project, "Financing Adult Learning: Spotlight on the States," Norman D. Kurland, Robert L. Purga, and William J. Hilton provided a comprehensive approach to the assessment of current funding of adult learning and a thoughtful look at the question of the state role for financing adult learning.[7] Based on the responses of the six pilot states and the twenty-seven other states participating in the project, the authors outlined five positions taken by states that finance adult learning, which follow.

*Laissez-faire.* A number of states take this position and have little or no specifically stated policy for dealing with financing the educational needs of adults. The theory is that the supply of educational services is sufficient for the demand.

*Federal retrenchment.* A policymaker who takes this position recognizes that "the total resources to the state are being drastically cut . . . hence . . . education, including education for adults, must take its share of the cuts."[8] A variation of this position came with the establishment of block grants to the states. As federal funds are cut and lumped together into block grants, continuing higher education must compete with other agencies at the state level to secure funds.

*Voluntary and forced retrenchment.* This position is best described in the example of the state that, when resources were plentiful, permitted funding for the education of adults to grow along with educational expansion for youth. However, as times became more difficult, the institutions were asked to reduce the commitment "to adult learning services that produce no clear public benefits."[9]

The most notable example of forced retrenchment can be seen in the state of California. When Proposition 13 was passed in a general referendum, tax cuts were mandated that had a major impact on education. Many community colleges, for example, had offered continuing education courses that were primarily underwritten by state funds. When these funds were lost, the community college system had to make substantial cuts in these programs.

*Decentralized control of funding.* Kurland and his associates use the term "decentralized control of funding"[10] to describe states that have a desire to increase state funds to meet the educational needs of adults but do not have the means or the desire to control, at the state level, the way institutions spend the funds. This approach suggests state advocacy for continuing higher education but the provision of only general guidelines to institutions and agencies with its allocations.

*Centralized control of funding.* This arrangement places the state in the position of "coordinating how adult learning is delivered and financed to assure that limited state resources are used efficiently and effectively, and that learning needs of underserved adults are met."[11] Such an approach, it is argued, discourages duplication and wasteful competition among institutions.

The continuing higher education administrator whose state government takes seriously its responsibility to educate older adults and provides funding for appropriate programs is fortunate. But no one wishes simply to ride the tides of fortune. Suggestions for organizing national constituent support for continuing higher education policies and funding initiatives apply at the state level as well. In fact, such efforts are more likely to prove fruitful at the state level than at the national level. For example, during a recent period of state income shortfall, personnel at one university targeted the firefighters' continuing education program for retrenchment. Many other programs were cut but none had such a dramatic effect. The state firefighters' association sent a strong message to state legislators. The legislators then urged the university to reconsider its decision and the university complied.

The continued success of the Cooperative Extension Service in most states is an excellent example of how a constituency can be organized to help a college or university achieve funding goals. In several states, representatives from the Cooperative Extension Service, the Agricultural Experiment Stations, and affiliated colleges conduct information sessions in each of the state's senatorial districts before the beginning of the legislative session. Inviting state senators, county commissioners, and other key citizens to a local meeting to discuss the university's budget is very effective. Rarely are these budget requests defeated in the state legislatures. Indeed, the internal university priority-setting process may be a greater hazard for such programs than state legislatures. It is important for leaders of continuing education programs to urge state policymakers to analyze the need for adult learning through programs in continuing higher education by studying current funding of adult learning opportunities and the relevant public benefit of such programs. Conducting such an analysis would also be helpful to continuing educators as they seek to influence policymakers in their states.

As the provisions of federal funding are viewed by educational leaders, gaps will be found that states must address. For example, in Minnesota, a state legislator learned that Pell Grants provided funds only for those pursuing degree credits at the half-time level or more. After several discussions with University of Minnesota continuing education/extension staff members and others, the legislator sponsored legislation that provided state funds to help students taking less than a half-time load. The bill passed and was funded. Funding for the first few years was modest. However, the 1985 legislature voted to increase the funding significantly. This example illustrates the value of keeping state officials informed about the effects of federal cuts and funding policies.

However, unless an analysis of the current funding situation is combined with a clear and compelling explanation of the public benefits to be derived from continuing higher education, success in the legislatures will be limited. As long as the benefits from a learning activity are purely personal, no claim can be made for public funds. Kurland and associates described a relatively simple but useful process for evaluating the public benefits from lifelong learning. They suggest it is possible to assign rank order or relative values according to the different mix of public and private benefits.[12]

Continuing educators should take the initiative and urge state postsecondary coordinating agencies and government leaders to analyze carefully their states' support for continuing higher education in relation to current funding levels and the public benefits to be derived from such programs.

## PRIVATE FUNDING

For years one of the most consistent supporters of continuing higher education has been private industry. Recent studies of continuing higher education students at the University of Minnesota revealed that nearly 75 percent of noncredit conference participants had their registration fees paid by their employers, and that 22 percent of the 35,000 annual credit class registrants had their tuition reimbursed by their employers. A discussion with personnel officers from seven major Minneapolis-St. Paul area employers and state personnel office representatives revealed that, without exception, the reimbursement policies of the state and the companies were liberal enough to pay employees for virtually any course that moved them toward baccalaureate degrees. Master's degrees were slightly more carefully monitored, with company officials generally directing their employees in Master's of Business Administration and Master's of Public Administration programs or other degrees directly related to their work.

On a national basis, a substantial proportion of continuing education student tuitions are reimbursed by private industry. The 1981 *Current Population Survey* carried out by the Bureau of Census includes a survey of participation in adult education every three years. One individual in each 58,000 American households is the focus of the survey, and the individual is asked if any courses were taken, why they were taken, and who paid the tuition. The results of the survey indicated that 21 million adults took 37 million courses and that employers paid for approximately 12 million of those courses. Of the 12 million courses, more than 9 million were provided by the employer, and approximately 3 million were offered by educational institutions and others. Professor Ernest Lynton of the University of Massachusetts in his book, *The Missing Connection Between Business and the Universities,* suggests that these results indicate the potential of employer support for adult education at one-third of the total courses taken and for continuing education programs from colleges and universities at less than 10 percent.[13] Lynton further estimated that direct expenditures for employee education were in the range of $20 to $40 million per year.[14] Clearly, the potential for corporate support of continuing higher education is enormous. Requests for increased state and federal funding to support continuing higher education must not diminish the importance of corporation support for continuing education programs by colleges and universities.

There are cases where corporations contribute directly to continuing higher education projects. This happens when the project either directly benefits the corporation or, to a lesser extent, when there is a perceived *pro bono publico* purpose to the project. When a degree program for engineers, for example, is offered by the university to employees, there is ample reason for it to be supported by the employer at full cost; however, there is no special reason to fund a university to offer noncredit programs that are readily available from other sources. It is important to remember that the incentive for corporate support of a college- or university-sponsored educational program is greatest when the program represents an otherwise scarce resource for the corporation.

FOUNDATIONS. An effort to raise money to offer courses for low-income persons or to provide start-up costs for less profitable ventures will be most successful through foundation funding. Again, as it is hard to identify long-term corporate funding, it is unusual to find foundations with enthusiasm for long-term commitments of any kind. But partnerships with colleges and universities are frequent, with the foundation providing start-up money and the institution promising to try to find other money, either from internal or external sources once the foundation money runs out. There are many examples of the success of this approach. Carnegie Foundation grants to women's programs not only initiated long-term programs at institutions that received the grants but stimulated the growth of successful women's programs at other institutions which have continued long after the start-up funds ran out.

A notable example of a foundation with a long-term commitment to continuing higher education is the Kellogg Foundation. No foundation in America has been more generous in its efforts to advance the interests of continuing higher education. The Kellogg Foundation has provided the funds for a number of residential conference centers at colleges and universities for the purpose of conducting continuing education programs and activities. The Kellogg Foundation has contributed a great deal to continuing education in the health sciences and has funded many programs and important experiments in the field of adult and continuing education. The Foundation's investment in the expansion of continuing education efforts at the University of Georgia stimulated a state match of over $5 million. More than any other foundation, the Kellogg Foundation has helped universities to reach out and meet community needs, both within and outside the boundaries of the United States. The Kellogg Foundation has also made funds available to the National University Continuing Education Association (NUCEA) to encourage the development of new leaders in continuing higher education.

INDIVIDUALS. Perhaps the greatest untapped funding resource for continuing higher education is in its own individual constituents. Many retirees greatly appreciate what their college or university has done for them or for their children. After they have assured a secure financial future for their families, they want to contribute to a worthy cause—"to perpetuate their value system," as one development professional stated. These people are looking for a cause and a program that they would be proud to support. There is no doubt that many continuing higher education programs can meet these criteria. Matching the program with the person takes some effort and know-how. Continuing higher education administrators who are discouraged by their low financial priority on campus, who are worn out from dealing with unsupportive state legislative committees, and who are tired of hearing they have brought the wrong package to the wrong foundation may find dealing with private individuals a more pleasant and profitable experience.

The continuing education organizations in a few institutions are concentrating on development through individual funding. North Carolina State, for example, built its Center for Continuing Education largely with private donations. Florida State University has an active continuing education development program, and the University of Minnesota has a development office in Continuing Education and Extension.

A touching, if not typical, story comes from the University of Minnesota. The school received a $1,000 check from a retired gentleman. In the 1920s he came to Minnesota from Germany and worked in the streetcar garage of the Twin City Lines. One day he saw a placard in one of the cars which said, "Improve youself—take an evening course at the University!" He enrolled in the course, took another, and then another. After two years of part-time study, he enrolled full-time and finished a degree. He taught German at another university, retiring after forty years in the classroom. He remembered the school that gave him his start and wrote, "Thank you." There are millions of others who would, if asked, give in support of continuing higher education.

## INTERNAL FUNDING SOURCES

### INSTITUTIONAL FUNDING STRATEGIES

Sources of funding outside the university have been the focus of this chapter. Federal, state, corporate, foundation, and other private donors offer some promise of help to the institution that seeks to serve the needs of adult learners. However, participants are by far the largest single source of funding for nonagricultural continuing higher education programs, and continuing education units on many campuses are often operated as profit centers. This situation is unlikely to change in the years ahead. Thus, it is important to focus on internal strategies that can provide funding.

It is the primary responsibility of the leaders of a continuing education program at an institution to determine the major program emphasis for their college or university. That decision should be made, not in the context of what programs will produce the best income, but on the basis of community needs and the appropriateness of the institution to respond to identified needs in its geographic service area. After the institutional direction is established by a process of market research and internal consultation, the dean or director of the continuing education program can then address the question of how programs are to be funded. Once it is clear what is expected by the institution from the continuing education program in relation to community needs, the leaders of the continuing education unit can develop a plan to fund the program.

An unfortunate if not crucial failure often occurs at this stage. Institutional officials may decide that a continuing education program should support itself. Unfortunately, that decision may rule out the kind of planning that could provide the best quality program. As entrepreneurial as the continuing education organization might be and as creative and energetic as the leaders may be, the necessity for the program to support itself could eliminate important programming that should be offered in the institution's service area. For example, research conducted at the institution that should be shared with the public might not be disseminated unless funds are available to develop a continuing education activity for that purpose.

The establishment of a division, school, or college of continuing education at an institution is often done on the basis that the operation will be self-supporting and that profits made by some programs will finance other programs unable to recover their costs. This approach introduces the "Robin Hood" philosophy: take from the richer clients and give to the worthy poor. Some institutions have effectively used this approach, allowing the continuing education unit to develop several levels of pricing. For example, A-level programs are of high institutional priority and are not expected to be self-supporting, and both direct and indirect costs are subsidized; B-level courses are also of high institutional priority and are expected to pay direct expenses, but the indirect costs are absorbed; C-level courses pay for both direct and indirect costs; and D-level courses pay all costs as well as subsidizing A- and B-level courses.

This method is familiar to most deans and directors of continuing education. It has weaknesses, however. With intense competition for the clients who can pay for the D-level courses, it is increasingly difficult to charge high enough prices for these courses to cover other offerings. This is particularly true when clients participate in the planning process, at which time there are continual pressures to reduce costs and keep prices competitive. Faculty members frequently do not help in these situations because they generally offer their services to the highest bidder, whether it be a continuing education unit on their campus or a professional association or other organizations. Another weakness of the "Robin Hood" method is that it requires the continuing education unit to serve client groups that may have easy access to numerous educational programs.

At this point the dean or director of a continuing education unit must mix and match various funding sources to develop a comprehensive program. A combination of agency and corporate funds mixed with registration fees and tuition income sufficient to cover direct and indirect costs becomes necessary to carry out a broad mandate for continuing education as a public service to the community.

For many years continuing education has been dependent on a patchwork structure of support systems to fund programs. But now with the expectation of declining enrollments among traditional-age students, there may be unexpected help on the horizon—from the academic departments themselves.

According to a survey done by Richard E. Anderson and reported in the book, *The Costs and Financing of Adult Education and Training,*[15] 45 percent of the cost of continuing higher education programs is in instruction. It has been discovered in some continuing education programs that it is most cost-effective to hire instructors on an overload basis. In this case, faculty members assume responsibility for a continuing education assignment beyond their regular teaching loads, or in the case of adjunct faculty members from the community, beyond their regular jobs. This method has advantages in that it allows continuing education units more flexibility in hiring and keeps instructional costs lower than if faculty members were hired specifically to do this teaching. At some institutions, faculty members are being forced to consider the alternative of "inloading" instruction in continuing education programs to save as much as 45 percent of the cost for teaching a course.

Inloading requires a close look. As enrollment of 18- to 22-year-old students diminishes on many campuses, courses taught off-campus and through continuing education units may need to be staffed by regular faculty as part of the required teaching load. Institutions that have allowed regular faculty members to teach these courses on an overload pay basis may now have to ask faculty members to teach them as part of their regular load. When this occurs it precipitates debate, some acrimonious, between academic administrators and faculty members. The opportunity may arise for the continuing education administrator to assume a leadership role in helping the institution develop inload models which help colleges and departments expand their outreach program efforts.

The wise continuing higher education administrator will assume the role of an institutional problem solver when it comes to diversifying the departmental instructional portfolio to include outreach instruction through inloading approaches. It is also important that the continuing education unit on campus be designated as the coordinating body for this realignment.

This approach to instruction is not new to continuing education. It has been used for many years by colleges of agriculture and home economics and by cooperative extension services at many colleges and universities in the United States. In most academic departments in the colleges of agriculture and home economics at land-grant institutions, faculty members have extension and continuing education assignments as part of their regular responsibility. Much of this activity is partially due to federal funding received by the Cooperative Extension Service. Its success, however, is proof that faculty members can work effectively to solve community needs and meet the educational needs of the general public.

An opportunity has been provided by declining enrollments for continuing education units that have been on the fringe of the institution to move to the center of the academic stage. In some instances, disciplines that face declining numbers of students in "regular" programs can be assigned to serve broader constituencies. In many instances traditional disciplines can participate in exciting new programs and activities offered by continuing education units. As an example, faculty members in the humanities can be used to provide instruction in programs specifically designed for the continued advancement and knowledge of professionals. As the continuing education administrator provides leadership in this effort, new programs can be devised with instructional costs covered as part of the regular faculty member's load.

## DEVELOPING BUDGETS

At the most basic level, the budgeting process for a continuing education operation in higher education is additive, that is, after assessing what should be done and how, the budgeting officer adds together the programs that are planned for the coming year. The income from those programs, combined with outside support, is joined with the institutional underwriting from tax funds, inloading, or other institutional resources for the total operation. This combination of funding sources equals the total resources available for the year. All program expenses and operational overhead must be considered when calculating total expenses. As it is not the purpose of this chapter to dwell on budget preparation, it is sufficient to identify the process and to suggest other resources where this process is discussed in greater detail.

Among resources concerning budget planning, one very useful work from a practitioner's perspective is *Achieving Success in Continuing Education: A Basic Financial Guide*.[16] Author George L. Talbott took a straightforward approach to costing out a program, including overhead and indirect expenses and added instructions on how to build the budget for a department. The book also contains useful suggestions for determining when it is financially feasible to proceed with a low-enrollment program or when it is advisable to cancel the program. The principles suggested in this publication are, with minor adaptations, applicable to both small and large institutions.

A book with a more comprehensive outlook is Richard E. Anderson and Elizabeth S. Kasl's *The Costs and Financing of Adult Education and Training*.[17] The book covers such topics as cost-benefit analysis and cost accounting and includes chapters dealing with educational providers such as public schools, colleges and universities, proprietary occupational schools, professional associations, labor unions, and employers in the private sector.

A recent text by Gary W. Matkin entitled *Effective Budgeting in Continuing Education*[18] shows continuing educators how to use the techniques of budgeting and financial control for managing continuing education organizations. The book includes how to coordinate budgets of different departments and provides advice on computerizing budget and reporting systems.

## CASE STUDY: THE ART SECURITY INSTITUTE

When studying the process of building a budget, it may be helpful to look at planning the individual course, the basic building block of program budgeting. The following case study is modeled after a three-day conference on art security.

> Dr. Ann Zimmermann of the Department of Conferences at the University of the Midwest has been working to assess interest in a program for museum directors on maintaining the security of collections. After concluding that such a program would be useful, Dr. Zimmermann sits down to assemble her budget for the program. She has a handbook for budget building that has been modeled after the *Financial Guide* of Brigham Young University and adapted to the needs of the University of the Midwest's Division of University Extension (UMEX). Using that handbook, Dr. Zimmermann is reminded that the elements of her budget consist of three major parts: expected income, direct expenses, and indirect expenses. She will need to consider fixed and variable income and costs, and should calculate what expenses will be encumbered even though the program might not materialize (sunk costs).
>
> As Zimmerman calculates expected expenses for this national conference, she has to estimate such fixed and direct expenses as brochures and mailing, transportation for and honoraria paid to faculty members, and telephone charges. Variable direct costs include meals, handouts and materials, size and cost of the meeting rooms, etc. UMEX requires that the overhead costs (level 1) of operating the Department of Conferences be calculated at 15 percent for all courses. In addition, the overhead for the operation of the overall administration of UMEX (level 2) is set at 10 percent. The university has required UMEX to identify, in all of its courses, an overhead figure (level 3) of 25 percent to reflect the real university costs of the operation of UMEX and its departments. However, because of state funds from tax sources, the institution has omitted the 25 percent charge in recognition of its responsibility for outreach programs.
>
> As income for the Art Security Institute, Zimmermann can calculate the 25 percent of expenses for the University of the Midwest institutional overhead as an item to offset the same figure in the expense column. She has also received

a $5,000 grant from the State Arts Council to cover some of the costs. Zimmerman and her program planning committee have established a target enrollment of 100 persons who will pay $200 each. Finally, the American Museum Association has also promised to underwrite any losses of the program up to $5,000.

Zimmerman then notes that information on one of the UMEX budget forms as shown in Table 6.1.

## TABLE 6.1. UMEX Program Budget

### Art Security Institute

**INCOME**
1. Institutional Overhead—forgiven @ 25 percent of expenses ...... $ 5,410
2. Registrants—100 @ $200 ........................................ 20,000
3. Grants—Arts Council ........................................... 5,000
4. Additional income: American Museum Assn. Program underwrite—
   *only if needed* to offset costs................................ $ 5,000

   TOTAL Program Income ...................................... $30,410

| DIRECT EXPENSES | FIXED | VARIABLE | TOTAL |
|---|---|---|---|
| 1. Honoraria | $ 4,000 | | $ 4,000 |
| 2. Parking | 600 | | 600 |
| 3. Telephone | 300 | | 300 |
| 4. Office travel | 500 | | 500 |
| 5. Participant travel | 7,000 | | 7,000 |
| 6. Mailing, advertising, promotion | 4,600 | | 4,600 |
| 7. Food and lodging | | $3,525 | 3,525 |
| 8. Program supplies | | 1,115 | 1,115 |
| TOTAL Direct Expenses | $17,000 | $4,640 | $21,640 |

**INDIRECT EXPENSES**
1. Departmental overhead—conference @ 15% of total expenses
   of $21,640 .................................................... $ 3,246
2. UMEX overhead expenses @ 10% of total expenses of $21,640 ... 2,164
3. University of Midwest overhead expenses (also entered as
   income) @ 25% of direct expenses ........................... 5,410

   TOTAL Indirect Expenses .................................... $10,820

   TOTAL EXPENSES ............................................ $32,460
   TOTAL PROGRAM NET (covered by up to $5,000 in underwrite
                      from AMA) .............................. (2,050)

In the above example, the program is planned to break even after all direct and indirect expenses are met. This placed the Art Security Institute in what was categorized as a C-level program. It is possible that UMEX administrators will want the program to be a D-level program (provide a surplus as well as cover all direct and indirect expenses) since it is national in scope and will draw participants whose registration fee will be paid by their museums. This would place an additional requirement for a UMEX net of perhaps 5 to 25 percent.

In the Art Security Institute example, all of the budgeting elements can be seen: the wide range of sources of funds from the state, the institution, from private sources, and from program income. Without being overly complicated, the variation in expense categories is suggested as well.

## SUMMARY

The task of the continuing education administrator in financing programs requires strategies for the devlopment of constituencies at the local, state, and national level. Matching institutional capability with the goals of federal and state agencies for continuing education is a complicated task but one that may pay off in solid funding for worthwhile efforts. Matching college and university courses to corporate needs for staff development and identifying and cultivating foundation support are also important responsibilities.

Financing continuing education is a complex matter. It is not unlike conducting an orchestra. As there are many instruments designed to make different sounds and to perform different functions, the continuing education administrator, as the conductor, must bring all facets of the organization together with timing and emphasis. Good harmonies can come from a skilled leader, both in orchestral music and in directing programs of continuing education. In the establishment of a successful program, the skilled leader must understand and exercise the various funding options that are available if a financially stable operation is to be achieved for a college or university program of continuing higher education.

## REFERENCES

1. Hofstadter, R., and Smith, W., *American Higher Education,* Vol. 2 (Chicago: University of Chicago Press, 1961), p. 568.
2. Ibid., p. 568.
3. Rositer, Margaret, "Organization of the Agricultural Sciences," *The Organization of Knowledge in Modern America 1860–1920* (Baltimore: Johns Hopkins University Press, 1979), pp. 217, 241.

4. National Advisory Council on Extension, Continuing Education, *A Measure of Success: Federal Support for Continuing Education,* 93rd Congress, 1st Session, House Document #93–73 (Washington, D.C.: U.S. Government Printing Service, March 31, 1973), p. 3.

5. Kurland, Norman D.; Purga, R. L.; and Hilton, W. F., *Financing Adult Learning: Spotlight on the States* (Denver, Colo.: Education Commission of the States, July 1982), p. 20.

6. National Advisory Council on Extension, Continuing Education, op. cit., p. 3.

7. Kurland, Purga, and Hilton, loc. cit.

8. Ibid., p. 7.

9. Ibid., p. 7.

10. Ibid., p. 8.

11. Ibid., p. 9.

12. Ibid., pp. 25–31.

13. Lynton, Ernest A., *The Missing Connection Between Business and the Universities* (New York: Collier Macmillan, 1984), p. 29.

14. Ibid., p. 29.

15. Anderson, Richard E., and Kasl, Elizabeth Swain, *The Costs and Financing of Adult Education and Training* (Lexington, Mass.: Lexington Books, 1982).

16. Talbott, George J., *Achieving Success in Continuing Education: A Basic Financial Guide* (Provo, Utah: Brigham Young University, 1983).

17. Anderson and Kasl, loc. cit.

18. Matkin, Gary W., *Effective Budgeting in Continuing Education* (San Francisco: Jossey Bass, 1985).

# -7-

# UTILIZING A SYSTEMATIC PROGRAM PLANNING PROCESS

## John H. Buskey

Program planning is a central function of any continuing education organization. The ability to conceive of a program, carry out the planning, deliver it in a suitable format to an appropriate clientele, and evaluate it are the primary tasks of continuing educators. The level of skill exercised in the performance of these tasks determines short-term as well as long-term success.

Practitioners tend to think of program planning as a short-term activity, particularly in relation to the planning and development of a specific program to be delivered in the next few months. However, program planning also has important long-range implications in terms of positioning the organization for future planning, programming, and growth. The programs planned and executed this year provide the programming and financial base for next year and the years that follow. Unfortunately, much of the literature about continuing education and program planning tend to deal with short-term issues rather than the longer-term positioning and strategic needs of the organization. Continuing education organizers need to look ahead to and plan for both the short-term (one to two years) and the mid-term (four to five years) future while operating an effective program in the present. The needs of continuing education programming change more rapidly than those in most academic areas; systematic program planning can be a key element in the long-term success of the organization.

The focus of this chapter is on the systematic planning and development of a wide variety of continuing higher education programs. The variety of continuing education programs offered by institutions of higher education has resulted in a diverse array of program delivery mechanisms and program planning approaches. The purposes of this chapter are to (1) describe the setting in which program planning takes place in continuing higher education; (2) describe the situations and circumstances in which the program planning process operates; (3) review the literature on planning models of particular relevance to continuing higher education; (4) describe a generic program planning model with potential for wide application in continuing education; and (5) suggest new approaches to financing program planning and needs assessment processes.

## THE SETTING

A strong argument can be made for the position that colleges and universities have a broad mandate to provide continuing education programming for their alumni, their community, their state, the nation, and the world. Yet institutions vary widely in the scope and nature of their interest in and commitment to continuing education. At some institutions, an attempt is made to serve as many constituencies and clientele groups as possible, utilizing numerous delivery modes and systems. At other institutions, personnel are extremely selective in the audiences they choose to serve and the mechanisms they use; still others choose to serve only their traditional resident student body.

### INSTITUTIONAL RESOURCES

Institutions of higher learning, individually and collectively, are unique in the assortment of resources available to address the multiple continuing education needs of society. No other provider—public schools, voluntary organizations, professional associations, consulting firms, business and industrial corporations, or government agencies— has the diversity of resources available through institutions of higher education. The most obvious resource is the faculty; this is perhaps the major advantage that colleges and universities have over other providers of continuing education. The interests of faculty members typically range widely across numerous disciplines and subdisciplines. The physical facilities and academic support services common to institutions constitute another significant resource for carrying out the continuing education mission.

While most continuing education programs rely heavily on the institution's faculty, specialists from other organizations are often secured as well. Professionals with special expertise in business and industrial firms, city, state, and federal government, professional organizations and associations, and consulting firms can also contribute to an institution's outreach program.

## CLIENTELE

A diverse clientele is usually served by institutions of higher education through their continuing education programs. Generally, the people served and the programs offered are related directly to the institution's academic programs and resources. It is certainly appropriate, however, for institutions to serve clientele in their service area by providing programs in subjects not available at their institution, particularly when other local agencies are not providing such services. For example, the absence of an engineering curriculum does not mean that programs should not be provided for local engineers. Resources from and arrangements with other institutions or organizations can be used to provide the programs.

Money is one of the limiting factors faced by institutions that desire to serve a broad clientele. In theory, institutional personnel can decide who they want to serve with what programs; in fact, the deciding factor is usually the client's ability and willingness to pay. If the client can pay for all costs, programs and services can be provided. Thus, by default, if not by design, the self-supporting nature of many continuing education operations forces the institution to serve a limited, if not elite, audience. A strong argument can be made for providing state appropriations or institutional support for continuing education programs, especially in publicly supported institutions.

## PROGRAMMING

There are many opinions concerning the position institutions of higher education should take in developing and offering continuing education programs. Programming can be characterized as primarily "reactive" in nature at some institutions; personnel wait for the telephone to ring and respond with programs designed specifically for the caller's needs. At other institutions, perhaps characterized as primarily "proactive" in their programming, extraordinary efforts are made to identify problems and needs, develop programming accordingly, and to recruit participants. Most institutions fall in the middle of the reactive-proactive continuum. Educators at such institutions are prepared to react and respond to the needs of specific groups, but also to initiate programs, recruit client groups, and develop their own curricula while matching institutional resources with clientele needs.

In developing programming, continuing educators can build upon the strong tradition of sequential curricular offerings inherent in every collegiate institution. While often seen in the programs of evening colleges, many other continuing education units, driven by the need to offer programming that "sells," do not take advantage of this strong tradition. The advantages of sequential programming (credit or non-credit programs leading to a degree, a certificate, or other formal recognition) are substantial. First, it creates a core of participants who will register for multiple events in the sequence and constitute a continuing clientele. Second, once developed, the sequences are relatively inexpensive to operate because the development costs can be prorated over multiple offerings. Third, family members commonly become more involved and committed to the continuing education enterprise. Fourth, sequences of programs provide more content and substance than "one-shot" programs, which are also expensive to conduct due to their one-time nature. A disadvantage of sequential programs is that not everyone who enrolls in the first program also enrolls in the subsequent events. Thus, a dropout factor must be considered in program and financial planning.

## THE PLANNING PROCESS

Numerous tasks must be accomplished by continuing higher education programmers before a program idea is brought to fruition. Programmers need to: (1) set priorities in selecting issues to address, (2) select from numerous options in designing the program, (3) select from several delivery systems at their disposal, and (4) incorporate the interests and capabilities of many people into the planning enterprise. Persons in the audience for whom they are planning hold expectations for what they want to learn or what problems they want to solve. The instructors have content expertise and instructional skills that must be matched with the program design and participant needs and expectations. The task of the continuing education programmer is to bring diverse needs, expectations, and skills together in a program planning process. A systematic approach to the planning process can be very useful.

### TYPES OF PROGRAMS

There are many ways to categorize continuing higher education programs. Perhaps the two most obvious categories, common to many institutions, are credit and noncredit programs. Several authors, looking for a more basic framework, have attempted to bring order to the field by developing classification schemes that could be used for conducting research as well as for administrative and programming purposes. One of the earliest attempts was Coolie Verner's effort to classify processes according to three levels: individual methods, group methods, and community methods.[1] Cyril O. Houle proposed eleven "categories of educational situations," ranging from independent study, through various group learning situations, the creation of institutions, and, finally, mass education processes.[2]

For the purposes of this chapter, a good way to classify programs is provided by Philip M. Nowlen's four-level classification system. The "individual setting" includes correspondence study, television courses, and computer-assisted instruction. The "temporary group" setting incorporates evening classes, conferences, workshops and seminars, satellite video conferences, and telephone network programs. The "organization setting" focuses on people who are members of an organization, such as a business, industrial firm, hospital, or school system, that provides in-service or employee development programs. The "community setting" focuses on problems and issues common to a neighborhood, community, or a broad geographical area. Community and development programs are the major example in this category.[3]

Another way to view types of programs is to consider the purposes of individual activities. In continuing higher education, instructional programs are typically perceived as having objectives that deal with the acquisition of knowledge, skills, or attitudes. Programs are often designed, however, to solve problems, help groups reach consensus or make decisions, develop a plan or produce a report, or analyze social or public issues or problems. Learning is certainly an outcome, perhaps a by-product of the program, but the major focus is on the accomplishment of some task.

The approaches discussed in this chapter are applicable to designing most types of programs delivered in a variety of formats through several kinds of systems. It should be noted that, in practice, the bulk of program planning in continuing higher education is directed toward the development of noncredit programs such as conferences, workshops, and informal classes; the majority of credit programs are usually versions of existing courses in academic departments, and major modifications or redevelopment are not required for delivery as in continuing education programs.

## PLANNING PERSPECTIVES

Program planning for adult audiences is a complex process and any planning activity should involve at least four perspectives: (1) the client or participant, (2) content, (3) instructional process, and (4) planning/design processes.

The *client* or *participant's* perspective is important because he or she has specific educational needs or problems that require a response. The client may be an individual, a formal or informal organization, or a cluster of people with identifiable needs. The *content* perspective concerns subject areas, broadly or narrowly defined, relevant to the needs of participants and the objectives of the program. The *instructional process* perspective focuses on the interaction that takes place between instructors and participants during the program. The procedures to guide the development and design of the program are emphasized in the *planning/design* perspective.

In some cases these perspectives will be provided by separate individuals; in other cases several people may represent one viewpoint; and in still other cases one person might represent more than one. For example, the client perspective might be provided by people who will receive the instruction, their supervisors, and/or their peers. The content perspective is often provided by subject-matter specialists, such as college and university faculty, external specialists, or consultants; interdisciplinary or multidisciplinary programs may require more than one content expert. The expertise for designing instructional processes may be provided by the faculty, by a consultant employed specifically for that purpose, or, in some cases, by a continuing educator. The continuing educator who is proficient in the management of the comprehensive program planning process should bring planning expertise to the group.

In general, every planning situation should include at least these four perspectives. However, it is often appropriate to include other viewpoints, such as the sponsor of a program, an expert in the delivery system to be used, or a "secondary client" of the program (e.g., an employer or potential employer of the participants).

The typical planning group is larger than four people, but each of the four major perspectives described above, as well as additional ones relevant to the particular program, is important in the success of the program design. Each representative has unique roles and responsibilities in the planning process which have been described by Tunis H. Dekker,[4] as they apply to planning in the college and university conference setting, and by Alan B. Knox.[5] The planning group can be established by selecting people who can contribute these perspectives to the process. Such persons should understand why they have been selected for the planning group and how they can contribute.

As good as the four-perspective planning method is, the program planner should be aware of two potential problem areas. The first is bringing the content expert perspective into the process too early before the nature of the problem, focus of the program, or need has been clearly articulated. This error can result in the problem, focus, or need being defined in terms of the content expert's expertise rather than in terms of the wide range of content expertise available throughout the institution. This type of premature closure can result in programs that fail to solve the problem or meet the need. A second problem arises if the client perspective is brought into the planning process too late. This can result in planners seeking final approval for a program that the client had no role in shaping.

## PLANNING SITUATIONS

In the programming environment of an institution, it is important to understand the variety of planning situations, many of which do not require that all steps in the typical planning process be accomplished in detail. The majority of individual programs offered by continuing education organizations are repeats of previously offered programs. Only a small number are new each year. The advantages of a "base" of programs that does not require major annual planning efforts are a reduction in overhead time and a fairly predictable financial base. The level of effort and the complexity of the task (in terms of the program planning steps that must be taken) suggest a range or continuum of effort.

The points along the continuum can be described in the following ways:

- *"Repeat"* programs that involve the same delivery system, the same instructor, and the same or a similar audience generally require the least effort and involve the least complexity. The primary focus is on fine-tuning the program based on the results of previous experience and evaluation reports. There should be periodic meetings with the instructor to discuss minor revisions in the program objectives, the description of the program, physical arrangements, and budget. A major task will be promoting and marketing the well-established program so that it continues to be placed in the "repeat" category.

- Another *"repeat"* program, the recurring annual meeting, commonly requires more effort and is more complex. There is usually a well-established planning process. The complexity of working with a planning committee and reviewing the participant needs, revising program objectives, selecting resources, and so forth, requires more of the continuing educator's time and skill than the program described above.

- A *new program* to be offered through an existing delivery system (e.g., an evening college, independent study by correspondence, or a conferences and institutes department) requires substantially more time and effort for program planning. All steps in the planning process should be carried out with strong emphasis on the identification of the participants and marketing the program for them. This program will require a major effort by continuing education staff members as they work with instructional resources, representatives of prospective participants, and any client organizations involved.

- The identification of a *new need* not previously addressed that requires development of a new program as well as selection of the delivery system, or perhaps the development of a new delivery system, requires the greatest effort. The needs assessment step is most important here, and the planning committee members will need to work through all the program planning steps. The continuing educator will be required to spend a great deal of time on the program. If a new delivery system is to be used, the research and development of the systems requires additional effort.

The typical continuing education organization probably is most efficient and effective when approximately 80 percent of its programming falls in the first two categories and approximately 20 percent of its effort is devoted to the latter two categories. This is referred to as the 80/20 concept: 80 percent repeat programming and 20 percent new programming. Members of an organization cannot afford to devote all of their resources to the development of new programs or delivery systems—overhead costs simply preclude such practice. Conversely, organization members that expend all their energy on repeating last year's programs soon become stagnant and will probably experience a gradual drop in clientele and programs and find themselves in financial difficulty. A solid program and financial base are needed in each continuing education organization; however, some risks in developing and offering new programs must also be taken.

An important related factor is the mix of programs within the total continuing education organization. Conferences and seminars, because of the detailed planning effort necessary, usually require more staff time than do evening classes for which the instructors take the major responsibility. For example, a conference coordinator who is thoroughly involved in the planning process and who has substantial support staff may plan and coordinate fifty conferences per year, but a single administrator with modest support assistance may coordinate more than 100 evening college credit classes per semester.

## PROGRAM PLANNING LITERATURE: RESOURCES FOR PROGRAMMERS

A substantial body of literature on program planning has been published over the last thirty years, especially since 1970. In addition to over ninety books and journal articles describing specific multistep program planning models, numerous articles and books have been written on individual steps in program planning. Planning techniques that may be useful in specific situations have been discussed in some journal articles; however, most articles in which an attempt has been made to describe an entire program planning process have limited usefulness because space limitations prevent the author from going into detail. Thus, as a format, books tend to be more useful to the practitioner and will be the major focus of this section.

Program planning models found in the literature are generally prescriptive in nature; they are meant to represent the essential characteristics of a process that may, could, or should exist rather than one that does or did exist. Most planning models are presented and described in linear fashion, and it is possible to justify and defend a linear sequence of steps. Nevertheless, the planning process is highly interactive and iterative and, although often unrecognized, feedback and feedforward loops are employed. It is a cyclical process; it is necessary to recycle to earlier steps frequently or to leap ahead to later steps to deal effectively with planning issues. Decisions reached in one phase may require modification later as new information is developed. To accomplish the design and delivery of the program, all steps must be completed.

The sheer quantity of literature makes it difficult for continuing educators to select the best program planning models for their specific needs. As part of a comprehensive project to examine the published literature on program planning models, John H. Buskey and Thomas J. Sork[6] developed an analytical framework to differentiate approaches to planning. In their framework characteristics of planning models that influence their theoretical or practical utility were compared and contrasted. Five distinguishing factors were developed to assist continuing educators in assessing and selecting program planning models to be used in specific situations.

## PLANNING CONTEXT

The environment or situation in which the author intended the planning model to be used is labeled the planning context. Authors have developed models for use in six major contexts: (1) adult basic education; (2) continuing education in the professions, including health and human services; (3) cooperative extension service; (4) general adult education, including public schools, religious education, and a variety of specialized areas; (5) training in business, industry, and government; and (6) continuing higher education. Authors writing for a specific context tend to use language and examples relating to that context. Programmers seeking a model relevant to their special area of interest should consider this factor when selecting a model, although some volumes written for a specific audience may be applied to other audiences.

Despite the fact that many of the program planning models have been written by college and university faculty members and administrators, only those by Dekker,[7] Elinor Lenz,[8] and George B. Strother and John P. Klus[9] have been written for specific application in continuing higher education. Other books and articles have been written for cooperative extension service programmers and administrators which are applicable to continuing higher education, especially in the area of community development.[10]

The largest body of literature is in the category of "general adult education," a descriptor used to categorize those documents written for continuing educators in any type of agency. The program examples in these books are drawn from a variety of agencies and subject matters; they are written in such a way that continuing educators in any agency can apply the espoused principles.

The authors of program planning models for continuing education in the professions have contributed a number of useful books. Among the more comprehensive volumes are ones by Armand Lauffer[11] in the field of social work and Helen M. Tobin, Pat S. Yoder Wise, and Peggy K. Hull[12] in nursing. Continuing educators who work in management development and training have a number of excellent publications from which to choose; this is the strongest literature as a group. The most comprehensive planning models include those of Leonard Nadler,[13] Dugan Laird,[14] and William R. Tracey.[15]

## LEVEL OF "PROGRAM" EMPHASIZED

As summarized by Verner,[16] three levels of programming are commonly discussed in the literature on adult education: (1) the design of an educational *activity,* such as a conference, class, or course; (2)

the composite of educational activities provided by a single *organization*, such as a YMCA, a church, a college, or an industrial firm; and (3) all of the educational opportunities for adults in a *community*. Although the planning steps may appear to be similar regardless of program level, the means used to accomplish a specific step often varies by level. Only one level of program is emphasized in most models, although equal emphasis is given to two levels of programming in several models. None deal explicitly with all three levels.

## CLIENT SYSTEM ORIENTATION

Some models are oriented toward planning situations where the prospective participants hold *membership* in a single formal organization, such as a corporation, a school system, or a professional association. Other models are designed for use in cases where the audience is general in nature and is not part of an identifiable membership client system or organization, hence the label *nonmembership* orientation.[17] Some models are designed for both situations. This factor is helpful in selecting a model because it implies the ease with which clients can be identified and has particularly important implications when planning needs assessments and designing strategies for recruiting participants. Planning models tend to have either a membership *or* a nonmembership orientation, although equal weight is given to both orientations in a few models.

## THEORETICAL FRAMEWORK

The extent to which a particular planning model is supported by an explicit theoretical or conceptual framework varies widely among current published works. At one extreme are the authors who make no attempt to provide a rationale for their specific planning process, while others describe in detail the theoretical framework or assumptions about adult learning, the planning process, or other factors upon which their work is based. In other cases, such assumptions are made, but they are not explicitly stated in the presentation of the model. With this factor in mind, users can select models with a level of theoretical explanation appropriate to their needs.

## COMPREHENSIVENESS OF THE PLANNING PROCESS

Each program planning model is unique, and individual models are composed of several steps. Although the number of steps varies from model to model, there are specific steps common to most models. Some authors describe in detail how each phase of their model should be completed, but other writers describe only a few steps comprehensively and barely mention others. In selecting a model for practical use, it is important to select one that provides enough information about each step in the process.

Among the more comprehensive books are ones by Houle,[18] which provides the strongest theoretical background and the broadest statement of program planning in the context of other literature; Malcolm S. Knowles,[19] which is the most practical book on program planning, particularly in the context of a specific theoretical framework; John R. Verduin, Harry G. Miller, and Charles E. Greer,[20] which is one of the few books written specifically from the perspective of the instructor; Alan B. Knox and Associates,[21] and Patrick G. Boyle.[22]

As the planning models are examined collectively, it is apparent that many models are similar and provide essentially the same guidance to the program planner. The major weaknesses of published models tend to be the absence of a theoretical base on which to found the planning model, the lack of information on budgeting and administration as it relates to the specific model, and inadequate information on marketing and promotion to ensure that participants are recruited to the program. Few published program planning models are comprehensive in their treatment of the individual steps of planning. In contrast, the major strengths of the published models appear in discussions of needs assessments, instructional processes, and evaluation procedures. A more detailed analysis of the literature upon which this discussion is based appears in Sork and Buskey.[23]

## A GENERIC PROGRAM PLANNING MODEL

The program planning models presented in the literature vary in the number of recommended steps or phases from five or six to over a dozen. In order to compare and contrast the variety of published program planning models, Sork and Buskey[24] developed a synthesized, or generic, nine-step planning model, labeling the individual steps with terms that can be related to most of the published works. Most published models include these steps; however, they are not always labeled the same or fully described in every model. The generic model is presented to suggest the scope and intent of each step in a comprehensive program planning model.

Each step of the planning process is briefly described in the following sections, along with additional sources of information. It should be noted that under each individual step are assumed a number of substeps that are not reported here.

## ANALYSIS OF PLANNING CONTEXT AND CLIENT SYSTEMS (STEP 1)

Program planning does not occur in isolation. The alternatives available to a continuing education planner and the criteria used to decide among alternatives are influenced by the philosophy, goals, traditions, structure, political environment, fiscal condition, and service orientation of the institution. Similarly, many planning decisions are also affected by the characteristics of the client system(s) to be served.

Analysis of the planning context involves the identification or review of important characteristics in the environment where planning is taking place. For example, the structure or tradition of an institution may limit the range of delivery systems or instructional formats that can be employed by the planner. Some institutional personnel may respond only to needs of certain client groups (e.g., doctors, nurses, lawyers, social workers) because of existing academic programs within the college or university. Developing a clear understanding of internal constraints to planning (philosophical, fiscal, political, and so forth) is one of two primary goals of context analysis. The second goal is to understand factors in the external environment that may influence the planning effort. Such factors include the existence of competitive programs, the public "image" of the college or university, and political or ideological currents that affect the institution.

Analysis of the client system should produce a clear description of potential participants. Among the characteristics that often have important implications are income, age, geographic distribution, level of formal education, history of previous participation, discretionary time available, sources of information, and work schedule. Each of these characteristics has important implications for later planning steps, such as selection of instructional processes, scheduling, budgeting, and recruiting participants.

Planning models that give considerable attention to this step include those of John R. Verduin,[25] Donald F. Michilak and Edwin G. Yager,[26] Irwin L. Goldstein,[27] and George M. Beal et al.[28]

## ASSESSMENT OF NEEDS (STEP 2)

"Needs" are commonly defined in the literature of continuing education as a deficiency, a gap, a discrepancy, or a difference between what is and what ought to be. The purpose of this step in the planning process is to determine the specific nature of the need or problem and make decisions about the type of intervention that will be most effective. Among continuing educators, it is commonly assumed that a proper response is the development of an educational program. Depending on the situation, however, the appropriate response might call for changes in an organization's reward or incentive structure, changes in or reassignment of personnel, changes in equipment, or modifications of policies and procedures.

The major steps in conducting a formal needs assessment include collecting data, describing the current situation or problem, projecting and describing the more desirable situation, and setting priorities. A key element in the success of this process involves making a series of judgments about, and interpretations of, the data in each phase of the process.

Needs assessments can be performed in a variety of ways; there are also alternatives that merit serious consideration depending on the resources available and the results of Step 1, the analysis of the planning context and the client system.

The major outcome of this step in the planning process is the development of information on which a decision can be based regarding the proper intervention. In some cases, it may be appropriate to stop the program planning process after the needs assessment and focus on other remedies as suggested above. In most instances, however, the needs assessment results in information and a set of priorities which can be used in developing program objectives and program design. The works of Michilak and Yager,[29] and Robert L. Craig[30] provide detail and useful guidance for the needs assessment step.

## DEVELOPMENT OF OBJECTIVES (STEP 3)

Program objectives are derived from the problems and issues identified in the analysis of the planning context and the assessment of client needs or problems. Typically they focus on the acquisition of knowledge, skills, or attitudes, although many programs have objectives that involve the accomplishment of some task, the production of a document, or the solution of a problem.

Usually it is appropriate to state program objectives at two or three levels: broad objectives (sometimes labeled goals) that indicate overall program outcomes; midlevel objectives that relate to major program components; and specific objectives that may relate to individual program sessions. It is useful to organize objectives in a hierarchical fashion in which their relationships to each other are clearly shown. Above all, objectives should clearly indicate the expected outcomes of the program, either in terms of learner behavior or expected products, depending upon the purpose of the program.

Ideally, during this step, and certainly prior to the start of formal design work, members of the planning group need to select the delivery system (e.g., a class, correspondence course, or other system) to be used to offer the program. By delaying the delivery system decision until this time, the planners will have a clearer picture of the planning context, participants' needs, and the objectives of the program; they will, therefore, be in a good position to select the most appropriate delivery system. Criteria that need to be considered prior to making a decision about the delivery system to use are discussed in Chapter 9. In practice, however, planning is often undertaken by persons already committed to a specific delivery system regardless of whether it is the best way to deliver the program. Additional sources of information include Verduin[31] and Ralph W. Tyler.[32]

## SELECTION AND ORDERING OF CONTENT (STEP 4)

The purpose of this step is to select content relevant to the program and to organize the content, based on previously stated objectives, into an appropriate sequence for the participants. There are numerous ways to organize content, including chronological sequence, the progressive development of concepts from simple to complex, the development of broad principles from a series of specific illustrations, and the application of simple concepts or principles to more complex situations as the program unfolds.[33] Verduin[34] also offered some especially helpful guidance on this issue.

## SELECTION, DESIGN, AND ORDERING OF INSTRUCTIONAL PROCESSES (STEP 5)

Attention is focused on the interaction among and between the program participants and the program's leaders that will result from the selection, design, and ordering of instructional processes. As with content, careful thought must be given to the sequence in which the processes are used in order to facilitate the accomplishment of the program's objectives.

Perhaps the largest single body of literature in the field is concerned with processes; there are many methods and techniques available to the creative programmer. Buskey,[35] Craig,[36] Warner W. Burke and Richard Beckhard,[37] and Paul Bergevin, Dwight Morris, and Robert M. Smith[38] provide a variety of perspectives on the topic.

## SELECTION OF INSTRUCTIONAL RESOURCES (STEP 6)

The category of instructional resources focuses on human resources, but may also include physical resources and program materials. Human resources obviously include instructors, program leaders and group leaders; depending on the program, such resources may include planning committee members, program coordinators, remote site monitors, and a variety of support staff members, such as secretarial, registration, food service, and physical plant staff. Every program will not require such an extensive list of human resources; some programs, such as the origination of a national satellite video teleconference, may require an even longer list of resources, many of whom will be technical specialists.

Criteria for selecting instructors and leaders vary from program to program. However, the two major criteria should be competence in the subject area and ability to communicate effectively with a specific audience. It is not unusual to find that faculty members who are effective in the traditional classroom have trouble orienting their materials and methods to adult students who wish to make immediate practical application of the information. Other selection criteria may involve local, regional, or national reputation, ability to use a specific instructional process, or ability to develop and design a session (or program) to deal with a specific problem.

Among the physical resources that may need to be considered are films, slides, transparencies, tapes, computers, projectors, easels, videotape machines, tables, chairs, telephones, meeting rooms, classrooms, television studios, dining facilities, and lodging facilities. Program materials may include textbooks, notebooks, program outlines, reference materials, group exercises, computer software, examinations, evaluation sheets, and study guides.

Program planners need to incorporate the scheduling and procurement of these resources into the planning process in such a way that the accomplishment of the program's objectives is supported and facilitated. Other authors that address these issues are M. Alan Brown and Harlan G. Copeland,[39] Ivor K. Davies,[40] Craig,[41] and Burke and Beckhard.[42]

## FORMULATION OF THE BUDGET AND ADMINISTRATIVE PLAN (STEP 7)

The formulation of the budget and administrative plan is an ongoing process. Decisions that affect the budget and have implications for administrative tasks are made at every stage in the planning process. Developing the budget requires creating a list of all cost items, both direct and indirect, and the identification of all sources of income, which may include participant fees, general institutional support, or external funding.

Creation of the administrative plan involves identifying the tasks that must be accomplished, when they must be completed, how they will be done, and who will do them. The plan must include all the

items indicated in previous steps, as well as those in the later steps
of the process. A key part of the administrative plan is the developing
of a planning timeline that includes deadlines.

## ASSURANCE OF PARTICIPATION (STEP 8)

The purpose of this step is to bring the entire planning process to
fruition by recruiting participants. This step is labeled promotion or
marketing in many models; however, it also includes securing participants for a wide variety of in-service programs conducted by
organizations. For "in-house" programs, participants are usually selected and invited by a central office or may even be assigned to
attend a training program.

Marketing and promotion have received increased attention in
recent years; marketing audits, marketing mix (product, price, place,
and promotion), marketing techniques, and target audience identification are now familiar concepts to continuing educators. Techniques
such as radio, television, and newspaper advertising; news releases;
direct mail; telephone marketing; and many other promotional methods are now used to sell programs to prospective participants.

## DESIGN OF THE EVALUATION PROCEDURE (STEP 9)

The basic purposes of evaluation are to find out (1) whether the
program accomplished what it intended to accomplish, (2) how well
it was accomplished, and (3) what could be done better next time.
Evaluation helps establish standards of accountability, provides feedback, assists with administrative and program decisions, provides
evidence for funding justification, and supplies evidence about learning.

Evaluation (and feedback) are integral parts of the entire planning
process; evaluative questions should be asked at every stage of the
process to provide a basis for proceeding to the next step. This
continuous process is typically labeled "formative" evaluation, and
it addresses the effectiveness of the planning process. "Summative"
evaluation is concerned with the final outcomes of the program: "What
did the participants learn? Did we accomplish that which we set out
to do?

The task in this step of the planning process is to design the
evaluation and feedback processes to accomplish the above goals. The
design should include specifications about what data are to be collected, how they are to be collected, from whom they are to be
collected, when they will be collected, how they will be analyzed,
and to whom feedback will be provided.

There are many approaches to evaluation, and it is probably fair
to say that formal evaluation processes are not used as frequently in
continuing education as they should be. Further information about
evaluation is provided by Craig[43] and Goldstein.[44]

## FINANCING PROGRAM PLANNING

Relatively few continuing education organizations have adequate funds
for carrying out comprehensive program planning processes. Yet the
lifeblood of the organization may depend upon its ability to develop
new programs and revise and refine current offerings.

As a result of the need for new programs, a number of mechanisms
to finance program development may be employed by institutions.
Perhaps the most common practice is to allocate a small amount of
staff time to new program development. In effect, a portion of the
annual budget is actually allocated to the program development function by the organization. The extent to which the allocation is not
labeled "program development" or "needs assessment" may limit
understanding of the actual allocation of time (dollars!) to these
functions. This practice of allocating a percentage of staff time works
well when new programs are modifications of, or closely related to,
existing programs. It may not be adequate, however, when the new
programs are major undertakings and a great deal of staff time is
required for each step of the program planning process.

A certain percentage of the total continuing education budget is
set aside at some institutions to finance needs assessments and program
development activities. In some cases if new programs show deficits,
the funds are allocated "after the fact." In other instances the funds
are allocated early in the program budgeting process and become a
part of the program's initial budget.

At other institutions, program development and related needs
assessments activities are carried out by a specific unit in the organization whose sole or major task is to conduct needs assessments and
perform the initial tasks in program development. The program or
the results of the needs study may later be turned over to operational
units for subsequent development and delivery.

External funds are sought through proposals written to public
and private granting agencies at some institutions. While the task of
writing the proposal may take a great deal of time, its major values
include the opportunity to clarify constituents' needs, elaborate the
scope and nature of the program, and examine the potential for long-
term programming. The major disadvantage is the length of time
taken to prepare the proposal and receive feedback from the pro-

spective funding agency. It can, however, be a useful way to acquire seed money for high-risk ventures. A variation of this approach, wherein the constituent group provides developmental funds or free services (e.g., staff time) that reduce the cost of program development, has been used successfully by some continuing education organizations.

A small number of continuing education organizations have begun to acquire endowment funds from private sources to produce annual interest or dividend income.[45] The income can be used to finance various parts of the program development process. The most valuable funds are unrestricted as to subject matter or clientele; however, it may be easier to acquire funds that provide for program development in a specific profession or group of people.

It is also possible to secure endowed funds for other purposes such as scholarships, libraries, staff development, building and capital equipment expenses, and occasionally for the operation of existing programs. The acquisition of seed money can relieve the annual operating budget of specific expenses, which become significant over time. For example, a program development endowed fund of $50,000 can generate $4,000 to $6,000 per year (depending upon interest and dividend income) for use in conducting needs assessments or providing seed money for new programming ventures that will, in turn, provide program services to adults and produce income. If the program is successful, the income may represent a substantial return on investment. On the other hand, if the new program is not successful, the impact on current operating funds is minimized.

Probably the best approach to funding the needs assessment and program development activities of an organization is a combination of the above methods. To rely on any one method is to court possible disaster because the individual circumstances of funding agencies change from time to time, and last year's agency may not be in business this year.

## SUMMARY

While the usefulness and desirability of using systematic planning processes have been emphasized, a note of caution is appropriate. Planning takes time and resources, and it is important to consider carefully how much time, effort, and resources can and should be devoted to planning a specific program activity, as well as to the planning of all acitivites. "Overplanning" may absorb resources that could be better spent on delivering current programs, while "underplanning" may result in restricting the development of programs necessary to sustain next year's program and financial plan. There are obvious dangers to both extremes, and a balance in planning efforts will be sought in the effective continuing education organization, ranging from the use of a comprehensive planning process for new initiatives to the judicious modification of well-founded, effective programs that will be repeated in the next program cycle.

## REFERENCES

1. Verner, Coolie, *A Conceptual Scheme for the Identification and Classification of Processes for Adult Education* (Chicago: Adult Education Association, 1962.

2. Houle, Cyril O., *The Design of Education* (San Francisco: Jossey-Bass, 1972), pp. 90–130.

3. Nowlen, Philip M., "Program Origins," in *Developing, Administering and Evaluating Adult Education,* ed. Alan B. Knox and Associates (San Francisco: Jossey-Bass, 1980), pp. 15–17.

4. Dekker, Tunis H., "The Conference Coordinator: Educator-Administrator," *Adult Education,* 16 (1) (1965), pp. 37–40.

5. Knox, Alan B., *Enhancing Proficiencies of Continuing Educators, New Directions for Continuing Education,* No. 1 (San Francisco: Jossey-Bass, 1979), pp. 30–35.

6. Buskey, John H., and Sork, Thomas J., "From Chaos to Order in Program Planning: A System for Selecting Models and Ordering Research," *Proceedings of the Twenty-Third Annual Adult Education Research Conference* (Lincoln: University of Nebraska–Lincoln, Department of Adult and Continuing Education, 1982), pp. 54–59.

7. Dekker, loc. cit.

8. Lenz, Elinor, *Creating and Marketing Programs in Continuing Education* (New York: McGraw-Hill, 1980).

9. Strother, George B., and Klus, John P., *Administration of Continuing Education* (Belmont, Calif.: Wadsworth, 1982).

10. Beal, George M.; Blount, Ross C.; Powers, Ronald C.; and Johnson, W.J., *Social Action and Interaction in Program Planning* (Ames: Iowa State University Press, 1966).

11. Lauffer, Armand, *Doing Continuing Education and Staff Development* (New York: McGraw-Hill, 1978).

12. Tobin, Helen M.; Wise, Pat S. Yoder; and Hull, Peggy K., *The Process of Staff Development: Components for Change* (2nd ed.; St. Louis: Mosby, 1979).

13. Nadler, Leonard, *Designing Training Programs: The Critical Events Model* (Reading, Mass.: Addison-Wesley, 1982).

14. Laird, Dugan, *Approaches to Training and Development* (Reading, Mass.: Addison-Wesley, 1978).

15. Tracey, William R., *Designing Training and Development Systems* (New York: American Management Association, 1971).

16. Verner, Coolie, "Definitions of Terms," in *Adult Education: Outlines of an Emerging Field of University Study,* ed. Gale Jensen, A. A. Liveright, and Wilbur Hallenbeck (Washington, D.C.: Adult Education Association, 1964), p. 34.

17. Schroeder, Wayne L., "Typology of Adult Learning Systems," *Building an Effective Adult Education Enterprise,* ed. John M. Peters and Associates (San Francisco: Jossey-Bass, 1980), pp. 52–56.

18. Houle, loc. cit.

19. Knowles, Malcolm S., *The Modern Practice of Adult Education: From Pedagogy to Andragogy* (rev. ed.; Chicago: Association Press/Follett, 1980).

20. Verduin, Jr., John R.; Miller, Harry G.; and Greer, Charles E., *Adults Teaching Adults* (Austin, Tex.: Learning Concepts, 1977).

21. Knox, Alan B., and Associates, *Developing, Administering, and Evaluating Adult Education* (San Francisco: Jossey-Bass, 1980).

22. Boyle, Patrick G., *Planning Better Programs* (New York: McGraw-Hill, 1981).

23. Sork, Thomas J., and Buskey, John H., "A Descriptive and Evaluative Analysis of Program Planning Literature, 1950–1983, *Adult Education Quarterly,* 36(2) 1986, pp. 86–96.

24. Ibid.

25. Verduin, Jr., John R., *Curriculum Building for Adult Learning* (Carbondale: Southern Illinois University Press, 1980).

26. Michalak, Donald F., and Yager, Edwin G., *Making the Training Process Work* (New York: Harper and Row, 1979).

27. Goldstein, Irwin L., *Training: Program Development and Evaluation* (Monterey, Calif.: Brooks/Cole, 1974).

28. Beal et al., loc. cit.

29. Michalak and Yager, loc. cit.

30. Craig, Robert L., ed., *Training and Development Handbook* (2nd ed.; New York: McGraw-Hill, 1976).

31. Verduin, loc. cit.

32. Tyler, Ralph W., *Basic Principles of Curriculum and Instruction* (Chicago: University of Chicago Press, 1950).

33. Ibid., pp. 54–67.

34. Verduin, loc. cit.

35. Buskey, John H., "Using Technology to Enhance Learning," in *Designing and Implementing Effective Workshops,* ed. Thomas J. Sork, New Directions for Continuing Education, No. 22 (San Francisco: Jossey-Bass, 1984).

36. Craig, loc. cit.

37. Burke, Warner W., and Beckhard, Richard, *Conference Planning* (2nd ed.; Washington, D.C.: National Training Laboratory, 1970).

38. Bergevin, Paul; Morris, Dwight; and Smith, Robert M., *Adult Education Procedures* (Greenwich, Conn.: Seabury, 1963).

39. Brown, M. Alan, and Copeland, Harlan G., eds., *Attracting Able Instructors of Adults,* New Directions for Continuing Education, No. 4 (San Francisco: Jossey-Bass, 1979).

40. Davies, Ivor K., *Instructional Technique* (New York: McGraw-Hill, 1981).

41. Craig, loc. cit.

42. Burke and Beckhard, loc. cit.

43. Craig, loc. cit.

44. Goldstein, loc. cit.

45. Atkinson, Maurice, "Fund Raising for Continuing Education," in *Attracting External Funds for Continuing Education,* ed. John H. Buskey, New Directions for Continuing Education, No. 12 (San Francisco: Jossey-Bass, 1981).

# –8–

# NEEDS ASSESSMENT AS PART OF PROGRAM PLANNING

## Thomas J. Sork

Continuing educators, who spend their time designing educational programs for adults, typically go about planning in some systematic manner. Decisions are made about which learners will be served, what goals will be sought, how activities will be organized and sequenced, what resources will be used, and when and where the program will be offered. With experience, these decisions become routinized and may eventually be expressed in the form of a "model" set of procedures or collection of steps. In Chapter 7, a generic planning model is described, the steps of which subsume many of the tasks associated with formal program planning in continuing higher education. The purpose of this chapter is to expand one step of the planning process that has received an impressive amount of attention in the literature and has achieved a venerable position in the rhetoric of continuing educators. That one step is *needs assessment.*

Neither in-depth analysis of the literature nor careful listening to the discourse of continuing education practitioners is necessary to reach the conclusion that the term *need* and the process known as *needs assessment* are well-entrenched in the language of the field. An analysis of program planning models completed by John H. Buskey and Thomas J. Sork[1] revealed that virtually every model published in the past thirty-five years contained a step, task, or element referred to as needs assessment or was labeled with an accepted synonym. It is clear from a review of this literature that a wide variety of means has become associated with the concept and that a wide range of practices and procedures has come to be described as needs assessment. Belle Ruth Witkin, in a recent comprehensive review of the literature, concluded:

There is no one model or conceptual framework for needs assessment that has been universally accepted, and there is little empirical evidence of the superiority of one approach over another. Moreover, there often appears to be an inverse ratio between the elegance and completeness of a model and its widespread acceptance and implementation.[2]

Any term that is associated with a variety of meanings is useful in general discourse but has limited theoretical and practical utility when used to label a specific conceptual tool or a particular technology. Some persons have gone so far as to propose that the concept be dropped from the language altogether. For example, Russell Mattimore-Knudson contended:

> Far too much time and space have been spent on the concept of need in adult education literature. The term does not seem worthy of such effort (literally dozens of articles have been printed on it), and surely such effort could be spent on much more important areas in adult education as a profession and as an educational system. The recommendation being made here is to discard the term altogether. Using the term "need" is not productive; it can only add work where more work is unnecessary.[3]

Adopting such a recommendation would, however, leave a void in the rhetoric of those engaged in continuing higher education unless a substitute concept and related process were introduced and accepted. A concept and process so entrenched in the literature, thoughts, and speech of a field and so central to the technology of program planning seems worthy of additional attempts to increase their utility. Bonnie Brackhaus, after identifying many of the conceptual and methodological problems associated with needs assessment, concluded:

> Although . . . it may appear that the prospects of needs assessment in adult education are poor, this is not necessarily the case, for needs assessment is a vital process for certain programs. Needs assessment is both cost-effective and essential for adult education programs which are very expensive to run. Accountability is increased because needs assessments provide a rational basis for decisions and increase the likelihood that programs will be successful. As the cost of programs increases, the importance of needs assessment increases.[4]

Consequently, the approach taken here will be to sharpen the definition of need and needs assessment, to propose a generic process of needs assessment with potential for wide application in continuing higher education, and to describe alternatives to needs assessment and the kinds of situations when each would be most appropriate.

## CONCEPTUAL ISSUES

A fundamental problem faced by anyone attempting to sharpen the definition of need is that it has, over the years, been misunderstood, misused, and maligned. Since virtually all program planning models contain a step either explicitly or implicitly referred to as needs assessment, there is the expectation that all good program planners will conduct a needs assessment. However, not all planning situations require a needs assessment, because the resources (time, energy, money) to carry out a proper needs assessment are not available, or because the planner has not distinguished needs assessment from other legitimate means to justify and focus programming efforts, all sorts of data gathering processes have come to be referred to as needs assessments. Since "good" planners always do a needs assessment, anything that is done to justify and focus programming efforts has come to be accepted as a needs assessment.

The position taken here is that needs assessment is *not* an essential step in designing effective and efficient continuing education programs. Some method of justifying and focusing programming efforts is often required, and needs assessment is one of the more powerful means for doing so, but there are legitimate alternatives to needs assessment that the thoughtful programmer should consider whenever the efficacy or feasibility of conducting a needs assessment is questionable.

Of the various conceptions of need found in the literature, the one most commonly presented is known as the discrepancy, gap, or deficiency definition. Although there are conceptual, philosophical, and practical weaknesses associated with this conception, its relatively wide acceptance and potential for application in a broad range of programming situations in continuing higher education make it worthy of more careful analysis. A number of authors have defined this conception in various ways. For example, J. Paul Leagans concluded:

> Needs represent an imbalance, lack of adjustment, or gap between the present situation or status quo and a new or changed set of conditions assumed to be more desirable. Needs may be viewed as the difference between what is, and what ought to be; they always imply a gap.[5]

More recently, Paulette T. Beatty proposed that "need is the measurable discrepancy existing between a present state of affairs and a desired state of affairs as asserted either by an 'owner' of need or by an 'authority' on need."[6] She drew a useful distinction between *prescriptive needs,* which are articulated by an "authority" and *motivational needs,* which are articulated by the "owner" of the discrepancy. This definition and distinction are useful for those involved in continuing higher education for several reasons. First, the discrepancy definition requires that the present state of affairs be clearly described and documented and that the corresponding desired state of affairs be specified so that the gap between the two can be clearly perceived. This requirement makes it impossible to proceed with programming until the planner understands what change is proposed, what new condition is expected at the end of the program, and where things stand at present.

Second, the distinction between prescriptive and motivational needs forces the planner to determine the source of the need. This information is useful in determining the priority of needs and has important implications for developing instructional and administrative plans. For example, a need that is purely prescriptive in origin (not acknowledged by those who are experiencing the need) requires a different instructional approach and marketing strategy than one that is purely motivational or has elements of both. It is possible there will be lack of agreement between "owners" and "others" about the present condition or, more likely, the desired condition. William S. Griffith indicated the inherently political nature of needs assessment; such lack of agreement represents a political problem that should be addressed before planning proceeds.[7] Either the parties must compromise, or the programmer must decide which viewpoint will be accepted for planning purposes. In the best of all worlds, all needs would reflect agreement between "owners" and "others."

Third, employing such a definition eases the task of proceeding from the needs assessment to the formulation of objectives because the specification of the desired state of affairs can often be directly converted into a program objective. Even complex desired states of affairs can be analyzed into component parts which then provide a basis for constructing objectives.

Fourth, the use of the word "discrepancy" accommodates both a remedial orientation in which the purpose of the assessment is to uncover *deficiencies* (discrepancies between actual and expected mandated standards) and a growth orientation in which the purpose of the assessment is to reveal *differences* between acceptable present conditions and more desirable future conditions. Adopting a definition that refers only to deficiencies assumes that the resulting program is purely remedial. Although remediation has its proper place in continuing higher education, to propose remediation as a basis for all programs is neither consistent with the philosophical foundations of higher education or congruent with the expectations of many client systems served by continuing educators.

Finally, employing this definition of need makes the task of evaluating program outcomes much less troublesome than in situations where the impetus for programming is not clearly articulated. This is based on the assumption that evaluation efforts should be beyond the use of a "happiness index," which too often represents the only type of program outcome assessed. A need statement provides focus for evaluation efforts and forces the consideration of higher level outcomes like learning, application of learning, and the consequences of application of learning.

## COMMON APPROACHES TO NEEDS ASSESSMENT

Although by definition needs assessment involves collecting information, the needs assessment process is conceptually distinct from data collection techniques. It is inconsistent to refer to questionnaires, interviews, critical incident analyses, job analyses, report and record reviews, community studies, and similar data collection techniques as needs assessment techniques. Such approaches to data collection are necessary but not sufficient to complete a needs assessment. The problem is similar to that found in evaluation; data collection is not evaluation because evaluation involves making a *judgment,* and without the judgment there is no evaluation. Similarly, if a procedure does not produce a description of a present state of affairs and specification of a more desirable state of affairs, it should not be called a needs assessment. Technically, since priority setting is the final task of needs assessment, the procedure should not be called a needs assessment unless it includes priority setting. The common approaches to needs assessment that follow meet these criteria because they all can result in (1) the description and specification of the present state of affairs and a more desirable state of affairs and (2) the placement of the resulting needs statements in priority order.

### THE SELF-ASSESSMENT

Relying on members of the client system to assess their own needs has a long history in continuing higher education. However, many self-assessment procedures reported in the literature are not strictly needs assessments. Some ask potential clients to identify program topics in which they have an interest; some ask clients to identify problems they are encountering that learning may help them solve; and some ask clients to indicate how relevant certain skills or competencies are to the work they perform, to rate their present abilities, and to reveal how motivated they are to increase their abilities.[8] Of these examples the last comes closest to revealing needs of the client, but it falls short on one important dimension—the desired state of affairs is not specified. All that is revealed is that the clients are motivated to increase their abilities, but it is unclear how great an increase they hope to achieve.

As in any needs assessment, the self-assessment should result in a clear description of the present state of affairs and a specification of the more desirable state of affairs. Effectiveness of the self-assessment depends on how well individuals assess their own abilities. Limited research on the competency of individuals to make such assessments suggests that it is unwise to assume that clients can conduct self-assessments. The primary strengths of the self-assessment are that it (1) places the programmer in direct contact with the client system, thereby increasing the chances that any program designed will be relevant to the client; (2) creates awareness in the client system that the provider is available and willing to provide educational services; (3) causes the client to examine the nature of the work he or she does and the relationship between learning and performance; and (4) places responsibility for making value judgments about the desirable state of affairs with the people who have to act to make it happen.

## THE ADVISORY COMMITTEE

When direct contact with the client system is not feasible, representatives of the system can be invited to participate in needs assessment. The questions asked would be similar to those in the self-assessment, but those responding would be presenting the views and perceptions of their peers. Advisory committees are an economical means of maintaining contact with a client system that makes it possible to monitor needs and to detect emerging needs early. A frequent difficulty with advisory committees is that they tend to move to solutions before clearly articulating the need; prescriptions are made before diagnosis is complete. Forming and maintaining a representative advisory committee requires a substantial investment of planning resources, but the potential benefits of continuous monitoring of needs are clear to those who employ this approach.

## THE PUBLIC FORUM

When the client system is not well-defined, self-assessments and advisory committees obviously have limited utility. Similarly, when the client system is large or made up of numerous subsystems with varied perspectives, a different approach to needs assessment may be required. The public forum represents an opportunity to focus attention on specific areas of concern and to involve quite diverse audiences in the assessment process. Organizing and managing a forum is resource intensive because unless the process is carefully planned and orchestrated, the outcome can become something other than a list of needs in priority order. Some may use the public forum to vent frustrations about the present state of affairs; some may use it to promote pet solutions to real or imagined problems; and some may use it as an opportunity to further their own political, economic, or social objectives. Nevertheless, a well-planned and carefully managed forum can produce a wealth of needs statements and clear priorities for programmers.

## A FRAMEWORK FOR NEEDS ASSESSMENT

Regardless of the approach used to assess needs, a framework must be provided to guide the process from the chaos that typically characterizes early stages of planning through the production of a list of needs statements in priority order, the desired outcome of the assessment process. The following proposed framework is based on the assumption that a careful analysis of the planning context and client system has been completed, resulting in a profile of important client characteristics and an understanding of the milieu in which planning takes place. Those interested in a more detailed explication of needs assessment tasks may find the six steps described by Carolyn W. Barbulesco useful.[9]

*Step 1. Specify the areas of concern.* By its nature, planning involves a progressive focusing of attention and narrowing the field of view. Before any data are collected, the programmer should specify the limits of the assessment. For example, an assessment could be limited to a narrow range of knowledge or skills, a set of competencies related to job performance, a subject field, a problem area, or a single goal thought to be valued by the client system.

*Step 2. Decide who will be involved in the assessment.* Whether one relies on the "owner" of the needs or on an "authority' on needs has important implications for later stages of planning. If only the "owners" are involved, only motivational needs will be revealed. If only "authorities" are involved, only prescriptive needs will be revealed. The programmer should consider the benefits of sequencing involvement in such a way that prescriptive and motivational needs are checked against one another so that disagreements regarding the present and desired state of affairs can be resolved early.

*Step 3. Describe how the present state of affairs will be determined.* This task involves deciding what means will be employed to determine the present condition. The data may already exist in records, reports, test scores, performance appraisals, and other documents. Resources should not be wasted to collect data that are already available. Care must be taken to select a data collection technique that is technically appropriate and feasible to apply and that produces valid and reliable information.

*Step 4. Describe how the desired state of affairs will be determined.* *Desired* states of affairs are based on value judgments and therefore cannot be determined by observation or analysis. The approach used to establish the desired state should acknowledge the judgmental nature of the process, seek some level of consensus among those who are making the judgments, and treat the data as value-based rather than as factually based. Desired states may be based only on beliefs about a "proper" or "more desirable" level of performance or set of outcomes, but they can also be specified by making reference to existing performance or outcomes in another similar client system. In other words, the desired condition may be determined by comparing performance or outcomes of two similar systems and then making a judgment about the relevance of the comparison to the client system of concern.

*Step 5. Plan how data will be processed.* A needs assessment involves collecting data that must be analyzed and summarized before it is of use for programming. The manner in which this is done should be decided prior to initiating the assessment. Unless the capacity and the desire to process the information into a useful form are both present, the assessment should not be initiated. Information about the present and desired states of affairs must be consolidated into needs statements that can serve as information for the priority-setting step. Although needs statements can take many forms depending on the nature of the information collected, they should always include a clear description of the present state of affairs (PSA) and a complete specification of the desired state of affairs (DSA). The hypothetical needs statements that follow illustrate the basic form that should be applied if the assessment is based on the definition of needs discussed above:

- *PSA 1.* Analysis of records reveals that during the past twelve months, 30 percent of the patients under treatment complied with less than 80 percent of their instructions for therapy.

- *DSA 1.* During the twelve-month period commencing January 1, the percentage of patients complying with less than 80 percent of their instructions for therapy will be no more than 15 percent.

- *PSA 2.* Forty percent of those responding to the survey reported they did not have the knowledge of skills required to properly administer CPR to a person experiencing cardiac arrest.
- *DSA 2.* Six months following a series of programs, no more than 15 percent of the respondents will indicate lack of knowledge of skills required to properly administer CPR.
- *PSA 3.* In a self-assessment completed two months ago, a majority of respondents (53 percent) indicated they were not aware of the legal and ethical implications of the recently amended Public Records Access Act.
- *DSA 3.* In six months, following a series of programs and other information dissemination activities, no more than 30 percent of the professionals will indicate such lack of awareness, and after two years no more than 10 percent will do so.
- *PSA 4.* Our advisory committee on business programs has indicated that a high percentage of small business failures (they estimated 60–70 percent) are attributable to lack of necessary capitalization during the first year of operation.
- *DSA 4.* After a series of programs focusing on how to determine capital requirements, how to locate sources of capital, and how to acquire capital, the estimated rate of first-year failures attributable to under-capitalization will fall by at least 25 percent.

Constructing needs statements of this general form can be a challenging task, but the examples should illustrate the clear focus for programming that needs assessment provides—a focus that may be missing when alternatives to needs assessment are employed in planning.

*Step 6: Decide how priorities will be determined.* A carefully planned needs assessment will usually reveal more needs than there are resources. Consequently, the programmer must decide which needs will receive attention first, second, third, and so on, until all available resources are committed.

Priority setting is the final step of needs assessment. It is given extended treatment here because it has generally received little attention in the literature. Although the common conception of *priority* is "that which is most important," it literally means "that which received first attention." Decisions about what received first attention are not always based on the importance of the activity or service. In continuing higher education, priority of needs may be based on several criteria that seem to fall into two general categories: those related to the importance of meeting a need and those related to the feasibility of meeting a need.

## IMPORTANCE CRITERIA

Importance criteria are related to the amount of value placed on eliminating the discrepancy between the present state of affairs and the desired state of affairs. There are at least five importance criteria that may be useful to the programmer in continuing higher education.

*Number of people affected.* This criterion can be used to establish priority based on the number of people who would benefit if the desired state of affairs were realized. The larger the number of people affected, the higher the priority of need.

*Contribution to goals.* This criterion can be used to establish priority based on the degree to which meeting the need would contribute to the attainment of institutional goals. It is quite likely that a needs assessment will reveal some goals that are unrelated to the goals of a college or university. Such needs would be of lower priority than needs that are directly related to the goals of the institution.

*Immediacy.* This criterion can be used to establish priority based on the degree to which each need requires immediate attention. Immediacy is determined by analyzing how the situation has been changing over time. If it appears that a need is becoming more acute as time passes, that need would be considered of higher priority than needs that are stable or are becoming less acute over time. Determining immediacy requires the collection and analysis of time-series data—information that indicates how the situation has developed historically and suggests how it might change in the future if no action is taken to eliminate the need.

*Instrumental value.* This criterion can be used to establish priority based on the degree to which meeting one need will have a positive or negative effect on meeting other needs. It is based on the assumption that certain needs, when met, will increase the likelihood the other needs will be met and should be considered of higher priority than needs that will decrease the likelihood that other needs will be met.

*Magnitude of the discrepancy.* This criterion can be used to establish priority based on the relative size of the "gap" (measurable discrepancy) between the present state of affairs and the desirable state of affairs. Since information used to describe a need is not always the same, determining magnitude of the discrepancy often involves making a "best guess" about the relative sizes of the gaps.

## FEASIBILITY CRITERIA

Feasibility criteria are related to the likelihood that the discrepancy can be eliminated. There are at least three feasibility criteria that are useful in continuing higher education.

*Educational efficacy.* This criterion can be used to establish priority based on the degree to which an educational intervention (program or series of programs) can contribute to eliminating the needs. Not all needs can be eliminated solely by providing a continuing education program. For example, some needs that appear on the surface to be amenable to an educational or training program may, on careful analysis, be found to be alterable only through changes in policy, procedures, personnel, or an adjustment in the systems of rewards and sanctions that exist in organizations, institutions, and communities. Continuing educators should be careful when claiming that change can be effected through education unless they have sufficient evidence to support such claims.

Using this criterion, needs judged to have high educational effectiveness will be considered to be of higher priority since the "tool" used by programmers is education. Needs judged to have low educational effectiveness would be of lower priority and might be referred to other institutions and agencies better able to address the need, or cooperative arrangements might be made to employ education and other means concurrently to eliminate a need requiring more than one approach.

*Availability of resources.* This criterion can be used to establish priority based on the degree to which the resources necessary to meet the need will be available if it is decided that the need should be addressed. Use of this criterion involves making a judgment about the potential availability of human, financial, physical, and other resources necessary to respond to a need. Needs for which all or most of the required resources are potentially available (or for which few or no resources are required) would be given higher priority than needs for which the necessary resources would not be available. It is true that resources required to address an otherwise high priority need can often be "created," so the judgment regarding availability should take into account the *potential* for creating the necessary resources.

*Commitment to change.* This criterion can be used to establish priority based on the degree to which "relevant publics" are committed to eliminating the need. "Relevant publics" are people or groups of people who have a vested interest in the success or failure of efforts to eliminate needs; they are often in a position to help or hinder the programmer's efforts to develop and implement programs. This criterion reflects, in part, the political realities of resource allocation decisions. For example, there may be strong political forces operating to assure that a certain client group is well-served by the institution. Programming efforts that benefit that client group will receive active support, while efforts that divert attention from the group may be actively opposed. Responding to such political realities in the priority-setting process is appropriate, but should be balanced by criteria related to the importance of meeting needs as well. Using this criterion involves identifying "relevant publics," deciding the relative importance of each public's commitment, and assessing the commitment to change of each individual or group. If the programmer is dealing with a purely prescriptive need, the client group would be an important relevant public since if the group does not acknowledge the need, commitment to change may be zero.

The preceding importance and feasibility criteria represent conceptual tools that programmers, directors, deans, and others can use to decide what needs will receive prior attention. The priority-setting process can, at one extreme, be informal, intuitive, and rapid or, at the other extreme, it can be formal, systematic, and time-consuming. The benefits to be derived from employing a process that falls on the formal/time-intensive end of the continuum should be clear before a decision is made to pay the costs.

## ALTERNATIVES TO NEEDS ASSESSMENT

Although it is possible—some would say desirable—to force a needs assessment paradigm on *every* situation requiring program planning, such a practice can distort the meaning of needs assessment, cause frustration among programmers who may feel satisfied with information obtained using other means, and ultimately discount the practical utility of the method for informing decision makers. *Alternatives* to needs assessment that can provide sufficient information for justifying and focusing programming efforts follow. These alternatives should be considered when either the resources are not available to conduct a proper needs assessment or when the nature of the planning task does not require the identification and validation of present states of affairs and the specification of more desirable states of affairs. They are considered to be alternatives to needs assessment, rather than different forms of needs assessment, because they do not result in the identification of gaps or discrepancies.

### THE INTEREST INVENTORY

When clients are asked to indicate their preferences among a listing of potential program topics, their responses are based on their interests. The expression of interest in program topics seems to have little power to predict participation in programs. However, the interest inventory can provide limited justification and focus for programming efforts, although the information is not as useful for developing objectives and evaluating programs as needs statements. The usual outcome of an interest inventory is a statement such as, "Fifty percent of those responding to our survey indicated they are interested in the program topic 'Selecting Computers for Small Business.' " A more direct approach to the assessment of potential demand for programs would ask the respondents either to indicate those programs in which they would likely enroll or to indicate on a scale their *relative* interest in the alternative topics presented. The analysis of past enrollment patterns is a natural, economical, and relatively reliable method of determining interest in various types of programs. Plotting enrollments, over time, for categories of programs can reveal topics or types of programs with an upward growth trend as well as those in decline that may be reaching the end of their life cycle.

The interest inventory and its variants are particularly useful in situations where a programmer must limit offerings to those with greatest potential *demand.* It provides a basis for selecting the offerings most likely to finish in the front of the field. It helps the programmer concentrate on preparing items for the "cafeteria line" with the best chance of being consumed. It is assumed that the programmer knows the recipes for the dishes that will be in greatest demand, so there is little point in asking the patrons for their opinions about either the ingredients or the method of preparation.

## THE MARKET TEST

In some situations it may be economically justifiable to design and offer programs and wait and see how many enrollments result. Philip M. Nowlen observed:

> This approach of offering a sample to test the market has the advantage of allowing potential participants to respond not only to a phrase in a list of topics [as in an interest inventory] but to a specific program description, resource person, day, time, location, and price. Furthermore, the commitment of time, money, and attention provides a much firmer basis for predicting future enrollments by similar adults than merely indicating a topic on an interest inventory.[10]

There are ethical issues related to the use of this approach that are often not acknowledged. Arranging to participate in an educational program is often a psychologically, socially, and physically demanding activity. If a person makes the commitment to attend a program and discovers that because of insufficient demand the program was cancelled, that person's motivation to enroll in future programs and confidence in the provider may be affected. Application of the market test alternative to needs assessment should be considered only after the ethical questions have been resolved. Deciding and arranging to "consume" an educational program is a very different process than buying a new product while strolling through a grocery or department store.

## THE COMPELLING MANDATE

The justification and focus for some programming activities come from a source or are presented in such a way that no further information is needed. In some cases the impetus and focus are provided by an individual in a position of power, influence, or authority; in some cases by a rule, regulation, or law; and in some cases by a large number of potential participants. Situations in which the compelling mandate drives the planning process are usually characterized by clear definition of direction and little or no disagreement about the appropriateness of the program. In fact, it is likely that an inquiry about conducting a needs assessment would produce rather puzzled reactions (verbal and nonverbal) from those responding to the mandate.

Conflicts can arise if the compelling mandate becomes the primary justification for programming primarily because of its highly political nature, as do many mandates that affect continuing higher education, or because of the highly reactive nature of such programming. Responding to mandates, if it becomes the institution's *modus operandi*, may result in conducting programs with good intentions while ignoring more serious problems that require immediate attention.

## THE TREND ANALYSIS

A disadvantage of the discrepancy definition of need is that it does not easily accommodate *projected* or anticipated conditions that would be undesirable, that is, situations in which the present state of affairs is satisfactory (no need exists) but where analysis reveals that the situation will soon change to one that is undesirable. In such cases it would be important to take immediate action to prevent the undesirable from occurring. Trend analysis is the process of monitoring conditions over time and projecting changes in the conditions based on knowledge of the past. Trend analysis requires the collection and analysis of time-series information, which is a resource-intensive activity. Trend analysis is especially resource-intensive if the information must be *collected* rather than *retrieved* from reliable sources.

Trend analysis is particularly important in fields where the rate of change is relatively high and in human affairs where changes in social, economic, or political structures have far-ranging consequences. Trends have a habit of changing direction without much warning; thus, projecting trends is a high-risk operation. But if the weaknesses are understood and the results presented in terms of probability of occurrence, trend analysis can be a potent antidote to the overly reactive stance taken by too many continuing educators and continuing education units in colleges and universities.

## THE PROBLEM ANALYSIS

Many planning models use problem analysis as an organizational paradigm. The impetus for planning activities comes from the realization that a problem exists and that some attempt should be made to resolve, eliminate, or moderate the condition. Problem analysis usually results in a clarification of the present state of affairs; it is assumed the desired condition is that the problem no longer exists or its impact is reduced. After the nature of the problem is clarified, attention shifts to consideration of means to eliminate the problem. Education is usually one of several means that might be used. As in the case of the compelling mandate, the problem might be so well-defined and the perceived need for action so clear that performing a needs assessment would be considered unnecessary.

What may begin as a problem analysis can easily become a proper needs assessment if the desired state of affairs is clearly specified in terms of knowledge, skills, performance, or other outcomes. However, if the classic steps of problem solving are followed, the analysis will not provide as specific a focus for programming as a needs assessment.

## THE PERIPATETIC PROGRAMMER

Some individuals seem to have a natural talent for identifying program ideas with great promise. It may be the product of an innate or intuitive sense they have developed; it may be the result of a free-ranging creative mind; or it could be the result of insights gained from past experience. Whatever the origin, this type of programmer will suggest a novel program idea that has great potential, not only for generating revenue but for addressing an important or emerging issue or capitalizing on a latent interest in a large number of people. It is not clear how the talents of the peripatetic programmer can be isolated or even how they can be cultivated. The important point is that their ideas are successful; the organization in which they work should be willing to accept promising ideas even if they are not documented by hard data and covered by the rhetoric of needs assessment.

## INTERNAL AND EXTERNAL RELATIONSHIPS

Needs assessment and the previously described alternatives are a means of improving the decision-making process in continuing higher education. The utility of the information obtained depends not only on the technical skills of those involved in collecting, processing, and reporting the information, but also on the truthfulness of information sources. Maintaining relationships with those in a position to provide information on needs, problems, interests, and demand is essential to the effective operation of a continuing education unit. In many cases, college or university faculty members will suggest program ideas based on their knowledge of a subject or on their interactions with potential clients outside the institution. In some instances, continuing education programmers will identify program ideas based on their contacts with professionals, community groups, associations, or on their analysis of current events, emerging trends, or technological developments.

A characteristic of successful continuing education units is the considerable energy devoted to the task of developing and maintaining open communication channels with groups inside their institutions and with client systems outside their institutions. By definition and choice, successful continuing education operations are often systems that seek and receive constant information from their environment and that react to that information by adjusting procedures, designing programs, and offering learning opportunities.

One note of caution concerns the effect that needs assessment has on the expectations of potential clients. By asking people to express their desires, goals, expectations, and hopes, expectations are raised that an institution intends to respond. In cultivating relationships with external groups, the intentions of the programmers should be made clear. If the intention is to plan and offer programs immediately in response to the information received from the client group, that intent should be communicated; if the intent is to use the information for long-range planning with little chance that any immediate benefit will accrue to the client system, that information should also be made clear. Otherwise, the motives of the programmer may be questioned and the image of the institution damaged. Using a needs assessment primarily as a public relations tool can have negative consequences. An assessment suggests an institution is interested in the clients it serves. However, if the institution fails to respond to the clients' needs or does so only on a superficial basis, those who have participated in the assessment can rightfully regard the continuing education unit and the college or university it represents as opportunistic and unreliable.

## SUMMARY

Needs assessment can be a very powerful tool for continuing education programs, but as is the case with any tool, it must be used for the right job and it must be used as intended if it is to have the greatest utility. Over the years, continuing educators have made needs assessment one of the standard implements in their tool chests but have different conceptions of what the tool looks like and use it to perform different jobs. If the tool is well-constructed, maintained properly, used for the right job, and is not abused, it should serve the programmer well. The ideas and perspectives presented in this chapter may help the apprentice, journeyman, or master craftsman of continuing education programs consider some of the issues associated with the selection, maintenance, and application of this tool.

## REFERENCES

1. Buskey, John H., and Sork, Thomas J., "From Chaos to Order in Program Planning: A System for Selecting Models and Ordering Research," *Proceedings of the Adult Education Research Conference* (Lincoln: Department of Adult and Continuing Education, University of Nebraska–Lincoln, 1982), pp. 54–59.

2. Witkin, Belle Ruth, *Assessing Needs in Educational and Social Programs* (San Francisco: Jossey-Bass, 1984), p. 29.

3. Mattimore-Knudson, Russell, "The Concept of Need: Its Hedonistic and Logical Nature," *Adult Education,* 33 (1983), p. 119.

4. Brackhaus, Bonnie, "Needs Assessment in Adult Education: Its Problems and Prospects," *Adult Education Quarterly,* 34 (1984), p. 237.

5. Leagans, J. Paul, "A Concept of Needs," *Journal of Extension,* 2 (1964), p. 92.

6. Beatty, Paulette T., "The Concept of Need: Proposal for Working Definition," *Journal of the Community Development Society,* 12 (1981), p. 40.

7. Griffith, William S., "Educational Needs: Definition, Assessment, and Utilization," *School Review,* 86 (1978), pp. 382–394.

8. Scisson, Edward H., "A Typology of Needs Assessment Definitions in Adult Education," *Adult Education,* 33(1) (1982), pp. 20–28.

9. Barbulesco, Carolyn W., "Components of a Major Needs Assessment Study," in *Assessing Educational Needs of Adults,* ed. Floyd C. Pennington, New Directions for Continuing Education, No. 7 (San Francisco: Jossey-Bass, 1980).

10 Nowlen, Philip M., "Programs and Origins," *Developing, Administering and Evaluating Adult Education,* ed. Alan B. Knox and Associates (San Francisco: Jossey-Bass, 1980), p. 31.

# -9-
# AN ANALYSIS OF DELIVERY SYSTEM ALTERNATIVES

## Mary L. Walshok

The term *delivery systems* refers to the means by which knowledge is communicated or delivered to a learner. There is a variety of means by which knowledge is communicated: in person, in print, through telecommunications. There is also a variety of formats in which knowledge is communicated: intensively in a few hours or days; over weeks, months, even years; in a lecture or discussion mode; through one-way or two-way communication. Delivery systems involve both the means for and format of the communication of knowledge to learners.

Continuing education is not characterized by any single approach to program delivery. In the varied college and university environments in which continuing educators work, continuing education programs are generally organized along academic discipline lines, which parallel campus departments, or by delivery systems, such as conferences, courses, or telecommunications, or by a combination of these. The form of delivery depends on the types of adult learners served by an institution and the role of the continuing education program within the overall academic mission of the campus.

In a discussion about delivery systems, it is useful to begin with the assumption that a continuing educator is in large part a "broker." The continuing educator is a link between the world of ideas—teaching, research, and scholarship—and the world of the adult student. Continuing education as an academic enterprise is highly diverse and multidimensional depending upon the characteristics of the learner being served, the characteristics of the knowledge or skills being shared, and the characteristics of the institutional context in which the learner and the knowledge are brought together.

When considering delivery systems, a continuing educator needs to be sensitive to a number of issues, such as whether or not to offer weekend, evening, and/or part-time programs and whether or not to utilize telecommunications for instruction or set up off-campus centers. Adult students, like traditional students, are highly differentiated in terms of their needs, motivations, and abilities by such factors as age, sex, education, occupation, income, religion, social and ethnic group, level of educational attainment, occupational or professional status, formal and informal peer group expectations, family status, economic resources, and what sociologists call their store of "cultural capital." It is necessary to consider such factors when planning continuing education delivery systems for adult learners.

It is not enough to differentiate sociologically adult students, however. The continuing educator must also consider the highly differentiated character of higher education systems as formal institutions functioning in a larger socioeconomic environment. Institutions of higher education vary in their primary "missions" or functions. They are structured in different ways and, equally important, they exist in very different environments. A teaching-oriented state university in a midwestern city with a declining population base and declining "smokestack" industries is "doing business" in a different environment than a university in a southwestern city where the population is exploding and economic growth is tied to a growing high technology and service economy. Perceptions of adult learners and the appropriate ways to reach them will be affected by demographic and economic environmental factors.

This chapter begins with a discussion of a series of issues continuing education planners need to address concerning the adult learners they wish to serve, the kinds of knowledge being offered, the institutional contexts in which it is being offered, and the larger sociological environment in which the institution functions. Addressing these issues is the first step in determining the appropriate delivery systems for specific audiences interested in specific topics. These issues are as important to the continuing educator as a knowledge of the range of delivery systems available for adult learners. Planners need more than knowledge of options; they need a set of guidelines and decision criteria related to important academic and student issues to apply when determining suitable delivery systems. The decision criteria will assist a continuing educator in the critical process of determining what kind of knowledge is needed for what specific type of adult learner and under what specific conditions. This information aids the educator in the determination of appropriate methodologies or delivery systems.

# FACTORS IN EVALUATING DELIVERY SYSTEMS: DECISION CRITERIA

There are a number of factors other than the special needs of adult students that must be considered when evaluating delivery systems: (1) the character of the knowledge/information to be transmitted; (2) the characteristics of the audience for whom the knowledge is intended and the purposes for which the knowledge/information is sought; (3) the core education emphases and standards of the college or university offering the program; (4) the material resources available to support specific forms of program delivery and costs relative to the number of students served; (5) the human resources available to plan and implement programs that serve the needs of the constituency while also serving the overall academic mission of the institution; and (6) the character of the surrounding environment, which includes the broad socioeconomic environment, the value placed on education, and what is being done by other providers in continuing education.

Once these issues have been addressed, the continuing educator is in a position to evaluate the appropriateness and feasibility of a variety of formats for delivering continuing higher education. The planner can also review the delivery options available and evaluate them in relation to their costs and benefits. The methods and systems used to deliver educational programs are described later in the chapter following a discussion of the various factors that need to be taken into account when reviewing delivery alternatives.

## THE CHARACTER OF THE KNOWLEDGE/INFORMATION BEING DELIVERED

Curriculum courses tend to be organized around different types of knowledge transmission in continuing education programs across the country, such as (1) building block foundation courses in the humanities, arts, mathematics, biological, physical, and social sciences; (2) applied knowledge as it relates to practice in the world of work and the solution of specific problems in vocational, technical, and professional realms; (3) basic skill and competency development at introductory or advanced levels; (4) values clarification, attitude development, and consciousness raising; (5) social and environmental analyses; and (6) "state of the art" offerings.

Different types of knowledge/information require different instructional approaches. It is not merely the circumstances of the learners and the experiences and parameters they bring to the learning situation that determine how knowledge should be delivered but the nature of the knowledge itself. In some cases, thirty class hours of notetaking on the lectures of a highly skilled specialist is the best approach; in others, hands-on opportunities with computers and in labs, case studies, or field work are essential. For some groups a one-day seminar will be sufficient to provide an intensive update for a disparate group of experts, while in some situations special materials and lengthy reading and writing assignments are necessary because of the building-block character of the knowledge or the complexity of the value and ethical issues addressed. For others, a short session on how to use a comprehensive reference book may be sufficient; for some, the use of audio/video delivery may be both efficient and effective. Program/course content is a critical factor in deciding the appropriateness of a given delivery system.

## THE CHARACTERISTICS OF THE ADULT LEARNER AND THE PURPOSES OF KNOWLEDGE ACQUISITION

Adult learners, like young adults, are highly differentiated in terms of their needs, motivations, and abilities. It could be argued that adults have even more pronounced differences because of the oc-cupational and economic consequences in their early educational attainment. People become tracked occupationally based on early levels of educational attainment. Different vocational and occupational sectors provide different opportunities for intellectual growth and personal development. It is not accurate to assume that an adult, by virtue of "life experience," is automatically a more motivated, capable learner. The knowledge, motivation, and social class differences of the adult learner must be assessed. The adult with a background in liberal arts coupled with a professional degree is a different kind of learner, and interprets both the utilitarian and symbolic values of further education differently than an adult in his or her middle thirties who is working toward a first degree. Such distinctions are important to planners. An understanding of such differences can facilitate pro-gram development responsive to the needs of different adult con-stituencies. To do this a continuing education planner must have a "feel" for, as well as data on, the central characteristics of the adult constituency in order to serve it effectively and make appropriate delivery system decisions. An example may be useful.

Supporters and advocates of general education have lamented the low level of utilization of "telecourses" at major research univer-sities in continuing education/extension programs. Many have attri-buted it to traditionalism and faculty resistance. However, a close look at the students enrolled in continuing education programs at institutions such as Harvard, New York University, or the University of California reveals a student profile very different from that of the community colleges and state universities, which make greater use of television instruction.[1] Nearly 80 percent of the adult students at research universities hold a bachelor's degree, and half of these students have an advanced degree or credential. Such students are generally pursuing professional advancement or personal enrichment; they are not seeking degrees. Surveys conducted at the University of California and Harvard indicated the two primary reasons for taking an extension course are: the opportunity to take a course on campus with high quality faculty members and the opportunity to interact with fellow students who are intellectual and professional peers.[2] The two elements valued most by these adult students are eliminated by television instruction.

In contrast, television instruction has been found to be very successful in research universities as a delivery system for highly specialized "state of the art" technical and professional update courses for engineers, doctors, and lawyers. This information is usually presented "closed circuit" in a very direct, low cost, "talking head" manner; student satisfaction is high because the information is pertinent to their immediate responsibilities.

There are profound differences in the level of preparation, motivation, and utilitarian and symbolic values that adults attach to their learning experiences. The successful continuing education planner will consider these elements when choosing delivery systems.

## CORE PURPOSES OF THE INSTITUTION: FOR WHAT IS THE INSTITUTION KNOWN?

There is no one system of higher education in the United States; there is an infinite variety of institutions of different types and with differing purposes. Geographic location, funding sources, and types of degrees offered are the most distinguishing characteristics. Some institutions of higher education, however, such as religious and evangelical colleges and women's or traditional black colleges, differ in their commitment to serve a particular constituency. Institutions may also be distinguished by their capacity to serve part-time and evening students or full-time day students; their provision of a broad liberal arts curriculum, preparation for the world of work, or preparation for further study in graduate and professional fields; their status as a teaching or research institution; or their designation as a residential or commuter campus.

Continuing education planners must have a clear sense of the particular "niche" their institution occupies in the educational marketplace. Three key questions about the institution suggest the issues that must be addressed: What is the primary academic mission? Who or what is the primary student constituency? To what set of political and economic interests is the institution accountable?

*What is the primary academic mission?* Here the issues are fairly clear and familar. Does the institution offer a vocational/technical program to certify persons for specific occupations, or does it offer a liberal arts education? An organization's position in the academic marketplace is determined by the undergraduate curriculum and the requirements for graduation. Persons interested in jobs and certification for entry-level work immediately upon graduation are more likely to attend an institution where they can concentrate on professional studies as an undergraduate. Students concerned about postgraduate work in engineering or medicine may be drawn to an institution where the emphasis is placed on a major. Those less pressed by occupational or economic concerns may prefer an institution where they can pursue a broad liberal arts curriculum. The continuing educator should know the structure of the institution's undergraduate curriculum and how to build on or transform the curriculum when attempting to serve the adult learner.

These distinctions apply to graduate education as well. Many institutions offering graduate programs do so only at the master's level and in such professional fields as teaching, business administration, and social work. They often serve the local professional workforce and schedule classes so that a full-time worker can do graduate work in the late afternoons and evenings. The state university college system in California is an excellent example of a system that provides high quality, flexible degree programs in professional fields for working adults. Doctoral-granting institutions, particularly those at major research universities, have not been as flexible in accommodating adult students in either their professional schools or academic departments. One reason for this is their strong commitment to the expansion and discovery of knowledge along with teaching.

*Who or What is the primary student constituency?* An institution's academic reputation has a profound impact on delivery systems. If the institution's reputation is primarily local (based on a local student body and alumni group) this may affect how well respected its certification and degree programs will be outside the immediate community and how willing local employers and industries will be to work with the institution on specific programs. This reputation will affect how exportable, whether through off-campus seminars and conferences or telecommunications delivery, the institution's programs can be. Because of its regional or statewide reputation, the institution's programs have a different potential for outreach. If an institution is a nationally known liberal arts college or research university, its program potential may be entirely different in character.

The success of residential summer programs for adults at nationally recognized institutions may be as much a function of the desire for adult students to be affiliated with a prestigious institution as a function of specific programs.

Admission standards are also related to student profiles. To adults, performance standards and selectivity are symbolically important. For example, the continuing educator planning an off-campus program or part-time degree option for adults at a highly selective institution may be wise to argue for selective admissions and a certain percentage of on-campus work with tenured faculty rather than to make a broad appeal for open admissions and a parallel degree. Strategically, faculty members may be more supportive of selective admissions because the admittance of adults does not represent a shift in admissions standards. Selective admisssion may also be regarded as a positive factor by potential adult learners who equate such standards with quality and leverage in the professional marketplace.

A clear picture of the demographic makeup of the student population is important when determining necessary and appropriate delivery systems to serve adult needs. Demographic data reveal what the main campus provides in student support services and what delivery systems have been established on which to build special programs for adults. They also represent a clue to the segments of the adult population the program might best serve and the potential points of entry and support for adult programs in the larger community.

*To what set of political and economic interests is the institution accountable?* At a research university—where less than one-third of the annual budget comes from state revenues (the remainder coming from fees, contracts, and grants),[3] where faculty members perceive themselves as part of a national and international community of scholars, and where a growing student body includes a large percentage of out-of-state and international students, particularly in graduate programs—the levers that stimulate interest in adult learners and elicit support for alternative delivery systems may be different than those at a privately funded liberal arts college. At the private liberal arts college, the need for accountability to alumni, carrying out the primary liberal education mission of the school, and embracing adults in the face of declining undergraduate enrollments may encourage the development of off-campus credit programs and innovations in the timing or sequencing of on-campus courses and degree requirements.

An institution that receives primarily tax-based funding and that is subjected to line-item budgeting by the legislature has a different set of opportunities and limitations when developing delivery systems to respond to adult learners. Such a system does not have as much discretion to experiment and innovate as a private institution. Even among private institutions, the political and educational values of the trustees and alumni may result in an open or closed system. A community college, based on local control and serving a local constituency through community service programs, will have a different set of political and economic interests than either a state university or private institution.

## MATERIAL RESOURCES OF THE INSTITUTION

The physical and material resources of institutions also vary. On some campuses classrooms are underutilized due to declining student enrollments; other campuses are bursting at the seams. Generally speaking, resources for maintenance, renovation, or building new facilities are limited and often nonexistent. These factors affect program delivery and explain some of the interest in the use of new teaching technologies (television, audio, videodisc, computers for off-campus instruction). Even the new technologies, however, require funds for installation and maintenance.

The physical plant—classrooms, faculty offices, labs, library facilities, and parking—is a major factor in determining what programs can be offered to adult learners and under what circumstances. An off-campus center or courses taught on-site at the workplace may be the only option for an overcrowded campus. Hotels and community centers offer good settings if poor parking or inadequate food services are a problem on the campus. Regionally offered courses may be appropriate because of the time spent driving to campus in rural or large metropolitan areas, and in some areas of the country inclement weather may pose obstacles to classes scheduled on campus. Depending on the conditions, telephone linkages, computer networks, or television courses by microwave, satellite, or cable to selected sites or individual homes may solve delivery problems. Continuing education planners must not depend solely on a particular delivery system or operate with a set of unexamined assumptions about the needs and preferences of their constituents. Flexibility and adaptability are required when the continuing educator makes decisions about program delivery systems.

The technological capacity of the campus is an important factor in the facilities issue. Campuses vary in their ability to tie into teleconference networks and deliver television instruction. Even closed circuit instruction in systems already in place, such as the Instructional Television Fixed Service or local cable networks, require studio space or "wired" classrooms. Computer education is in great demand, but campuses may be limited in the extent to which they can provide hardware and software resources. Engineers working with sophisticated program languages need different technological supports than consumers interested in personal computers. In the case that an institution lacks resources, a continuing educator may be forced to take a program off-campus in order to offer the appropriate instruction.

Two additional items that may be pertinent to continuing educators, depending on their objectives, are the campus administrative system and the status of the campus budget. The more freedom given a continuing education unit to develop its own management systems—registration, accounting, income and expense tracking, purchasing and contracting with external agents—the more flexibility there will be in the types and forms of delivery systems that can be developed. Off-campus programs involve leasing, purchasing, liability arrangements, and contracts with companies and vendors, all of which require staff time, expertise, and flexible administrative systems. Discretion should be allowed in the pricing of programs and dispersing of revenues. Generally, innovative, varied continuing education programs are seen at institutions that allow a great deal of administrative flexibility and budgetary discretion. A continuing educator must take these managerial factors into account before committing the unit to a plan of action.

## HUMAN RESOURCES

Delivery systems are closely tied to the character and quality of human resources on the campus, within the continuing education unit, and in the broader community. Human resources must be considered in a broad context, for they are possibly *the* most critical variable to assess when making a decision about delivery systems. Human resources include the depth and breadth of the instructional personnel, the continuing education staff, academic and general support, campus advocates, community boosters, and networks. They are affected by staff size and diversity.

Faculty strength, range of expertise, and availability are critical parts of the continuing education programming equation. The challenge of identifying and recruiting appropriate instructional staff for evening, off-campus, or mediated instruction programs may be quite different in various parts of the country. There must be sufficient faculty resources, a broad range of topics in which competence is demonstrated, and a large, well-educated pool of off-campus professionals to mount a program with a variety of delivery systems. It is not easy to find highly qualified persons who will accept evening or weekend commitments. It is even more difficult to find persons able to take on daytime assignments at industrial sites or provide in-service education at schools and hospitals. Travel time to remote sites is often a problem as well.

The supply of human resources depends on the particular institution and the specific setting. If faculty members are underutilized or looking for additional income, they are often willing to participate in continuing education activities. However, if they have heavy teaching loads or are busy with other activities, such as private consulting, a national lecture circuit, or research grants and fellowships, they will be less accessible. There are many qualified master's-level and doctoral-level humanists, researchers, lecturers, lab technicians, and computer programmers who are potentially excellent instructors at a major research university. In an industrialized or urban area, the continuing educator can draw on the well-educated professional workforce in human resource departments, research and development units, and finance and marketing divisions. Instructors can also be found in law, accounting, or advertising firms. Personnel available to teach various programs at a given time and location will vary from place to place. The human resource base for instruction is a major issue for continuing educators and must be carefully assessed before decisions are made about program delivery.

Each delivery system carries special requirements. Student registration and recordkeeping are relatively easy as long as students enroll on campus. However, off-campus students often have problems with on-campus enrollment. At many institutions, students are allowed to enroll by mail or phone and to pay with credit cards, adding to the cost of registration. When students register at off-campus centers or on-site programs in schools, hospitals, or businesses, off-campus proctors, security precautions, and increased auditing measures are necessary. Thus, while off-campus programs and alternative delivery systems are highly responsive to adults, they do require special resources.

## ASSESSING THE COMPETITION

A final consideration in evaluating the potential effectiveness of a specific delivery system is an assessment of the competition. This assessment should include an investigation of formats used by other continuing education providers, the service area, subject areas, level of instruction, and targeted adult audiences. If no one is offering a program a continuing educator believes needs to be provided in a certain format for an adult group, and if the need is there, the price is right, and the previously mentioned issues have been addressed, the planner should proceed. If the marketplace for continuing education is overrun with providers, continuing education planners should be certain that some distinguishing characteristic of their program will appeal to currently served adult students or that there is some segment of the adult student market still unserved. An evening program will not be the solution to declining daytime enrollments if it fails to find a "niche" in an already well-served community. Planners of on-site education programs must give industry officials something they are not already receiving from their own training departments, professional education groups, or other colleges and universities. A series of intensive business seminars at local hotels is an excellent approach as long as three other colleges are not doing the same thing for the same audience at the same time. Success in the academic marketplace cannot be assured soley by the delivery approach. Each delivery approach must be evaluated in respect to what is offered by other providers, the size of the total adult student audience available for a given subject area, and the institution's potential market share.

## SUMMARY OF DECISION CRITERIA

Continuing educators need to take more than a "cookbook" approach to programming. Programs should not be designed on the basis of what is being done by other continuing educators, and planners should not jump on the innovative delivery system bandwagon as a way of flexing their professional muscles. Continuing educators work in unique institutions, in different environments, and with particular resources. The various delivery alternatives exist in order to communicate increasingly complex bodies of knowledge to the growing and diverse population of adult students in a dynamic learning society. Informed delivery decisions can be made if continuing educators have a critical understanding of: (1) the character of the knowledge that is transmitted; (2) the characteristics of the adult learners served; (3) the core purposes of their college or university; (4) the available material resources; (5) the available human resources; and (6) their institutional position vis-à-vis the competition. Delivery alternatives should be evaluated and selected on the basis of appropriateness for the specific audience learning a specific topic from an institution of higher education.

## ALTERNATIVE DELIVERY SYSTEMS

The variety and combination of formats and technologies available to the continuing educator for the delivery of educational programs are diverse and rapidly expanding. For example, students taking a broadcast television course may also be required to participate in on-campus discussion groups. Engineers in a flexible master's degree program may take a combination of on-campus course work, Instructional Television Fixed Service broadcast courses at their worksite, and intensive courses in the summer. An evaluation of alternative technologies and formats must be appropriate and feasible in light of the students' needs and educational objectives. Program delivery options available to the planner are described in this portion of the chapter.

For purposes of discussion, the various delivery options have been organized into five general categories: (1) on-campus instruction; (2) off-campus instruction; (3) independent study and self-paced learning; (4) telecommunication technologies; and (5) specialized learning communities. A matrix is presented at the conclusion of the chapter that shows delivery system alternatives and decision criteria discussed previously.

## ON-CAMPUS INSTRUCTION

A review of a number of college and university catalogs reveals that on-campus instruction in class sessions of 50–90 minutes over a 12- to 18-week period appears to be the dominant form of educational delivery in institutions of higher education. Continuing educators have been critical of this "rigidity" in many postsecondary institutions. Evening programs and intensive weekend or summer programs have introduced some flexibility at many institutions for both degree and nondegree oriented adult learners. However, recruiting regular campus faculty members to teach such courses is often difficult; at many institutions such teaching is considered an overload rather than a regular component of the professor's teaching load. Also, the increasingly technical nature of many academic subjects requires access to laboratories, facilities, and equipment that must be staffed, maintained, and secured.

On-campus instruction can be highly effective in the format of conferences, seminars, or workshops. These formats are characteristic of on-campus program delivery for selected interest groups and professional groups. Since researchers and leading faculty members are involved, such formats often create a bridge between the world of theory and research and the world of practice. Continuing educators can make a major contribution to the public service role of their institution by utilizing these short formats as a forum for intellectual exchange and professional networking between the campus and its environment. The suitability of different formats depends on program objectives and represents a major human resources commitment and marketing challenge.

The following descriptions of various types of program formats provide the continuing educator with a range of options from which to plan a short-term learning experience. The descriptions are synthesized from a review of program formats made available to the conference planner by Quentin H. Gessner in *Priorities in Adult Education.*[4]

- *Conference.* A conference is a planned and orderly series of educative experiences designed to achieve an educational objective.
- *Workshops.* A workshop can be defined as a meeting in which people work together in small groups and in which each person has an opportunity to participate in and contribute toward the achievement of the group goals.
- *Seminar.* A seminar involves a small number of persons who share experiences, with a high degree of participation among members of the group.
- *Institute.* An institute can be characterized by its general function, that is, the training of the participants by staff members who provide most of the resources. This type of program is usually of longer duration than other short-term programs, possibly one to two weeks or longer in length.
- *Symposium.* In a symposium a group of experts or well-informed persons deliver prepared speeches for the benefit of an audience. Following the speeches, questions may be asked or a panel of peers may discuss the content of the message.
- *Forum.* The forum generally applies to a meeting or that portion of a meeting in which members of the audience may participate in the discussion.
- *Clinic.* The clinic provides an opportunity for the audience to listen to experts speak on a specific topic or problem.
- *Panel.* A panel is a discussion, generally informal, that is held before an audience and involves a free interchange rather than prepared speeches. The distinctive feature of the panel is the communication pattern.
- *Dialogue.* The dialogue is a free interchange involving two communicating participants.

In developing these types of formats, continuing educators should be prepared to work with faculty members in the planning process, identify reachable and interested markets, handle logistical arrangements, promote effectively, and provide budgeting expertise.

Flexible, intensive formats for degree programs also should be considered, particularly where adult student demand is high and teaching is a central mission of the institution. Being "on-campus," and "going to college" can be important motivators and symbolic statements for many adults. By restructuring the hours, days, or weeks required to master certain subjects into evenings, weekends, and intensive sessions, adult students can have the on-campus learning experience they desire.

## OFF-CAMPUS INSTRUCTION

Off-campus programs, whether held at educational centers established by a college or university, hotels or motels, community centers, or worksites, have become an increasingly popular way of delivering instruction to adult learners. Off-campus programs can be offered in the same range of formats described in the preceding section: daytime, evening, short courses, etc.

There are many benefits of off-campus instruction. Perhaps the greatest benefit is convenience for the adult learner, who often works full-time. If the campus is remote or lacks sufficient classrooms, instructional equipment, or adequate parking, crucial facilities problems can be solved by off-campus programs. However, using and/or managing off-campus space can be costly, and special approaches to program marketing are often required. It may prove difficult to find both appropriate and acceptable instructors for off-campus programs. Continuing educators should evaluate, from the perspective of student needs and the priorities and capacities of their institution, what off-campus programs are appropriate.

Education for adults at the worksite is the fastest growing educational activity in the country today. Prior to divestiture, the education budget of AT&T exceeded that of the entire University of California system.[5] Many industries have established their own colleges on-site. College Board officials estimate that while higher education serves about 12 million students, close to 46 million adults are engaged in systematic learning in business, industry, government, and volunteer settings. Most of this education is offered "in-house" rather than by colleges and universities.[6] However, in-house educational programs offer many opportunities for the progressive continuing educator to collaborate with industry.

## INDEPENDENT STUDY AND SELF-PACED LEARNING

Independent study by correspondence has been a key component of continuing higher education for decades. Independent study by correspondence has been provided by colleges and universities to allow students to take courses while physically separated from the professor and the institution. The role of independent study has diminished with the rise of telecommunications technologies, the growth of community colleges, and flexible university academic programs for adult learners. On the other hand, what many consider the functional equivalent of independent study, now termed self-paced learning, has expanded significantly. This is due to the growth of packaged learning systems using computer-aided instruction and audio and video technologies.

Traditional forms of independent study rely on correspondence courses as the primary method of instruction. A professor's course syllabus is expanded into a series of lessons; each series usually has a set of learning objectives, readings, and self-assessment tools. In addition, written assignments are mailed regularly to the campus for review and feedback from the instructor. Reading, writing, and the postal service are utilized to create an interactive experience between an off-campus learner and the campus. The series of assignments numbers from eight to ten in the average correspondence study course and allows for continuous feedback from an instructor. Independent study departments are staffed by curriculum designers as well as administrative personnel who are responsible for course development and the interface between faculty members and the distant learner.

The decision to establish a correspondence study program on various campuses with diverse constituencies is a function of the program needs of particular constituencies, the academic priorities of the institution, and competing alternatives. Some correspondence study programs offer a high school diploma program. In California, which has a system of community colleges in all areas of the state, independent study serves college-educated adults more interested in personal enrichment and professional enhancement. This form of distance learning has been in existence for over 100 years and has served many adult learners.

Self-paced learning can be differentiated from independent study on the basis of the technologies employed and the less frequent, often nonexistent, interaction between student and instructor. The prototype of this mode of educational delivery is the PLATO system developed by Control Data Corporation. In this system of programmed learning, the student interacts on a computer terminal with a series of lessons and self-testing assignments. Such self-contained computerized instructional systems have been successful in the military and at off-site locations where the number of learners exceeds the resources available for study in the more personalized interactive mode of correspondence study.

The increasing availability of audio and video technologies has opened the door to self-paced learning alternatives. A form of media as a central component of instruction is utilized. The media component functions as a motivator and pacer for the student. As with independent/correspondence study courses, the learning objectives, reading and study assignments, and self-testing materials accompany the instructional materials. The interactive component is usually a final examination on paper that is evaluated by a certifying or accrediting group offering the course. Publishers and professional development associations, such as the American Management Association, use self-paced learning programs extensively. They are also used in many off-site, remote educational programs at military installations.

The costs of producing self-paced educational programs are significant, and a high volume of use or sales is required to justify the investment. In contrast, the "up-front" development costs of correspondence study are more reasonable and allow for the inclusion of academically important courses in a balanced liberal arts curriculum. Depending on the position of an institution in a particular marketplace, its geographical outreach, and the attitude of its faculty members, one or more independent study options may represent an appropriate alternative.

## TELECOMMUNICATIONS TECHNOLOGIES

Telecommunications technologies are becoming increasingly diversified and, as a consequence, delivery services are becoming more accessible for continuing educators. Prior to a discussion of the relative merits of telecommunications for instruction, it may be useful to review briefly the variety of available technologies. The descriptions of the following technologies have been adapted from an unpublished paper by Marcia Bankirer of Colorado State University.[7]

### AUDIO TECHNOLOGIES

- *Radio.* Most educational programs that use radio rely on public FM stations (most university licensees). Subsidiary Carrier Authorization (SCA) is utilized to provide reading services to the blind and to deliver formal course presentations. Delivery of courses by radio requires prerecorded lectures that must have general entertainment as well as educational value. Print materials, such as readings, study guides, and regular assignments, which supplement the listening sessions, are usually required.
- *Audiotapes.* Many institutions that offer radio courses also give students the option of taking the course on an independent study

basis by listening to audiotapes and completing other course requirements, such as readings and assignments, at their own pace. Audiotapes are often used to supplement correspondence courses and serve to pace the student or to provide illustrative material. With audiotape instruction, students have control over the delivery time, but there is generally no provision for faculty or student interaction.

- *Telephone/teleconferencing.* Telephone/teleconferencing consists of voice-only communications, using various equipment options for voice amplification and transmission. A conference telephone call is the simplest form of audio teleconferencing. Educational teleconferencing is a long party line connecting students in a number of locations and allowing them to interact with each other and with an instructor.

VIDEO TECHNOLOGIES. Although not as portable as radio and audiotapes, video technologies have the advantage of providing visual images of people, places, events, and ideas that may be difficult or impossible to convey through audio. Commonly, institutions, particularly many community college systems, use public and/or commercial open-broadcast television as their primary video technology because large numbers of students can be reached. Video tapes and cable television are often used as a supplement to repeat video programming for the convenience of students. The expense of utilizing any of the video technologies is high compared to that of the audio technologies.

- *Video tapes.* Next to the telephone, videotape is the most frequently used telecommunications technology. Tapes may be used to supplement other delivery systems, or they may be used as a primary mode of delivery. At some institutions, graduate courses in management and engineering are delivered to business and industry by means of videotapes. This technology has become increasingly accessible to students because of the availability of video cassette playback equipment. Students are allowed to work at their own pace.

- *Open-Broadcast TV.* Broadcast television, like broadcast radio, is available in nearly every home and has been used to provide instruction since the mid-1950s. It is the most effective technology for reaching large numbers of people; however, it is the most expensive to produce. Coursework accepted for broadcast on commercial or public broadcast stations must be of high quality and have a broad appeal in order to entertain as well as instruct. Although it may not be possible for a continuing education unit to produce its own broadcast courses, there are many sources where high quality, appropriate television courses for adult learners can be found. Each semester the Adult Learning Service of the Public Broadcasting Service makes a wide variety of courses available nationally. The International University Consortium is another source of excellent broadcast programming adapted from the British Broadcasting Corporation/Open University materials.

- *Cable TV.* Educators have generally used cable systems as a primary medium of delivery and to supplement broadcast TV by replaying programs. Cable is attractive to educators because it offers more time for programming than is available from commercial or public broadcast stations. Many cable or license agreements provide free or reduced rates for educational access channels.

- *Instructional Television Fixed Service (ITFS).* ITFS is a broadcast technology whereby locations equipped with the appropriate antennas receive audio and video signals. A closed-circuit form of delivery for either live lectures or videotaped programming is created. ITFS is only functional over short distances and is used extensively in continuing professional education for such groups as engineers and medical professionals. The University of Iowa uses ITFS successfully to deliver undergraduate liberal arts courses to off-campus students.

- *Satellite TV.* Programs that utilize satellites for delivery of instruction to institutions of higher education are currently provided by the Public Broadcast Service, the Appalachian Community Service Network, and the International University Consortium. This is generally in the form of prerecorded television courses which may or may not fit the curriculum or instructional needs of a user or instituion. Satellites can also be used interactively. They have the capability to transmit video and audio signals from a single point of origin to two or more earth stations scattered over a large geographic area. Interactive programming is possible if an audio technology like the telephone is used, which permits feedback from the receiving sites. The cost of buying time on existing communications satellites or of launching a satellite for institutional use may be prohibitive.

- *Slow-Scan/Freeze-Frame TV.* Transmission of video images, which are captured as a series of single pictures over telephone circuitry, is accomplished by the use of slow-scan/freeze-frame technology. It is less expensive than full-motion video and typically used in combination with other technologies.

TWO-WAY OR INTERACTIVE TELECOMMUNICATIONS TECHNOLO-
GIES. Such technologies, in addition to satellite, have become increasingly interesting to educators and include:

- *Point-to-Point Microwave.* Point-to-point microwave is a broad-
  band technology capable of transmitting both video and audio
  signals in two directions. In such systems programming can
  originate from any participating location, but students have access
  only at specially equipped sites and there must be no natural
  barriers (such as mountains) to the receiving site.

- *Electronic Blackboard.* The electronic blackboard is a telephone-
  based technology capable of transmitting graphics over long or
  short distances. It is generally used with the telephone, which
  creates an interactive system. Each site must be specially equipped
  with the blackboard, TV monitor, and telephone line for audio
  transmission.

- *Teleconferencing.* Through a combination of two-way video connections, by means of satellite or other video technology, and
  two-way audio connections (usually by telephone), it is possible
  for a number of sites to communicate.

Although various telecommunications technologies are becoming
increasingly accessible, the costs of producing courses, transmitting
broadcasts, marketing audio or video learning packages, and managing
related support services are still prohibitive for many institutions.
Rather than establishing their own free-standing telecommunications
delivery system, continuing educators have a variety of available
options. There are numerous educational telecommunications consortia at the regional and national level with which one can affiliate.
There are technological capacities and resources within public schools
and business and industry locations that can be utilized. An increasing
resource, because of the growth of the cable industry over the last
decade, is the local media. Even with the technological resources in
hand, however, the continuing educator needs to consider all decision
criteria when selecting the best delivery medium for the subject to
be offered to a particular adult constituency.

## SPECIALIZED LEARNING COMMUNITIES

A popular approach to serving the educational needs of specialized
constituencies, whether professional groups or interest groups, is the
establishment of semiautonomous institutes, programs, and centers.
This approach is most appropriate when learning objectives are longer
term, when developing a strongly identified "community of learners

is a central objective, and when there is a desire to provide varied services and experiences.

One example of specialized learning communities resulted from the interest in the quality and training of public school teachers combined with a concern that teacher education has failed to keep teachers up-to-date in fields that are central to the public schools, such as mathematics and science. Many institutions responded to this interest and concern by establishing special education programs for teachers that are multidimensional and involve regular and long-term interaction between a university and teachers. Teachers in mathematics, for instance, may spend part of their summer in an intenstive four- or five-week mathematics program followed by on-campus classes scheduled over the semester and short seminars in which topical issues are addressed. The teachers may receive a newsletter during the year and have occasional social events. This approach provides for the development of a community of learners who receive the benefits of continuing professional education and build a sense of increased professionalism as a group while learning from and with peers. Similar programs can be and have been developed for other professional groups that need an increased sense of "professionalism" and renewed commitment as well as additional skills and knowledge in a specific subject area. One of the more notable programs is the San Francisco Bay Area writing program, which has become a national model.

The increasing number of programs for retired persons on college campuses is another example of specialized learning communities. The objective is more than skill building or knowledge acquisition. Many retirees see retirement as an opportunity to explore new ideas and study topics they were unable to pursue in early and midlife because of family demands. They are interested in interacting on a regular basis with peers who have similar intellectual interests and often look for opportunities to participate in the design and execution of their own educational programs. Many colleges and universities have established institutes, centers, or societies for retired persons that include courses and seminars taught by retirees, access to campus courses, lectures by campus faculty and community leaders, theatrical and music groups, art exhibits, international travel opportunities, and social events. These approaches are usually self-contained and self-generating programs within a larger continuing education unit, but they are comprehensive in the range and character of offerings and fully academic in their emphasis. The Division of Continuing Studies at the University of Nebraska initiated a University Learning Society as a membership organization for people interested in learning. As a result many retirees have joined the Learning Society.

A final example of specialized learning communities is the Centers for the Continuing Education of Women that are operating on many campuses. The continuing education needs of women going from traditional roles as wives and mothers into the world of work or university study have a number of unique features. Many women seek a supportive community of other"older" women, opportunities for personal career and academic counseling, access to role models and a more positive sense of their abilities and contributions, and a physical place to meet their peers. Centers, such as those at the University of Minnesota and the University of Michigan, pioneered such activities and continue to flourish.

The foregoing examples represent a type of delivery system because they involve the creation of mini-learning communities within the larger community—the university. Diverse services are provided that are usually organized around a specific space with its own identity and program delivery structure. Such a method of offering a variety of educational opportunities and academic services to adults can have positive and long-term effects on the university and the community as a whole. However, significant commitments of human and material resources are necessary, and there must be evidence of a constituency underserved educationally by other sources.

## SUMMARY

Five general types of delivery alternatives available to the planner in continuing higher education have been described: (1) on-campus instruction, (2) off-campus instruction, (3) independent study and self-paced learning, (4) telecommunications technologies, and (5) specialized learning communities. These five categories, although not generic or exhaustive, represent a beginning point when thinking about alternatives. There are other ways of providing educational opportunities for adults beyond those discussed in this chapter such as travel study programs, foreign language institutes, research internships, and tutorial degree programs. The alternatives described represent the more typical and widespread delivery systems in the field.

Continuing educators need to understand the variety of available approaches for planning and delivering programs characteristic of higher education. In many institutions, the needs of students, the climate, and the material and human resources available make it possible to serve a number of constituencies with a variety of delivery modes; for other institutions, the audiences and resources may be more restrictive. The effective continuing educator is able to analyze the environment, assess resources, and commit to programs for which

## TABLE 9.1. Decision Criteria

| DELIVERY SYSTEM ALTERNATIVES | Character of Knowledge | | | | Character of Learner | | | Institutional Mission | | | | Material Resources | | | | Human Resources | | | Competition | | |
|---|---|---|---|---|---|---|---|---|---|---|---|---|---|---|---|---|---|---|---|---|---|
| | Found-ation | Compe-tency | Values | State of Art | Begin. | Inter-med. | Advanced | Lib. Art. | Voc. Pro. | Research | Teaching | Phys. Plant | Tech. Capa-city | Systems | Budget | Faculty | Staff | Off-campus | Type Pro-vider | Type Student | Type Program |
| On-campus Instructor on-site Courses | | | | | | | | | | | | | | | | | | | | | |
| Seminars | | | | | | | | | | | | | | | | | | | | | |
| Conferences | | | | | | | | | | | | | | | | | | | | | |
| Off-campus Instructor on-site Courses | | | | | | | | | | | | | | | | | | | | | |
| Seminars | | | | | | | | | | | | | | | | | | | | | |
| Conferences | | | | | | | | | | | | | | | | | | | | | |
| Independent Study/ Self-Paced Learning Correspondence Study | | | | | | | | | | | | | | | | | | | | | |
| Computer Aided Instruction/Com-puter Networks | | | | | | | | | | | | | | | | | | | | | |
| Audio/video Learn-ing Packages | | | | | | | | | | | | | | | | | | | | | |
| Specialized Learning Communities Retired Persons Organizations | | | | | | | | | | | | | | | | | | | | | |
| Women's Center | | | | | | | | | | | | | | | | | | | | | |
| Specialized Institutes | | | | | | | | | | | | | | | | | | | | | |
| Telecommunications Technologies | | | | | | | | | | | | | | | | | | | | | |
| Audio | | | | | | | | | | | | | | | | | | | | | |
| —Telephone | | | | | | | | | | | | | | | | | | | | | |
| —Broadcast | | | | | | | | | | | | | | | | | | | | | |
| —Cassette Tape | | | | | | | | | | | | | | | | | | | | | |
| Television | | | | | | | | | | | | | | | | | | | | | |
| —Open broadcast | | | | | | | | | | | | | | | | | | | | | |
| —Cable | | | | | | | | | | | | | | | | | | | | | |
| —ITFS | | | | | | | | | | | | | | | | | | | | | |
| —Satellite | | | | | | | | | | | | | | | | | | | | | |
| —Teleconferencing | | | | | | | | | | | | | | | | | | | | | |
| Video | | | | | | | | | | | | | | | | | | | | | |
| —Cassette | | | | | | | | | | | | | | | | | | | | | |
| —Microwave | | | | | | | | | | | | | | | | | | | | | |
| —Slow Scan | | | | | | | | | | | | | | | | | | | | | |
| —Electronic Blackboard | | | | | | | | | | | | | | | | | | | | | |

Note: When using this matrix, the planner should check those boxes in which criterion columns match with delivery alternatives as a way of quickly assessing the constraints and opportunities within the institution.

the institution has the necessary and available academic talent and material resources. By this approach the continuing educator ensures the program will successfully serve a targeted constituency and be a source of pride for the institution.

The matrix shown in Table 9.1 provides a checklist to evaluate current options and add emerging alternatives when they become viable. The decision criteria are relevant regardless of the available delivery system because they represent the central concerns and constraints facing academic institutions.

## REFERENCES

1.  The data were obtained from empirically based student profiles from Harvard University and two large University of California Extension programs at Berkeley and San Diego and are contained in the following reports: Fulton, Oliver, *Report of a Survey of Continuing Education Students* (Berkeley: University of California, University Extension, June 1983); Knoth and Meads Company, *Marketing Continuing Education: A Marketing Plan for the University of California* (San Diego, Calif.: Knoth and Meads, September 1981); and Shinagel, Mike, *Harvard University, Office of Continuing Education, Annual Report* (Cambridge: Harvard University, 1982–83).

2.  Ibid (Fulton, Knoth and Meads Company, and Shinagel).

3.  President's Office, Systemwide Administration, *Annual Budget of the University of California 1984–85* (Berkeley: University of California, 1984).

4.  Gessner, Quentin H., "Planning Conferences, Seminars, and Workshops for Large Groups of Adults," in *Priorities in Adult Education* (New York: Macmillan, 1972).

5.  Hawthorne,, Elizabeth M., et al., "The Emergence of Corporate Colleges," *The Journal of Continuing Higher Education,* 31 (4) (Fall 1983), pp. 2–9.

6.  Hodgkinson, Harold, "Demographics and the Economy: Understanding a Changing Marketplace," *The Admissions Strategist,* Special No. 3 (Winter 1985), p. 106.

7.  Bankirer, Marcia, "Innovation in Outreach: A Plan for Distance Education at the University of Wyoming" (unpublished paper, University of Wyoming, Laramie, February 1982).

# -10-
# SUCCESSFUL MARKETING STRATEGIES AND TECHNIQUES

### Richard B. Fischer

As competition increases among institutions of higher education, marketing has become an important activity on campus. From alumni tours and undergraduate admissions to continuing education programs, careful marketing analyses and planning are required.

Professional seminars and "how-to" material surround administrators and program developers searching for the best way to market their programs. The answer is elusive, for there is no "one best way." Marketing continuing higher education is more art than science. However, there is a base of knowledge, procedures, and strategies that, if understood, can help focus management decision making and increase the likelihood of successful marketing in continuing higher education.

## THE ROLE OF MARKETING IN CONTINUING HIGHER EDUCATION

Marketing should not be confused with selling, advertising, or promoting. It is a broader concept. In the context of higher education, marketing can be defined as: *A combination of activities required to direct the flow of educational programs and services from the higher education institution to the consumer in a form, place, time, and at a price that is best able to satisfy the consumers' needs.*

It should be noted that the last four words, "satisfy the *consumers' needs,*" are the most important part of the definition. This definition is based on two philosophical tenets set down in Philip Kotler's *Marketing for Nonprofit Organizations:*[1]

Tenet 1: Continuing education programming is developed to meet some identified consumer need or want.
Tenet 2: One of the measures of an organization's success is the efficiency with which it distributes its products and services.

Thus, from an educational institution's viewpoint, some of the goals of successful marketing are to maximize the use of facilities, make the most effective use of human and financial resources, and to find ways to distribute the education product efficiently and effectively. One marketing approach that can be used is based on the following five factors:

- *Marketing Research.* Determine the size, location, and characteristics of potential participants.
- *Emphasis on Planning.* Clearly state goals in terms of objectives, costs, timing, and results.
- *Emphasis on Management.* Manage all operations, coordinating activities toward the same goal, and ensure that events conform to plans.
- *Cost-Effectiveness.* Efficiently use resources to meet financial objectives.
- *Consumer Satisfaction.* Provide services and educational programs for user needs and wants.

It should be noted that most programs do not fail because of poor marketing. They fail because of poor marketing research. The subject of marketing research deserves considerably more attention than can be devoted to this chapter. Topics such as market segmentation, sociographics, concentration, differentiation, and group evaluation, to name a few, are key concepts in market research with which the reader should become familiar.

## COMPONENTS OF MARKETING CONCEPT

Five components of the broad concept of marketing are shown in Figure 10–1. These five components have been identified by one name or another by many writers, including Kotler.[2] These factors are identified as the "five P's" of marketing—product, price, place, promotion, and people. The *product* is that activity or service that satisfies some need. *Price* is the cost to the consumer of obtaining

FIGURE 10.1. Five Components of the Marketing Concept.

the product. *Place* is the physical location where the consumer uses or obtains the product. *Promotion* is the persuasive and/or informative communications that are initiated by the supplier of the product. *People* refers to actions and reactions of both the supplier and the purchaser of the product.

## COMPARISON OF MARKETING PROCESS WITH PROGRAM DEVELOPMENT PROCESS

The elements of the marketing concept are similar to the elements of the program or curriculum development process. The primary difference is that the former is market driven having been developed based on the expressed needs of the consumer. The latter is driven by administrators or teachers who believe they know what the student needs and how he or she learns best. While the program/curriculum approach may be appropriate for traditional college-age youth, it is not appropriate for adults. It fails to capitalize on one of the major strengths of continuing education programs—the background and experiences of the participants. This approach also fails to acknowledge that continuing education in the 1980s is a buyer's market, not a seller's market. The buyer has many sources from which to continue his or her education, and institutions of higher education represent only one source. It is important for higher education administrators and traditional academic faculty to recognize the similarities and differences between the two processes, as they occur in their institutions, in order to initiate successful marketing.

## UNIQUE PRODUCT CHARACTERISTICS

It is important to understand what is unique about the continuing education "product" when developing a marketing strategy. There are ten special characteristics of a continuing education "product."

1. The product is intangible.
2. The rewards for using the product are not always immediate and often not valued by the general public. Continuing education programs in the liberal arts and humanities often fail to attract sufficient participants, while other fields (e.g., accounting and computer science) turn participants away.
3. Use of the product requires two commitments—time and money—and the time commitment may be the more important of the two. Frequently adults comment that they could not attend because they could not spare the time.
4. The product is diversified in terms of content, format, benefits, and delivery system. The term "continuing education" is not easily understood. To some it means "night school," to others "corporate training," and to others "professional development."
5. Consumer use of the product is affected by many outside forces over which the institution has little or no control. Weather, economic conditions, public transportation, location, tax laws, and professional certification requirements are among the factors that impact participation in continuing education programs.
6. Most institutions of higher education have limited channels for distribution of their product. For example, many institutions schedule on-campus evening classes, but do not provide correspondence instruction, computer-assisted learning situations, off-campus centers, teleconferencing equipment, or educational broadcast networks.
7. The institution's public image affects consumers' willingness to purchase the product.
8. Continuing education products also are restricted by institutional constraints related to semesters, terms, hours, course credit, or degree requirements.
9. Many potential consumers are intimidated either by the complexity of a higher education institution or by their own fear of failure.
10. There are no common quality measures for consumers to use in judging relative worth of alternative educational products or suppliers. No consumer guide exists for continuing higher education. Word-of-mouth has become the basis for a significant number of consumer decisions.

Given the unusual nature of the continuing education product, why do people participate in such large numbers, and why do many seek out institutions of higher education as primary providers? The answers to these questions are important keys in planning a marketing strategy.

# FACTORS THAT MOTIVATE PARTICIPATION

Psychologists believe that all behavior is the result of needs satisfaction; therefore, participation in continuing education obviously satisfies some needs. What are these needs? Any discussion of needs satisfaction that contains only a few paragraphs is a gross oversimplification of a complete set of behaviors; however, a brief overview of basic motivators is valuable in planning a marketing strategy. Those persons wishing to study motivational typologies in depth should review the research and writings of Roger Boshier.[3,4] Maslow's five-step hierarchy of needs (physiological, safety, love and belonging, esteem, and self-actualization) is important in determining the basic motivations for participation in continuing education.[5]

*Incentives for adult learning.* Another way to analyze what motivates people to buy the product known as continuing education is shown in Figure 10.2. Based on Boshier's Educational Participation Scale, Mortsain and Smart[6] found six clusters of incentives for participation in continuing education. From the consumer's viewpoint, these incentives can be reduced to a key question at the end of the continuing education experience: "What will I be able to do that I cannot do now?" In marketing, this is often referred to as "benefits copy." The benefits of a continuing education activity should be clearly communicated to and understood by the prospective participant. This is crucial to the success of any marketing strategy.

*Ego involvement.* A third set of motivations focuses on ego needs. How will participation affect the ego of the consumer? Will he or she gain status or prestige from participation? Continuing education programs held at Harvard may attract participants because of the status of the institution. Programs marketed for "leaders in the field," "fast track managers," and "rising executives" all use ego involvement as a motivation for participation. There is also a negative side to ego-based motivation if the focus is on people's anxieties who may be "left out" or "not moving ahead in their jobs."

*Response to change.* Change is also a motivator. Change motivations appear to be grouped into five broad areas:

- Technological change (e.g., the computer revolution
- Economic change (e.g., shifting of population to the Sunbelt; the move from a production to a service-oriented society)
- Legislated change (e.g., mandatory continuing education for licensing and relicensing)
- Social change (e.g., the changing role of women in United States society and the increase in the number of two-income families)

### Factor I. Social Relationships

- To fulfill a need for personal associations and friendships
- To make new friends
- To meet members of the opposite sex
- To improve my social relationships
- To participate in group activity
- To be accepted by others
- To become acquainted with congenial people
- To maintain or improve my social position
- To gain insight into myself and my personal problems
- To share a common interest with my spouse or a friend

### Factor II. External Expectations

- To comply with instructions from someone else
- To carry out the expectations of someone with formal authority
- To carry out the recommendation of some authority
- To comply with the suggestions of someone else
- To comply with my employer's policy
- To meet with some formal requirements
- To take part in an activity which is customary in the circle in which I move

### Factor III. Social Welfare

- To improve my ability to serve mankind
- To prepare for service to the community
- To improve my ability to participate in community work
- To gain insight into human relations
- To become more effective as a citizen of this city
- To supplement a narrow previous education

### Factor IV. Professional Advancement

- To give me higher status in my job
- To secure professional advancement
- To keep up with competition
- To increase my competence in my job
- To help me earn a degree, diploma or certificate
- To clarify what I want to be doing five years from now
- To obtain some immediate practical benefit
- To keep up with others
- To acquire knowledge that will help with other courses

FIGURE 10.2. Incentives for Adult Learning. From "Reasons for Participation in Adult Education Courses: A Multivariate Analysis of Group Differences" by B. R. Morstain and J. C. Smart. Copyright 1974 by *Adult Education*. Reprinted by permission.

FIGURE 10.2. (continued)

---

Factor V. Escape/Stimulation

- To get relief from boredom
- To get a break in the routine of home or work
- To provide a contrast to the rest of my life
- To have a few hours away from responsibilities
- To overcome the frustration of day to day living
- To stop myself from becoming a "cabbage"
- To escape the intellectual narrowness of my occupation
- To escape an unhappy relationship
- To escape television

Factor VI. Cognitive interest

- To learn just for the sake of learning
- To seek knowledge for its own sake
- To satisfy an inquiring mind

---

- Life event changes (e.g., lifestyle changes such as marriage, divorce, childbirth)

Some good developmental studies have been published in this area by the College Entrance Examination Board.[7]

*Source of behavior.* When designing a market strategy, it is important to identify the source of the expected behavior. Is the decision to participate in continuing education made *by* the participant or *for* the participant? Should marketing be targeted at the potential student or at his or her employer? The answers to these questions greatly influence the promotional approach.

Subject matter may be a secondary motivation. People often attend continuing higher education programs as a means of obtaining further credentials to advance in their job and because participation shows initiative on their part. Employees are often sent to continuing education programs as a reward for good performance; others attend out of habit or tradition or as an escape from day-to-day activities.

Thus, in designing a marketing strategy, it is important to understand the motivations of a target audience.

## DEVELOPING A MARKETING PLAN

In the development of a marketing plan, the eleven-step process that follows is appropriate whether one is planning a small one-time program or a comprehensive multiyear project involving a wide variety of continuing education activities. Neither the size of budget nor the size of staff should alter the process. The plan should help use available financial and people resources efficiently and effectively.

*Step 1. Define marketing objectives.* In specific and quantifiable terms, state goals or desired outcomes for the marketing campaign. Is it to increase enrollment in a specific program? If so, by how much? Is it to increase the institution's visibility? Increase awareness? Generate inquiries? How will success be determined? What hard data will support conclusions?

*Step 2. Examine the program that is being marketed.* Be brutally honest! What are its weaknesses? How does the program differ from other programs? What is the competition? Look at enrollment trends, special features of the program, and gather data to identify the market demand.

*Step 3. List all potential audiences.* The more a program is targeted to a specific audience, the greater the likelihood of success. But don't overlook other potential audiences. Start by listing every potential audience, and then narrow the list as necessary. Consider why someone would be interested in the program. The answer to this often leads to new audiences. For example, a program on computer crime may be of primary interest to data processing managers but could also attract law enforcement personnel, accountants, internal revenue auditors, and lawyers as potential participants.

The first three steps should not be conducted in the vacuum of a program planner's office. The marketing plan will be improved by involving potential participants in the planning process. They are often in a position to assess program strengths and weaknesses more accurately than the program planner or teaching faculty. Members of the target audience can also identify communication channels through which potential participants seek information.

*Step 4. Design ideal marketing plan.* Forget personnel and financial limitations and design the best plan that can be devised. The plan might include any of the following:

| | |
|---|---|
| direct mail | public service announcements |
| bulletins | media events |
| display advertising | posters |
| billboards | free course previews |
| exhibits | telephone marketing |
| open houses | t-shirt giveaways |
| talk shows | personal visits |
| VIP presentations | |

*Step 5. Modify to fit needs.* After the ideal marketing plan has been designed, it should be modified to accommodate available funds, personnel, and institutional policies.

*Step 6. Prepare timeline and budget.* The nature of the program and audience will determine how much lead time is needed to market the program. The more widely dispersed the potential audience, the more lead time is necessary for the communication process.

One of the most frequently asked questions in marketing is "How far ahead should fliers or brochures be mailed?" It is generally recommended that direct mail material be sent fourteen to sixteen weeks prior to the event. An initial mailing six to eight weeks before the program should be the absolute minimum lead time. Some audiences, such as self-employed professionals, may need longer lead times to avoid conflicts on their calendars. It is important to remember that time not money is usually the major motivation or, conversely, limitation for participation.

When preparing a marketing budget, list all obvious costs, such as printing, postage for mailings, purchase of newspaper advertising space, and graphic design charges. Be aware of hidden costs such as: additional postage (e.g., fliers returned for address correction); copy changes after type has been set; stationery and duplicating costs (e.g., materials for first class mailings, registration and confirmation forms, correspondence with speakers); mailing preparation costs (e.g., personnel to seal, stamp, sort, tie, and bundle bulk mailings); and add-on costs (e.g., page proofs, rough versus finished design sketches, pick-up and delivery charges, shipping charges, photographic services, overrun printing allowances). A detailed billing should be required from all suppliers that itemizes each item and service provided.

Universal cost standards are difficult to calculate because of regional differences in wages and printing costs; however, as a guideline, college and university direct mail fliers cost in the range of twelve to sixteen cents each, including postage. Continuing education bulletins and catalogs are much higher, ranging from thirty-five cents to one dollar each.

*Step 7. Implement the plan.*

*Step 8. Monitor responses.*

The person who has the responsibility for implementing the marketing plan should personally monitor initial responses. This might include answering some of the telephone inquiries or reviewing early mail-in responses. Monitoring will provide immediate clues as to whether the plan is attracting the intended target audience and if additional information should be communicated.

*Step 9. Track responses.* It is important to know what strategies are generating responses. Are some mailing lists getting better responses than others? What direct mail flier or display advertising is working the best?

*Step 10. Calculate cost effectiveness.* The success of a marketing strategy can also be measured by calculating what it costs to obtain each individual response. What did it cost to get the inquiry? How many inquiries actually resulted in program registrations? What did it cost to generate each registration?

*Step 11. Evaluate the plan.* Were the marketing objectives set out in Step 1 achieved? What problems occurred? What improvements can be suggested for the next plan?

## BASIC MARKETING APPROACHES

There are three general approaches that can be taken in implementing promotional and advertising strategies, regardless of the specific marketing plan that is developed. They are: direct mail, mass media advertising, and personal contact. Most continuing education marketing involves either direct mail or mass media advertising or some combination of the two. There is an important difference between these two methods. Direct mail usually focuses on a well-defined audience with the intent of obtaining registrations, whereas mass media—television, radio, newspaper display advertisement—is often used when the audience is not well-defined or when programs have universal appeal. The use of mass media normally results in inquiries as opposed to registrations. Therefore, mass media has the disadvantage of requiring at least one major follow-up step to convert inquiries into actual registrations.

It can be argued that direct mail and mass advertising strategies will be increasingly unsuccessful in the 1980s and 1990s. There is growing resistance to "junk mail," and the costs are increasing significantly as a result of higher postage rates and printing costs. There is also the advertising "saturation" factor, which suggests that the public is overwhelmed with an ever-mounting number of advertisements each day. However, despite these problems, direct mail and mass advertising techniques will continue to be a significant part of most continuing education marketing plans.

### DIRECT MAIL MARKETING

Direct mail marketing techniques are used in most continuing higher education programs because:

- Direct mail can eliminate wasted circulation by focusing on target audiences only. By comparison, mass media advertising, such as display advertising in local newspapers, can result in large wasted circulation, since the newspaper will be read by many individuals who are not prospective students.

- Direct mail can provide more space to describe the program. Mass media, on the other hand, is usually limited by time (30- to 60-second commercials) or higher space cost.

- Direct mail advertising responses usually take the form of registrations. Advertising in the media generally results in inquiries that need to be converted to registrations.

- There are many aspects of a direct mail piece, such as the quality of the paper, photographs, and graphics, that can be used to enhance the message and reflect favorably on the program. If the brochure or letter is well designed and well written, the reader will expect the same quality in the program.

- It is easy to track and measure responses from direct mail. By using simple coding techniques on the registration form or mailing label, one can determine the mailing list that was used, the response to a type of mailing piece, and, in some instances, the best timeframe for receipt of the message.

- Most direct mail promotional pieces are either institutional- or program-focused. Institutional pieces provide general information and try to build the image of the sponsoring institution. Often no attempt is made to elicit a response of any type. Program-oriented direct mail focuses on a specific event or activity, usually gives a specific date, and asks the reader to respond in a relatively limited timeframe.

- The typical direct mail piece consists of an outside envelope, a letter and/or brochure, and a reply form. The advantage of this piece is twofold. First, there is usually adequate space to present extensive details about the continuing education activity. Second, it gives several chances to communicate the message. The primary disadvantages can be the expense of producing such a piece; resistance from the client who considers it junk mail or, at the other extreme, from the client who considers it too slick or too "hard sell"; and the difficulty of acquiring appropriate mailing lists.

- The other common form of direct mail is a self-mailer. This is usually a two- or threefold panel piece with a mailing label printed on the back panel and bulk mailed. This form of direct mail has the advantage of being relatively more cost effective and has greater flexibility in size and graphics. The disadvantage is that it is less personal or exclusive in nature.

The major problem in the preparation of any direct mail advertisement is the writing of copy. Much direct mail tends to be wordy and poorly organized. To increase the effectiveness of written copy, several suggestions are given:

1. Keep it simple. Avoid jargon.
2. Think message and purpose. What are you trying to accomplish? What are you trying to communicate? Why should anyone bother to read it?
3. Think audience. At whom is the program aimed? What is the tone, level of sophistication, and word choice to which this audience will respond?
4. Think action. What action should readers take? How soon must they respond and how do they do it? Make it easy to respond.
5. Think benefits. Why should someone attend? Prove it is worth the time and money.

DIRECT MAIL CATALOGS VERSUS FLIERS.   If the institution is offering many programs, a direct mail catalog may be a better choice than individual program fliers. Catalogs usually cover longer timeframes (four to twenty weeks) and are intended as reference pieces that remain around the office or home for some time. Fliers, on the other hand, usually focus on a specific activity happening at a specific time and request immediate action.

Most successful marketing plans require multiple strategies. This might include a semester catalog, follow-up fliers on individual courses or groups of courses, display advertising focusing on areas of general interest, and some form of personal contact to follow-up on program inquiries.

MAILING LISTS.   Personnel at many institutions spend a great deal of time designing direct mail pieces but fail to spend time on identifying, developing, compiling, and merging mailing lists. A well-organized and well-designed flier or catalog is of no value if it is mailed to a disinterested person. It is perhaps even worse for a local citizen to receive multiple copies of the same flier or to have fliers mailed to incorrect addresses, deceased persons, or community leaders whose titles and addresses are inaccurate.

The time spent on selecting, reviewing, and updating mailing lists is time well spent. There are many sources from which to acquire mailing lists. Internal sources include the alumni office, development office, or public relations office. External lists that are available for rent or purchase include magazine subscription lists, membership lists of professional and social organizations, local business directories, and census data. When developing the marketing plan, acquisition of mailing list resources should be given high priority. The person assigned to this task must be familiar with terminology such as *cheshire labels; one-up, two-up,* and *three-up labels; merge purge,* and postal regulations and bulk mail preparation requirements. Ralph Elliott's *How to Build and Maintain a High Quality Mailing List* is an excellent guide on the subject.[8]

The cost and effort of maintaining in-house mailing lists can be high. Because of the proliferation of mailing list sources, mailing lists can be rented from outside firms at costs ranging from ten to eighty-five dollars per thousand names. The cost of maintaining lists in-house may be considerably higher, particularly when one calculates the expense of personnel and computer time necessary to carry on this function. In addition, even the best list may be 20 to 30 percent obsolete on the day it is created, and the process of keeping lists up-to-date is a continual problem. Serious consideration should be given to seeking outside commercial sources for all mailing lists rather than maintaining in-house lists.

There are several questions that should be included in program evaluation forms to help build mailing lists:

- Which professional periodicals do you read?
- To which professional associations do you belong?
- Please list the names and titles of other persons who should receive information about similar programs.

TIMING. Knowledge of the target audience leads to more accurate predictions about the lead time participants need to make a decision about attending a continuing education program. In most situations, planning does not begin early enough. Direct mailing should occur, on the average, fourteen to sixteen weeks prior to the event. Six to eight weeks lead time should be considered the absolute minimum. *It is better to reschedule a program date than to mail too late.*

No matter when the mailing occurs, direct mail response seems to occur in two patterns—right away or just in time. On the average, half of the registrations will arrive immediately following initial distribution of the mailing piece. The balance will come in within one week prior to the start of the program and a few will arrive piecemeal in between. This pattern wreaks havoc on the planning process and can result in expensive last-minute adjustments. There do not seem to be any successful incentives, including price discounts or late payment charges, to encourage participants to discontinue this last-minute registration pattern. It is a situation program planners must learn to work around.

MULTIPLES STRATEGY.   Increasingly, one of the strategies being used to increase the effectiveness of direct mail is to increase the number of options provided for any specific program. This is often referred to as the "multiples strategy." The possible advantages of this strategy are shown in Figure 10.3.

The first block represents one program offered one time and at one location. Let's say the registration response is equal to 100. If the options are increased by one—for example, the same program offered on *two* dates or the same program offered at two different locations—there should be a significant increase in the responses. A 40 percent increase in registrations would not be unreasonable. The strategy can be increased to three or four options. For example, the same program could be offered in two different locations on two different dates. However, there seems to be a diminishing return with more than four options, as confusion of choice sets in with participants.

The advantage of the multiples strategy is that it does not increase the base cost of marketing. It costs the same to print and mail the brochure whether it has one program date or two program dates. The only additional cost is that of the program when it is conducted the second, third, or fourth time. The idea is that incremental registrations received from multiples strategy will more than offset the additional cost of operating the program more than once. If the registration response is not sufficient to run multiple sections, there is the option of condensing registrations to a single session. Experience suggests that once a commitment is made to attend a particular program, most people will follow through on this decision even if the program date and location are changed.

## MASS MEDIA ADVERTISING

Mass media advertising can take two forms—either paid advertising, such as newspaper display ads and/or radio and television spots, or free publicity such as public service announcements, news stories,

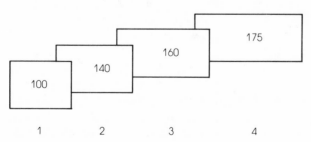

FIGURE 10.3. Multiples Strategy.

and press conferences. In recent years, recognition of the income potential of advertisements from colleges and universities has severely reduced the availability of free public service announcements and news stories. In most cases, it is necessary to purchase advertising space or time to assure that the message will appear. It should be kept in mind that it is the frequency of exposure, not the size of the newspaper ad or length of the radio spot, that is most effective. All media can provide demographic information on their audience profile. Once the demographics of the media have been matched with the demographics of the target audience, advertisements should be run frequently in the same newspapers or on the same radio station. This is referred to as purchasing vertical advertising.

Television, on the other hand, is normally viewed on a horizontal basis, that is, the public tends to watch specific programs as opposed to specific channels. Therefore, if the institution can afford television advertising, it should be purchased in relationship to specific programs regardless of the channel on which they are aired.

PRINT ADVERTISING. Newspaper display advertising is usually purchased on a column-inch basis. A column inch is a space one newspaper column wide and one inch in length. If plans are for continuous advertising over a long period of time, the possibility of purchasing yearly or monthly space contracts to obtain a lower per column inch cost should be investigated. Persons should not hesitate to use small local weekly newspapers as opposed to the large metropolitan dailies. Small weekly papers tend to have loyal followings, and their advertising rates are usually only a fraction of larger newspapers. Newspaper advertisements are placed in the paper at the discretion of the editor. If special placement is desired (e.g., placement on the business page or inside front page), there is usually an extra charge. Display advertisements should be *simple* and should contain a minimum of copy. The same logo should be used each time. Emphasis should be on frequency, not size. It is better to have a small ad run five or six times than to run one large ad once. Specialized journals and professional publications should not be overlooked. Although advertising rates tend to be high in these journals and their deadlines are often three to six months before publication, they do target specific audiences, thus reducing wasted circulation.

NEWSPAPER INSERTS. A popular form of distribution for catalogs or minicatalogs is the multiple page insert in local newspapers. Commonly called "throwaways," these inserts can provide wide distribution of a catalog in a selected geographical area. The advantage of this approach is that it places the catalog in the hands of people who might not normally request it or are unaware of the programs offered by the institution. The disadvantage is that it can result in expensive wasted circulation and, depending on the size of the newspaper, can be lost among other advertising throwaways. Newsprint also may not contribute to the image of the institution. This type of catalog is seldom kept for reference and either receives immediate attention or is discarded in much the same manner as a direct mail flier. In addition to printing expenses, the cost of a newspaper insert depends on the number of pages and the circulation of the newspaper. In some metropolitan areas, these costs can exceed those of direct mail postage.

RADIO ADVERTISING.  The principle of frequence applies to radio as well as newspapers. A radio station audience profile will help the advertising planner select the right station to reach a particular target audience. Radio spots are usually purchased for 30- or 60-second periods. Advertising rates will depend on the number of spots and selected air time. Commuter hours are considered prime time and carry the highest rates. Since most institutions of higher education are nonprofit, they may be able to obtain special rates and use public service announcements along with their paid advertising.

SUBMITTING PUBLICITY ITEMS TO THE MASS MEDIA.  Publicity information submitted to the mass media should include a brief statement about the activity that can be used "as is." The key is to be brief—one page, double spaced. Be sure to cover the "five W's and H" (who, what, when, where, why, and how, in this order) at the beginning. It is wise to check ahead on deadlines and desired format. Be sure to include the name and telephone number of a reliable contact person.

BILLBOARDS.  A new source of publicity is computer billboards. Many local computer clubs have computer bulletin boards that are accessed by phone line. Most clubs are willing to post course notices and other information that may be useful to members. Local cable television companies have similar arrangements for their news and weather channels, and most are available to nonprofit groups.

## PERSONAL CONTACT MARKETING

Nothing appears to be more effective as a marketing strategy for adult learning than personal contact. Direct field sales involving personal visitation—personal contact marketing—is increasing in a dramatic fashion in continuing higher education. One-on-one field work and the development of ongoing personal communication linkages will be more important than ever in the ultimate success of continuing education marketing. Development of a personal contact marketing strategy has several advantages:[9]

- Personal contact provides ongoing needs assessment. Despite all the literature on formal needs assessment, most adult learning programs are based on informal needs assessment techniques. Personal contact strategies focus on listening to potential clients and evaluating their problems in terms of higher education learning solutions.
- It demonstrates initiative and commitment from an educational institution. Personal contact strategies involve a major labor-intensive commitment.
- It provides an opportunity to capture the undivided attention of the client, if only for a brief moment.
- It supports the educational analyst role of the adult educator in a college and university environment.
- It results in an ongoing intellectual and practical awareness of the environment in which continuing education programs operate. It acts as a silent smoke alarm that can alert program planners to needs and problems, which in turn provide opportunities for future programming.
- It provides feedback on current programs and activities.
- It allows for a multidimensional feedback system involving both verbal and nonverbal communications.
- It enhances the adult educator's knowledge base of area activities of businesses and organizations.

Personal contact marketing requires institutions of higher education to:

- Be proactive rather than reactive
- Spend more time listening to those they serve, visiting work sites, and establishing personal communication linkages
- Establish an externally oriented communication system which focuses on contacts in the public and business domains
- Rethink routine communication patterns and practices, such as how telephone calls are handled and how registration confirmation requests are followed up within the institution
- Commit to a planning process that will facilitate personal contact
- Review the marketing communications cycle to establish ongoing dialogue and to coordinate personal contact marketing activities

## MANAGING THE MARKETING FUNCTION

Management of marketing activities must be timely and thorough because of the financial costs involved and the potential for positive or negative impact on the image of the institution. The cost of continuing education marketing activities, including personnel salaries, can range as high as 18 to 24 percent of the total budget for a continuing education operation.

In determining the appropriateness of alternative marketing approaches, it is useful to separate the marketing function into two components. In the planning component, the total marketing plan is developed including communication methods and budget. The production component includes printing, graphics and design, photography, and mailing. Some institutions have facilities for the production component in-house; others do not. Institutional policies and local costs will dictate whether production resources are purchased in-house or from outside vendors. There are three basic organizational designs for the management of the marketing function. In a decentralized operation, each college or unit is responsible for its own continuing education programs. Such a design permits each unit to have immediate control and access to its own marketing resources, provides for quick turnaround of publications, stimulates the ongoing dialogue between program developers and marketing professionals, and encourages creative approaches depending on the particular audience the college or unit is serving. Disadvantages of a decentralized operation include potential duplication of effort, loss of a single institutional image, and lack of marketing expertise.

Some institutions centralize the marketing function in one administrative office that serves the entire college or university; often this is referred to as the public information or public relations office. The highly centralized approach has the advantages of providing professional direction, strong quality control, and lower production costs based on volume. Disadvantages include the possibility of scheduling delays, since publication requests must be consistent with other university printing and publication needs. It requires a staff with marketing skills in addition to editorial know-how.

A third organizational design provides for coordination between individual continuing education operations on campus with contracts outside the institution for all graphic design, typesetting, and printing services. This allows continuing education marketers more design options and competitive benefits in pricing and deadlines.

In most instances, institutions separate the functions involved with media, press, and public relations from those concerned with publications and paid advertising. The division seems to be a logical one that permits an institution to engage in an extensive program of paid promotional and advertising activities for continuing education, while at the same time pursuing the positive public, political, and press relations that are important for the institution's image and its relationships with various constituents.

## USE OF AGENCIES

Increasingly, there is a trend toward using outside agencies to assist in the continuing education marketing function. Although there may be several benefits to this approach, including greater creativity and shorter turnaround time, a continuing educator must know how to select the right agency for the job.

*Full-service advertising agencies.* These agencies usually provide total marketing services, including planning and consultation, layout and design, editing and copywriting, in-house typesetting, media buying and placement, and photographing. Some agencies provide market research and rebate all or part of agency discounts received from large newspapers and radio and TV stations.

*Design agencies.* These firms are primarily production houses with graphic design staff and in-house typesetting capabilities. They usually are not strong in media placement, copywriting, or marketing strategies.

*Printers.* Many printers have graphic designers who can assist with layout and design on relatively simple jobs. The costs are minimal and are often included in the printing charges. Creativity may be limited however.

*Freelance graphic designers.* There are many graphic designers who work on a piecework basis. Generally, their rates are lower than an advertising agency, but the client must coordinate and supervise the work. Depending on a particular designer's workload, response time may be erratic.

There are three major reasons for considering use of an outside agency:

1. *Cost.* Outside agencies may be less expensive than employing a full-time staff and equipping a graphic studio.
2. *Response time.* Internal publication offices may require long lead times. For most continuing education operations, it is important to respond quickly to program opportunities, and the use of outside agencies is usually faster.
3. *Individual styles of designers.* The use of only one or two designers can produce a specific "design style" that may or may not be

desirable. On the other hand, an internal designer may communicate the institution's goals more effectively.

In selecting an outside agency it is advisable to:

- Invite bids. Estimate the volume and type of work desired and ask area agencies to bid on the work for a six- to twelve-month period, or on a product basis.
- Have the agencies make a formal presentation. Determine if your work will be a large part of a small firm's business or vice versa. How they represent themselves is a good indication of how they will represent the college or university.
- Visit the agency to meet the staff and inspect the facility. Determine the size of staff, capabilities for in-house typesetting, and photographic service.
- Obtain a list of the agency's clients and discuss the agency's capabilities with them.
- Review prices carefully and look for hidden costs that are not included in the bid, such as the costs for headline type, statistical tables, pick-up and delivery charges, and placement fees. Find out whether the firm will rebate advertising agency discounts.

The key factor in selecting an external agency is personal rapport. The account representative must be someone with whom the continuing educator feels comfortable and who shows interest and enthusiasm for the project. There must be a willingness, on both sides, to share ideas and criticism openly and to function as a team.

## BUDGET CONSIDERATIONS

Regardless of the marketing strategy selected or the design of the management function, the "bottom line" is how much it costs to market the program. Do the results justify the cost? There are no adequate guidelines to indicate whether too much or too little is being spent on marketing. Each institution must evaluate its costs against the criteria established to measure marketing success. The important thing is to keep detailed records of all costs, including salaries, fringe benefits, postage, typesetting, printing, and all other related services.

Cost can be measured in several ways. It may be measured as cost per enrollment or per participant by dividing marketing expenses by total enrollments. This can be done for individual continuing education activities or for the total program. Or, the cost can be measured as a percentage of the institution's total budget. There are no helpful national norms in either of these cases. Beware of hidden costs. Careful monitoring, especially of publications, can often lead to significant savings.

## SUMMARY

Several approaches to the marketing of continuing higher education programs have been provided. Marketing is above all a communication process with both an informative and persuasive dimension. Every time personnel in an institution of higher education mail a flyer, place a display advertisment, answer the telephone, or send a letter, they are advertising the school, its programs, and their potential worth. For most potential continuing education participants, these activities form the image they have of the educational institution. Such advertising should be clear, concise, complete, correct, convincing, and honest. The list of additional readings at the end of the book provide more detailed information on marketing techniques and strategies.

## REFERENCES

1. Kotler, Philip, *Marketing for Nonprofit Organizations* (Englewood Cliffs, N.J.: Prentice-Hall, 1975).
2. Kotler, Philip, *Marketing Management—Analysis, Planning and Control* (Englewood Cliffs, N.J.: Prentice-Hall, 1976).
3. Boshier, Roger, "Motivational Orientations of Adult Education Participants: A Factor Analytic Exploration of Houle's Typology," *Adult Education,* 21 (1971).
4. Boshier, Roger, "Motivational Orientations Revised: Life-Space Motives and the Education Participant Scale," *Adult Education,* 27 (1977).
5. Maslow, A. H., *Motivation and Personality* (2nd. ed; New York: Harper and Row, 1970).
6. Mortsain, B. R., and Smart, J. C., "Reasons for Participation in Adult Education Courses: A Multivariate Analysis of Group Differences," *Adult Education,* 24 (2) (1974), pp. 83–98.
7. Aslanian, Carol B., and Brickell, Henry M., *Americans in Transition—* (New York: College Entrance Examination Board, 1980)
8. Elliott, Ralph D., *How to Build and Maintain a High Quality Mailing List* (Manhattan, Kans.: Learning Resources Network, 1982).
9. Fischer, Richard B., *Personal Contact in Marketing* (Manhattan, Kans.: Learning Resources Network, 1984).

# -11-
# A REVIEW OF RESEARCH AND EVALUATION IN CONTINUING HIGHER EDUCATION

## Carl A. Lindsay and H. Leroy Marlow

The evolving status of the broad field of adult and continuing education and the more narrow field of continuing higher education dictates that this chapter be a selective overview rather than a comprehensive literature review of research and evaluation studies. The major purposes of the chapter are to provide sources of research and evaluation studies, to examine the current status of studies, and to point to future directions for research and evaluation.

## RESEARCH

Many forces have shaped the field of adult and continuing education and its research base during its brief history. Positive forces include the increase in doctoral programs and students in adult and continuing education; the availability and stability of research forums such as the Adult Education Research Conference and the Lifelong Learning Research Conferences; and journals such as *Adult Education, Continuum,* and *Continuing Higher Education.* Negative forces that have slowed the growth of research in adult and continuing education are the practice-oriented nature of the field, the field's newness, and the reliance on other disciplines for its theoretical foundations. Much of the research in adult and continuing education has been borrowed from other fields and disciplines, such as sociology, psychology, history, management, anthropology, and communication.[1]

## SOURCES FOR ADULT AND CONTINUING EDUCATION LITERATURE AND RESEARCH STUDIES

There are two methods of gaining information on research and practice in the field that are available to continuing educators: reading the professional literature and interacting with other practitioners and researchers. Accessing the professional literature is a formal means of enhancing proficiencies, while interacting and exchanging information with peers is an informal method. In this section, major publications in the formal literature are discussed, and the professional associations and publications that contribute to adult and continuing education as a field of practice and research are identified.

Although its scope is broader than continuing higher education, Huey B. Long's *Adult Learning: Research and Practice* is the most comprehensive summary of research in adult and continuing education.[2] Phillip E. Frandson's *Power and Conflict in Continuing Education*[3] and Milton R. Stern's *Power and Conflict in Continuing Professional Education*[4] are highly readable sources that identify and discuss major issues in the field. An intensive analysis of the issues and literature regarding continuing professional education is provided in Cyril O. Houle's *Continuing Learning in the Professions*. This book includes a discussion of the roles of professional schools, associations, and higher education institutions in providing continuing higher education.[5] Two books focusing on the health professions, but that discuss continuing education issues such as needs assessment, program planning, and research implications, are Christine H. McGuire's *Handbook of Health Professions*[6] and Joseph S. Green's *Continuing Education for the Health Professions*.[7] Quarterly sourcebooks entitled "New Directions for Continuing Education" are published by Jossey-Bass. The first volume, published in 1979, by Alan Knox, contained information about enhancing the proficiencies of continuing educators.[8] Subsequent volumes included such topics as staffing by M. Alan Brown and Harlan G. Copeland;[9] teaching by Knox;[10] and attracting external funds by John Buskey.[11] "The Higher Education Research Reports," published by the Association for the Study of Higher Education-Educational Resources Information Center (ASHE-ERIC), frequently contain articles of interest to the continuing higher education community. The monograph *Public Service in Higher Education: Practices and Priorities* by Patricia Crossin is a good example.[12]

Continuing higher education is served by three national professional associations with associated regional and state affiliates. The most comprehensive association is the American Association for Adult and Continuing Education (AAACE). AAACE, located in Washington, D.C., is an individually based professional association whose membership consists of continuing educators from a wide variety of organizations, agencies, associations, and corporations. AAACE publishes a monthly magazine, *Lifelong Learning, An Omnibus of Practice and Research,* and a research journal, *Adult Education Quarterly.* It also has a division of continuing professional education that publishes a periodic newsletter.

The National University Continuing Education Association (NUCEA), located in Washington, D.C., is primarily an institutionally based professional association that offers individual memberships for continuing educators from colleges and universities. NUCEA publishes the monthly *NUCEA Newsletter* and a research journal, *Continuum.* NUCEA also has a division of continuing professional education that publishes its own newsletter and a division of research and programs.

The Association for Continuing Higher Education (ACHE), headquartered in Evansville, Indiana, offers both institutional and individual memberships for continuing educators from colleges and universities. ACHE publishes the *Journal for Continuing Higher Education,* a quarterly publication of research, program information, and papers on continuing higher education issues.

Other professional publications include *Mobius,* a journal for continuing education professionals in health sciences and health policy, published by the University of California Press. The American Educational Research Association (AERA) has two divisions for members interested in continuing education, and each publishes a newsletter. Division I, Education in the Professions, publishes *Professional Education Research Notes,* and Division J, Postsecondary Education, publishes *Postsecondary Education Newsletter.* The *Educational Record,* the journal of the American Council on Education (ACE), publishes research articles and conceptual pieces on broad issues that impact on higher education.

There are also two nationally known annual conferences devoted to research and practice in adult and continuing education: the Adult Education Research Conference, sponsored by AAACE, and the University of Maryland's Lifelong Learning Research Conference. Both publish proceedings that are beginning to have an impact on literature in the field.

Each continuing educator has his or her own approach toward maintaining, enhancing, and learning new proficiencies. The above listings can assist practitioners to discover, through formal and informal means, ideas, resources, and strategies that can be used to obtain a better understanding of the field and more competence in the performance of their responsibilities.

## ADULT AND CONTINUING EDUCATION LITERATURE RESEARCH AREAS

There are no standard topic categories in the literature that provide the continuing educator with information concerning the parameters used to describe and examine the major research areas of the field and the relative emphasis each receives in the literature. However, three schemes have been developed.

The first and most detailed scheme, consisting of thirty-one categories, is the subject index developed by J. Lance Kramer for *Continuum* articles.[13] Kramer noted that, while the continuing education literature is becoming increasingly relevant to practice and to the general development of the field, it has yet to be systematically delineated in any fashion that might be useful to the field. Consequently, he developed a scheme to encourage greater use of the literature related to continuing education practice.

Long, who tracks and summarizes the material published in the *Adult Education Quarterly,* the Adult Education Research Conference, and the Lifelong Learning Conference, developed a more manageable ten-topic categorization system that includes: adult learning; program planning and administration; institutional sponsor; adult education as a field of study; instructional materials and methods; philosophical concerns; program area; personnel and staff; international perspective; and other. Long's scheme was developed to provide a framework to characterize the content of adult and continuing education research. To develop his system, Long examined 355 papers presented at the Adult Education Research Conference over a ten-year (1971–1981) period. He found that 28 percent of the papers focused on program areas, and 24 percent were concerned with program planning and administration. Taken together, program areas, program planning and administration, and adult education as a field of study accounted for 68 percent of the papers.[14]

Long also developed a more abstract, five-category topic classification system to summarize research findings in his book, *Adult Learning: Research and Practice.* The categories, including representative research conclusions from each are:

> *Learning Ability.* Age does not seem to be an important variable in the learning ability of adults.
>
> *Enrolling the Adult.* Participation of blacks and other minority members does not appear to be a factor of race per se; low

participation among these groups seems to be associated with socioeconomic factors.

*Program Building.* Although there is general agreement in the literature concerning the broad outlines of the program planning procedure, the procedure itself remains a complex constellation of many action steps that are difficult to evaluate.

*Teaching-Learning Transactions.* Usefulness of the learning activity appears to be associated with interest in specific programs.

*Field of Practice and Philosophy.* There is increasing acceptance of adult education as a field of professional practice that has a distinctive body of knowledge, and there is increasing agreement that professionals engaged in the education of adults require specific competencies.[15]

## NEEDED RESEARCH AREAS

In a recent study, Robert Boyd surveyed deans and directors of continuing education/extension units in member institutions of the National Association of State Universities and Land-Grant Colleges. Respondents were asked to identify their research needs and those professional journals they found most helpful in keeping current on research in adult and continuing education.[16]

The respondents suggested a number of needed areas for research, and Boyd found it convenient to summarize their responses utilizing Long's five-category topic classification system. The most popular broad area for research suggested by the respondents was program building (62 percent). The category of teaching-learning transactions totaled 16 percent, followed by enrolling the adult, learning ability, and field of practice, which accounted for a total of 12 percent.[17]

By collapsing Long's ten-topic category into a five-topic category, one can compare needed research with current practice. At this relatively high level of abstraction, there seems to be reasonable agreement between the areas of needed research (practice/problems) and that which is being conducted. Long found that program areas and program planning and administration, both practice-oriented areas, accounted for 52 percent of the Adult Education Research Conference studies,[18] while Boyd found that program building accounted for 62 percent of the needed topics.[19] Boyd also reported his respondents found the following publications, in rank order of preference, most helpful in keeping up-to-date on research in the field: *Continuum, Journal of Higher Education, Lifelong Learning, Chronicle of Higher Education, Adult Education Quarterly,* and *Change.*

## FUTURE ISSUES AND DIRECTIONS

If research is to continue its important role as an information base for the practice and study of the education of adults, the emerging issues that confront the field must be addressed. While recognizing that numerous problems and issues compete for attention, the focus is given in this section to issues that have some salience for a rapprochement between research and practice. Given an emerging consensus that research is a major force in shaping the field and informing practice, two issues are examined: quality assurance and the need for syntheses of research findings from both the same and different areas of the field.

QUALITY ASSURANCE. The issue of quality assurance stems from a growing demand for accountability—a general social phenomenon that has increased over the past twenty years. It is related to developments such as consumerism, management by objectives, and widespread dissatisfaction with and distrust of all professionals and elites.[20] Houle stated:

> As the amount of educational services has increased, following the general principle that more is better, so has the skepticism. . . . In profession after profession . . . efforts of teaching and learning seem to have had too little effect on practice. A sense of despondency is sometimes expressed even by those who have devoted much of their lives to lifelong learning.[21]

K. Patricia Cross observed:

> Many educators and policy makers are calling for new forms of quality assessment of programs designed to serve the unique needs of adults. The question "what is quality?" appears to be straightforward and objective when in fact it is neither.[22]

Joseph S. Green and associates noted that recent experience in several health fields has shown the lack of demonstrable impact of continuing education is due to the design of the educational experience or its evaluation rather than to the failure of continuing education per se. Notably, the more general the learning objectives of a given educational activity, the more difficult it is to assess and evaluate impact.[23] By contrast, the use of a systems approach on a limited, clearly described set of objectives can result in a measurable impact on a specified area of competence.[24]

Demands for quality assurance in continuing education are increasing, and methods for assessing effectiveness are available to the practitioner. Examples are G. L. Andrew's *Principles of Good Practice in Continuing Education*[25] published by the Council on the Continuing Education Unit and the "Continuing Education Systems Project."[26] An assessment model was developed by project members, and a list of 141 quality elements were divided into five areas: setting directions, organizing the continuing education provider unit, providing continuing education activities and products, providing educational assistance and services, and administering the continuing education provider unit. It would appear that the demands for demonstrating a causal relationship between instruction and practice behavior are more stringently placed on continuing education than they are on the preparatory phases of professional training. While acknowledging the issue of educational quality assurance, Richard Caplan was very direct as to its source and resolution:

> This question and others of its type seem to place on the educator the burden of delivering education that assures improved patient care. The time has come, I believe, to assert that such an assurance is not the proper charge to educators or to education alone. It is proper for educators to work toward practical and patient-oriented goals, but they should no longer docilely accept blame and develop feelings of guilt when their educational labors cannot be shown in every instance to have produced the desired perfection in the process or outcome of care.[27]

Given the continuing societal demand for accountability and the fact that it permeates nearly all aspects of a continuing education enterprise, the issue of quality assurance will not diminish in importance. The tasks of defining the issue and its implications provide opportunities for researchers and continuing educators to work together.

NEED FOR RESEARCH TRANSLATION AND SYNTHESIS.    Another issue affecting both researchers and practitioners is how to make research findings more useful to continuing educators. There is some consensus among researchers and practitioners that research in adult and continuing education has not been particularly helpful in influencing practice; however, there is not any consensus on how to improve the situation. It has been suggested that research, to be more useful in the future, should emphasize development of theory over application and basic research. Others argue the development of theoretical positions is not the answer, rather that the translation of theory and research findings into applied practice holds the most promise.[28]

This important translation task, to which the authors subscribe, leads to the need for synthesizing frameworks and the conduct of meta-research. Meta-research is a technique for summarizing in a systematic fashion the conclusions and trends from a number of different studies in a given area. Tom Sork identified six types of meta-research for adult and continuing education: inventories of research, general reviews of research, critical reviews of specific topics, research agendas or taxonomies of needed research, focused critiques of research methodology, and frameworks or paradigms for understanding and, improving research.[29]

The chief value of these suggested types of meta-research studies is to inform both practitioners and researchers of the development of research trends and methods.

There is an additional dimension to the overall need to translate research into practice—the need for analysis and synthesis of other broad areas of research for application to adult and continuing education. Long proposed a list of needs in this regard. He believed the field needs to integrate past research with more recent findings; review selectively recent research in the fields of psychology, anthropology, vocational education, and communications for findings pertinent to the process of educating adults; integrate the adult education literature with relevant material from other fields; and relate the integrated research literature from other disciplines to existing theory in adult education.[30] Progress toward meeting these needs to help make research more useful to practitioners will continue with the development of the field of adult and continuing education.

## EVALUATION

A review of the literature on evaluation in adult and continuing education reveals there is no shortage of philosophies or ideas for procedures and techniques applied to the topic. Despite the great amount of literature on evaluation, an effective continuing education guideline has not emerged, and it remains an elusive educational tool.

This section emphasizes the pragmatic aspects of evaluation. It is aimed at the practitioner working in a college or university setting who wishes to create an effective evaluation tool for current programs.

### WHY PROGRAM EVALUATION?

There are five basic reasons why evaluations are conducted:

1. To determine if the program or public service activity is meeting its stated objectives. The persons responsible for the activity need proof the program is accomplishing what it was designed to do.

2. To learn participants' opinions of the program. Their responses can be useful in making future program decisions regarding such things as program content, frequency of offerings, geographical locations, fee structure, what faculty should be used, and preferred type of facilities.

3. To calculate results and determine the cost/benefit ratio. This type of evaluation appears to be increasing in importance for continuing education programs.

4. To provide data to meet reporting requirements. This can be as simple as reporting the number of attendees, or it might require significant amounts of information.

5. To justify the program to funding sources—foundations, government agencies, professional associations, industry—that require proof of the value of the educational program.

The reasons for program evaluation must be kept foremost in the design of the evaluation procedure and instruments. A variety of information can be obtained through the evaluation procedure; however, the most significant goal is to justify the existence of the program. An evaluation is relevant only if it provides practical data regarding achievement of the program's stated goals. Effective evaluation produces a bottom line rather than blue-sky appraisal.

Some higher education programs can be evaluated and financially quantified by demonstrating economic benefit to the state and citizens. For other programs it is difficult to determine dollar amounts because of the nature of the service. In some programs results will produce immediate results. For example, new knowledge acquired at a workshop is a benefit available for immediate use. On the other hand, productivity improvements may not be realized for several years. Changes in attitudes are more difficult to measure and may never be fully documented to everyone's satisfaction. While short- and long-term results are crucial to the program, its growth, or even survival, they are often overlooked as continuing educators design evaluation forms to be distributed to program participants. Often, little thought is given to the real purposes for conducting the evaluation; in many cases it is only a perfunctory, meaningless activity. Evaluation forms that merely indicate the participant "liked" the program are often the rule. These data may be comforting to the presenter, but provide insufficient information to justify the program's existence or to obtain future support.

Continuing education programs are designed to improve the knowledge of adult learners, to upgrade or update them in their work or professional area, to prepare them for new or different jobs or for entry or reentry into higher education, or to kindle their interest in further educational advancement. The axiom is that the more education a person has, the more likely he or she will become a higher wage earner, will pay higher taxes, and will contribute more to the community as an enlightened citizen.

Studies examining the benefits of the G.I. Bill showed that money spent on education for veterans produced greater benefits for the United States.[31] Large numbers of veterans were educated in critical areas such as science, engineering, and medicine[32] and also in the humanities and other subjects essential to any democracy.[33] As anticipated, the G.I. Bill produced higher wage earnings, greater tax revenues, and a better educated and informed citizenry. Many continuing education offerings provide benefits that cannot be measured financially but do have a profound effect on the individual, state, and nation.

Some programs can be measured in terms of direct financial benefits. An example is the Pennsylvania Technical Assistance Program (PENNTAP). Its purpose is to assist business, industry, and public sector agencies in solving a wide variety of technical problems by using the resources of higher education. Program officials use university resources to share knowledge and research data in order to solve the problems of specific organizations. A broad cross-section of the community is served. Historically, small business and industrial clients compose more than half of the users. Government agencies, institutions of higher education, and school districts make up another 20 percent. Consultants, engineers and entrepreneurs account for 12 percent, and the balance is made up of health care facilities, nonprofit associations, quasi-governmental groups, and similar users. The latest technical information is gathered, stated in understandable terms, and applied to the particular problems presented by the various organizations. An example is the comprehensive preventive maintenance program developed by the U.S. Navy at its Dahlgren, Virginia, base. With the help of Navy personnel, technical data were rewritten and disseminated to organizations that could apply the information to reduce their physical plant operating costs. An evaluation system designed to gain data on benefits achieved, not services performed, showed that the economic impact of this service—as reported by users—over a twelve-year period (1971–1983) was $69.1 million.[34] As a benefit versus cost measurement, for every dollar invested in this program an average of $17.20 was returned to the state's economy.[35]

## THE EVALUATION PROCESS

To organize an evaluation, the following tasks must be implemented. They are the same as for any problem-solving effort.

1. Determine the goal. What is the objective? Precisely what is to be measured? What is the evaluation to accomplish?

2. Define the kind of data that are needed to reach the objective. To develop a cost/benefit ratio, there will be a need to define benefits clearly—jobs created, processes improved, sales increased, productivity improved. To prepare a year-end statistical report, in addition to economic-type information more generalized activity data will be needed.

3. Decide how and when the data are to be collected. Should it be collected through questionnaires? Through interviews? Will it be at the end of the seminar, semester, or course? Will it be after participants have had time to apply the new information?

4. Analyze the data. How is this to be done? What will be done with the results? In what form will they be presented?

5. Develop conclusions. What are the implications of the evaluation results? What should happen next? Should changes be made in future programs? With whom should the evaluation data be shared? What results of a tangible nature have been verified? What has been learned about the program as a result of the evaluation? What conclusions can be drawn?

6. Implement a plan of action. How will changes be initiated that have been identified by the evaluation? What can be done to ensure the data are used? Develop a schedule of what needs to be done, when it will be done, and by whom. Build mechanisms into the plan to ensure that the plan is implemented and carried out.

The evaluation process may range from a simple questionnaire to elaborate follow-up studies. It should not be initiated without considerable planning. Some of the questions that need to be asked are, What is the program expected to accomplish? What is to be measured? What type of information will be useful? How are the data to be collected? What will be done with the information after it is received?

Maintaining the proper perspective when considering these questions is vital. If participants are asked the right kind of questions about the program's impact, secondary information also falls into place. For example, when a recipient indicates an educational program or activity was useful, he or she also suggests the instructor or transfer agent was effective.

For whatever reason, program participants are not usually inclined to respond to an evaluation with enthusiasm. Participants seldom volunteer information or reactions beyond what is requested on the form. Consequently, when it is important to know if or how information from a course or workshop has been or will be useful, that question must be asked. When appropriate, the question might be asked in several ways. What benfits did you/will you achieve in dollars? In time saved? How did it benefit your company? Your community?

Too frequently, there is not a definite plan for using the results of evaluation, which may mean it becomes a worthless activity. At the other extreme, there may be a highly developed analytical procedure for using the data as a decision-making tool. Most program evaluations fall somewhere between these two extremes.

## CATEGORIES OF EVALUATION

No one form can meet all evaluation needs. Evaluation forms must be designed to meet specific program objectives. However, there are certain basic questions that will appear in any evaluation category. All evaluations of continuing higher education programs and activities can be included in one or more of the following three categories.

*Category 1. Evaluation of programs and facilities.* There is an attitudinal evaluation by participants of their perceptions of the program, faculty, or facility. It is used primarily to evaluate informal and credit programs—those falling into the "course" type of offerings. It is usually conducted at the conclusion of the program as a measure of the participants' satisfaction or dissatisfaction with the educational program or the facility. Questions in this evaluation category will ask participants to rank such items as the effectiveness of the instructor, the length of the program, room arrangements, etc. This evaluation is usually considered in planning future programs and is widely used in developing and executing a marketing program. It is most often used for conferences, workshops, seminars, and evening school programs. A sample typical evaluation format used in Category 1 is shown in Figure 11.1.

*Category 2. Evaluation of program activities.* The volume or number of activities that the program has generated is measured by this evaluation. It may be used to prepare a year-end report or to document the activity level of a typical classroom program or an outreach activity. The extent of involvement rather than the quality of the programs or the accomplishments generated is recorded. This type of evaluation is often used by small business centers to report their client level of activity and by program specialists or others who are interested in the quantitative aspects of evaluation with little or no concern for quality or results. A sample form, listing the type of questions included in a Category 2 evaluation, is shown in Figure 11.2.

## FIGURE 11.1. Sample Form: Category 1

THIS EVALUATION FORM WILL BE OF ASSISTANCE TO YOUR PROGRAM COMMITTEE. PLEASE COMPLETE IT AND RETURN IT AT THE END OF THE MEETING.

### Program Evaluation

Please list the names of speakers and rank their performance by circling the number which most accurately describes your impression:

| Names | Quality of Presentation | | | | | |
|---|---|---|---|---|---|---|
| | Poor | Fair | | Good | | Excellent |
| _____ | 1 | 2 | 3 | 4 | 5 | 6 |
| _____ | 1 | 2 | 3 | 4 | 5 | 6 |
| _____ | 1 | 2 | 3 | 4 | 5 | 6 |
| _____ | 1 | 2 | 3 | 4 | 5 | 6 |
| _____ | 1 | 2 | 3 | 4 | 5 | 6 |
| _____ | 1 | 2 | 3 | 4 | 5 | 6 |
| _____ | 1 | 2 | 3 | 4 | 5 | 6 |
| _____ | 1 | 2 | 3 | 4 | 5 | 6 |
| _____ | 1 | 2 | 3 | 4 | 5 | 6 |
| _____ | 1 | 2 | 3 | 4 | 5 | 6 |

This year's conference theme is " _____ ." Circle the number below which describes how well you think this meeting embodied this theme:

| Poor | Fair | Good | | Excellent | |
|---|---|---|---|---|---|
| 1 | 2 | 3 | 4 | 5 | 6 |

The characteristics listed below are usually considered to be essential to any effective educational program. Please indicate how effectively you think these characteristics were by circling the number which most accurately describes your experience:

| | Poor | Fair | | Good | | Excellent |
|---|---|---|---|---|---|---|
| I. Content | | | | | | |
| Interesting | 1 | 2 | 3 | 4 | 5 | 6 |
| Useful | 1 | 2 | 3 | 4 | 5 | 6 |
| II. Process | | | | | | |
| Well-organized | 1 | 2 | 3 | 4 | 5 | 6 |
| Thorough | 1 | 2 | 3 | 4 | 5 | 6 |
| Creative | 1 | 2 | 3 | 4 | 5 | 6 |
| Clearly presented | 1 | 2 | 3 | 4 | 5 | 6 |

Were handouts used in this meeting?  Yes ____  No ____

If handouts were used, how useful were they? (Please circle the number which best expresses your impression.)

| Poor | Fair | Good | | Excellent | |
|---|---|---|---|---|---|
| 1 | 2 | 3 | 4 | 5 | 6 |

FIGURE 11.1. (continued)

If handouts were not used, how helpful would they have been to you?
\_\_\_ Probably not helpful             \_\_\_ Very helpful
\_\_\_ Somewhat helpful              \_\_\_ Essential for proper understanding

Were charts, films, slides, tapes, or other audio and/or visual aids used in this meeting? Yes \_\_\_    No \_\_\_

If audio and/or visual aids were used, how useful were they? (Please circle the number which best expresses your impression.)

| Poor | | Fair | | Good | | Excellent | |
|------|---|------|---|------|---|-----------|---|
| 1 | 2 | 3 | 4 | 5 | 6 | | |

If audio and/or visual aids were not used, how helpful would they have been to you?
\_\_\_ Probably not helpful             \_\_\_ Very helpful
\_\_\_ Somewhat helpful              \_\_\_ Essential for proper understanding

How helpful was this meeting in strengthening your feeling of membership in the group?

| Not Helpful | | Somewhat Helpful | | Very Helpful | |
|-------------|---|------------------|---|--------------|---|
| 1 | 2 | 3 | 4 | 5 | 6 |

Was there ample opportunity for audience participation during the meeting?
Yes \_\_\_    No \_\_\_

Would you want to attend another meeting of this group?
Yes \_\_\_    No \_\_\_

Would you want to participate as an active member of this group?
Yes \_\_\_    No \_\_\_

---

*Category 3. Evaluation of accomplishments.* This is the most difficult and least-used evaluation category. There is a growing demand by educational and business leaders, legislators, and other decision makers for this type of formal evaluation. This evaluation can be conducted for a credit course or informal program but generally is not used for this purpose. It is most often used to measure the results of a public service activity. Evaluators seek to learn what has been accomplished as a result of participation in the activity. While this type of evaluation could be employed to measure behavioral change as a result of a management development program, it is generally used to measure tangible benefits (e.g., the number of new jobs

## FIGURE 11.2. Sample Form: Category 2

I. CASE RECORD

Submitted by: _____ Date _____
              (Signature)

Case Number _____

Case _____

    Status (Circle One)    A — Active    C — Closed    Unit Number ____

      Start Date _____
               Mo.      Day      Year

_____      _____
Estimated Completion Date         Close Date

II. Person Requesting Service

Name _____ Title _____ Telephone _____
      (Last)       (First)

Address: _____
          (Street)        (City)      (County)      (State)

_____
   (Zip Code)

Organization _____ Initial Contact _____

III. Personal Data

| Sex | Ethnic Background | Veteran Status |
|---|---|---|
| ___ 1. Female | ___ 1. Am. Indian or Alaskan Native | ___ 1. Pre-Vietnam Vet |
| ___ 2. Male | ___ 2. Asian or Pacific Islander | ___ 2. Vietnam Vet |
| | ___ 3. Black, not of Hispanic origin | ___ 3. Non-Veteran |
| Type Case | ___ 4. Hispanic | |
| ___ | ___ 5. White | |
| ___ | ___ 6. Other | |
| ___ | | |

| Type of Firm | Handicapped | Category of Management Concern |
|---|---|---|
| ___ 1. Pre-venture | ___ Yes | ___   ___ |
| ___ 1. New | ___ No | ___   ___ |
| ___ 3. Mature | | ___   ___ |
| ___ 4. Liquidation | | ___   ___ |

Year started _____

## FIGURE 11.2. (continued)

Industrial Code

—  —  —  —  —
—  —  —  —  —
—  —  —  —  —

Resources
\_\_\_\_ 1. Employees
\_\_\_\_ 2. Faculty
\_\_\_\_ 3. Graduate Student
\_\_\_\_ 4. Consultants
\_\_\_\_ 5. Professional Association
\_\_\_\_ 6. Other

IV. Financial Data

| Initial Contact | Date | Gross Sales | Export Sales |
|---|---|---|---|
| | Profit (Loss) | Number of Employees \_\_\_\_ Full-time    \_\_\_\_ Part-time | |
| | Owner's Compensation | Capital Investment | Payroll |
| Follow-up Contact | Date | Gross Sales | Export Sales |
| | Profit (Loss) | Number of Employees \_\_\_\_ Full-time    \_\_\_\_ Part-time | |
| | Owner's Compensation | Capital Investment | Payroll |

VI. Comments:

_____

created as a result of an economic development project or benefits generated through technology transfer). It is predicted that in the not-too-distant future, all continuing education programs and many resident instruction programs will be required to document *real* accomplishments. A brief form that may be used to demonstrate benefits to the clients is shown in Figure 11.3.

The timing and distribution of the form is determined, to some extent, by the evaluation category. Forms in Category 1 may be distributed, completed, and collected immediately upon completion of the program. This process allows for the participant's initial reaction and gives immedite feedback to the instructor/administrator.

Data in Category 2 are usually collected from a number of individuals at the time of the initial contact and may be updated with subsequent meetings. The sum of each individual activity report can be combined to form a quarterly or annual report of activity.

The use of a questionnaire for Category 3 is quite different. Since this type of evaluation reports results, the questionnaire is not sent

Name _____    Date Evaluation Sent _____

Organization _____    If information not as yet implemented, please indicate projected
date of implementation.

Address _____

_____

Name of Transfer Agent _____ Campus Contact _____

Classification of Question/Problem:

Accounting and Taxes ___    Energy ___    Engineering ___    Finance ___
Government Regulation ___ Marketing ___    New Business Start-Up ___
Personnel Management ___
Production Management ___    Safety ___    Other ___
Please Explain: _____

I. Did the assistance provided result in a ___ one time; ___ monthly; or
year economic benefit?  (Please check only one.)

II. Please indicate (1) the estimated dollar amount and (2) form of
benefit based on the assistance provided. (You may check one or
more.)

A. $ _____ Revenues of Sales Increased

B. $ _____ Cost of Goods or Services Reduced

C. $ _____ Operating Expenses Reduced

III. If **not already included** in answers above, were _____ jobs created or
jobs saved as a direct result of the assistance provided?

IV. Additional Comments (You may attach letter describing more detail if
there is not enough room provided.):

FIGURE 11.3. Sample Form. Category 3

to the client until such time as the individual has been able to apply
the new knowledge and determine whether it has been useful. This
time lag may be as short as several months or may require several
years.

## GROWING IMPORTANCE OF EVALUATION

For many years educational institutions used the evaluation procedure
primarily for administrative control—to help make decisions concerning which program should be repeated and which faculty members

should be retained. Evaluations have generally been used to measure a participant's perceptions of whether or not the program was satisfactory. In such evaluations, questions center on which luncheon menus were most favorably received, whether or not the physical arrangements of the room were satisfactory, and if the participants were comfortable.

Based on experience in producing measurable benefits from continuing education programs and observation, it appears there has been a change in the focus of evaluation procedures. While the administrative aspects of good evaluation are still important, evaluation has taken on a more serious goal. More and more continuing higher education programs are being asked to demonstrate that they achieve results. Continuing educators must prove that the money and time spent by participants were beneficial and that the program was conducted in a businesslike manner. Legislators now question long-term programs that have been conducted for years, asking those persons responsible to prove their usefulness. There have been cases where long-established programs and service projects did not provide results-oriented evaluations. The evaluation instruments collected administrative data, such as attendance levels, calls made, and cases handled, but provided no evidence of positive results from the years of program activity. Sponsors could not substantiate the program contributions to the social or economic welfare of their institution's service area.

Economic pressures leading to prudent management accountability are causing persons with oversight responsibilities to ask questions about programs and budgets that have escaped previous scrutiny. Suddenly, many program administrators must provide evidence of results or face program elimination. Under these circumstances, evaluation becomes an extremely important tool. Evaluation can no longer be a tranquil exercise but must be made an integral part of program design. Continuing education administrators and faculty members must be prepared to substantiate claims of the impact a program has on its clientele.

## FUNDING SOURCES

University funding patterns are changing as the role of state and federal support takes on new characteristics. Funding limitations in state legislatures are reducing appropriations for education. Institutions of higher education are especially vulnerable to the whims of lawmakers as they search for ways to justify budget cuts. Institutions are being forced to seek other funding sources through special development and endowment campaigns. Private business and foundations provide new opportunities for support to higher education through outright contributions or cooperative programming. Since corporations survive on the basis of profit and loss accountability, there is a growing attitude by federal and state governments and the general public that institutions of higher education should also be accountable for the money they receive.

It is expected that the current trend by funding agencies (e.g., Rural Technology Assistance Program under the Federal Highway Department, the University Center Program from the Federal Economic Development Administration, U.S. Department of Agriculture) to require a strong, useful evaluation as part of all projects will continue. It can be expected in the future that little, if any, funding will be made available for continuing higher education programs that do not require a results-oriented evaluation component.

## COST/BENEFIT ANALYSIS

It is difficult to develop a cost/benefit analysis for many continuing education programs. Such data are costly to collect and analyze, but cost/benefit analysis can be done. Forward-thinking practitioners should develop evaluative techniques to do so. In public service projects, such analyses have been made for almost two decades. As previously mentioned, the Pennsylvania Technical Assistance Program was created as a results-oriented activity that required such evaluations. Similar programs in the states of California (Western Research Application, University of Southern California), Oklahoma (Center for Local Government Technology, Oklahoma State), Georgia (Engineering Experiment Station, Georgia Tech), Iowa (Center for Industrial Research and Services, Iowa State University), and Tennessee (Center for Industrial Services, University of Tennessee), to name just a few, have made similar efforts. For a program in continuing higher education, a cost/benefit ratio of 10:1 to 20:1 is attainable. This ratio should be determined on a statistically sound basis. It is not sufficient for a project administrator to estimate the program benefits. To obtain proper credibility, program evaluations must have documented evidence from the participants.

Each institution should determine what factors are to be included in a cost/benefit analysis. In its simplest form, a cost/benefit analysis is determined by dividing the actual cost of operating by the determined financial benefits. Thus, an operating budget of $500,000 producing $10 million in benefits generates a 20:1 cost/benefit ratio. Not only will all cost factors need to be determined but the role that residual benefits will play in year-to-year comparisons should be decided. Some of the questions that may need to be asked are: Will a production improvement savings be counted for only the year it occurs or for a longer period? How is a fair percentage of overhead costs to be calculated? What standard accounting principles should be used to make the analysis accurate as possible?

The National Association of Management and Technical Assistance Centers reported that each of the centers has instituted some type of an evaluation program that will provide a cost/benefit ratio.[36] This approach to evaluation can be expected to occur more frequently in the future as state and federal governments, the private sector, and foundations demand an accounting of program results by colleges and universities.

## SUMMARY

The practice and study of adult and continuing education did not grow from careful study by theoreticians and researchers. It emerged and continued to develop as a result of contributions from practicing continuing educators and researchers in the field. Researchers in other academic disciplines and individuals concerned about the major issues in adult and continuing education have also contributed to the field. This mixed-heritage trend will probably continue as adult and continuing education moves toward greater maturity. As the field matures, an important task for professionals in continuing higher education is to develop a collective sense of mission and identity.

The approach to accomplish this goal is best expressed through dynamic professionalization.[37] Toward this end, continuing learning is necessary for the development of professional effectiveness of the individual practitioner. Therefore, a major challenge facing the field of adult and continuing education involves determining and increasing the professional proficiency of those directly related to the field, including administrators, teachers, counselors, policymakers, and researchers. One method for enhancing practitioner proficiencies that can also contribute to the professionalization of the field is to encourage more professionals to become actively involved in the research, evaluation, and publication process.

In this chapter, research was approached on the basis of any kind of disciplined study and reporting, including interpretive literature reviews, prescriptive, and "how-to" reports. This has been done to place research and evaluation activities, which should involve both practitioners and researchers, into the proper role in the professionalization of the field. Issues and questions remain, but they must be viewed in the context of the progress made in the strengthening of the foundations for the practice and continued development of adult and continuing higher education.

# REFERENCES

1. Long, Huey B., *Adult Learning: Research and Practice* (New York: Cambridge University Press, 1983).

2. Ibid.

3. Frandson, Phillip E., ed., *Power and Conflict in Continuing Education* (Belmont, Calif.: Wadsworth, 1980).

4. Stern, Milton R., ed., *Power and Conflict in Continuing Professional Education* (2nd ed.; Belmont, Calif.: Wadsworth, 1983).

5. Houle, Cyril O., *Continuing Learning in the Professions* (San Francisco: Jossey-Bass, 1980).

6. McGuire, Christine H., et al., eds., *Handbook for Health Professions* (San Francisco: Jossey-Bass, 1983).

7. Green, Joseph S., et al., eds., *Continuing Education for the Health Professions* (San Francisco: Jossey-Bass, 1984).

8. Knox, Alan B., *Enhancing Proficiencies of Continuing Educators,* New Directions for Continuing Education, No. 1 (San Francisco: Jossey-Bass, 1979).

9. Brown, M. Alan, and Copeland, Harland G., *Attracting Able Instructors of Adults,* New Directions for Continuing Education, No. 4 (San Francisco: Jossey-Bass, 1979).

10. Knox, Alan B., *Teaching Adults Effectively,* New Directions for Continuing Education, No. 6 (San Francisco: Jossey-Bass, 1980).

11. Buskey, John H., *Attracting External Funds for Continuing Education,* New Directions for Continuing Education, No. 12 (San Francisco: Jossey-Bass, 1981).

12. Crossin, Patricia, *Public Service in Higher Education: Practices and Priorities,* ASHE-ERIC Higher Education Research Report No. 7 (Washington, D.C.: Association for the Study of Higher Education, 1983).

13. Kramer, J. Lance, "The Literature of Continuing Education," *Continuum,* 48 (2) (1984).

14. Long, Huey B., "Characteristics of Adult Education Research Reported at the Adult Education Research Conference, 1971–1980," *Adult Education,* 33 (2) (1983), pp. 79–96.

15. Long, *Adult Learning,* loc. cit.

16. Boyd, Robert H., "State of the Art in Research in Extension and Continuing Education—One View" (paper presented at the meeting of the National Association of State Universities and Land-Grant Colleges, Washington, D.C., November 12, 1984).

17. Ibid.,

18. Long, "Characteristics of Adult Education Research," loc. cit.

19. Boyd, loc. cit.

20. Caplan, Richard M., "Continuing Education and Professional Accountability," in *Handbook of Health Professions,* Christine H. McGuire et al. (San Francisco: Jossey-Bass, 1983).

21. Houle, op. cit., p. 4.

22. Cross, K. Patricia, and McCartan, Anne Marie, "Adult Learning: State Policies and Institutional Practices," *Higher Educational Research Reports,* Report No. 1 (Washington, D.C.: Association for the Study of Higher Education, 1984).

23. Green et al., loc. cit.

24. Cervero, Ronald M., and Rottet, Suzanne, "Analyzing the Effectiveness of Continuing Professional Education: An Exploratory Study," *Adult Education Quarterly,* 34 (3) (1984).

25. Andrews, G. L., *Principles of Good Practice in Continuing Education* (Silver Spring: Council on the Continuing Education Unit, 1984).

26. Green et al., loc. cit.

27. Caplan, op. cit., p. 326.

28. Long, *Adult Learning,* loc. cit.

29. Sork, Tom J., "Meta-Research in Adult Education: An Historical Analysis of Critical Appraisal" (paper presented at the annual Adult Education Research Conference, Vancouver, British Columbia, 1980).

30. Long, *Adult Learning,* loc. cit.

31. Johnson, Donald E., "Veterans Benefits a Quarter Century of the GI Bill," *School and Society,* 90 (April 1970), p. 226.

32. Yarborough, R. W., "Six Precedents on Federal Aid to Education," *The American Teacher,* 45 (April 1961), p. 9.

33. Emens, John R., "Education Begets Education: The GI Bill 30 Years Later," *American Education,* 2 (Summer 1965), p. 11.

34. *PENNTAP Update,* Pennsylvania Technical Assistance Program (University Park: The Pennsylvania State University/Pennsylvania Department of Commerce, 1983).

35. Ibid.,

36. National Association of Management and Technical Assistance Centers, Annual Meeting, University of Maryland, September 26–27, 1985.

37. Houle, loc. cit.

# -12-
# SPECIAL CHARACTERISTICS OF CONTINUING EDUCATION FOR THE PROFESSIONS

## Philip M. Nowlen

Apprenticeship once seemed an indispensable preparation for occupational life, yet it was succeeded by technical and professional schools. Similarly, professional schools' monopoly for qualifying persons for professional life has been narrowed to qualifying persons to enter professional life. The issue of keeping professionals qualified is now addressed by many resources and systems. Continuing education is provided to professionals by universities and colleges; scholarly societies; professional associations; foundations; employers; federal, state, and local governments; voluntary groups; proprietary schools; churches and synagogues; individual, self-employed consultants; for-profit corporations whose only "products" are seminars for professionals; and, the largest provider group, individuals who organize and carry out learning activities for themselves. It is the individual professionals who are ultimately responsible for maintaining or enhancing their proficiencies and for integrating new skills of mind and action.

Insisting that professionals remain qualified is an objective of state licensing bureaus, some professional associations, and employers that mandate (with a wide range of persuaders that range from subtle to coercive) participation in continuing education or that compel participation in periodic reexaminations. Professionals who share a practice setting and carry out formal and informal peer review processes heighten motivation for lifelong learning. A variety of societal trends has served to increase public demand for professional accountability; one has only to look to medical malpractice insurance rates for a reminder that professional competence is increasingly the object of judicial inquiry. Maintenance and enhancement of performance are now not only functions of professional commitment, they have become matters of self-defense as well.

Dentists may find it convenient to tune in to their continuing education network. Lawyers and chemists find themselves attending programs that blend on-the-scene lectures and discussions with "live" televised presentations. Law enforcement officials can access programs through cable or UHF channels. Accountants may keep up through interactive computer terminals. Nurses and social workers are offered audiotape recordings. Professionals' needs are also addressed within their national, regional, or state professional association meetings, over brown-bag lunches in industry, in evening and weekend courses on campuses, and daily in conferences and seminars in hotels throughout the United States and Canada.

Consider higher education itself. Those in the scholarly professions hold multiple memberships in societies reflecting one or more disciplines or fields of research, in associations that reflect professional support systems (computer societies, for example), and in national groups that address the common interests and problems of scholar administrators. These societies and associations are organized both nationally and regionally and reflect further variables such as institutional size, mission, and values. Whether it is the Modern Language Association, the Council of Independent Colleges, the National Council of University Research Administrators, or the American Society for Engineering Education, every one of these organizations has a considerable investment in the continuing education of its membership—the most highly degreed and self-directed learners that one can find. In addition, the scholarly professions are addressed by foundation- and government-sponsored continuing education programs and by the offerings of planning consultants, accounting firms, and manufacturers whose advertisements and announcements fill pages of the *Chronicle of Higher Education.*

Midsized associations offer 150 to 200 programs a year, based on budgets of $1.5 to $2 million and staffed by ten to twenty-five persons. Larger associations typically have continuing education budgets in excess of $10 million, offer 300 or more programs per year, and have staff members (or access to associational staff members) that include marketing and telecommunications specialists.

It has been estimated by the American Society for Training and Development that employers make an annual investment of $60 billion in continuing education for their executives and professional personnel as well as for other white and blue-collar employees. Approximately

$3 billion is spent on professional development by the Department of Defense. A significant portion of the Bell System's $1.7 billion training budget is devoted to professional development. Employer-paid registrations outnumber self-paid registrations in university- and college-based continuing education programs by more than four to one. Crain's *Chicago Business* reported that of more than 3,000 organizations offering some 40,000 seminars in business and management topics alone, 700 were colleges and universities. Dorothy C. Fenwick, former associate director for educational credit and credentials of the American Council on Education, stated that in 1983 more than 200 employers offered 3,000 or more accredited courses, forming a kind of shadow education system.[1] Bell and Howell had an accredited program in which there were 35,000 students.[2]

Figures such as the above are not in short supply, but the larger and more precise they are, the less reliable. Why is this so? There is disagreement between inclusivists and exclusivists about which groups (MBAs, for example) are or are not professions. Definitional clarity is lacking, with one school's seminar being another's institute, course, or program. There are narrow and broad approaches to what should be counted as continuing professional education. Some include only content related to professional curricula, for example, "New SEC Regulations for Accountants." Others count whatever programs might be, by intention, related to professional performance, for example, "Approaches to Counseling Professionals Impaired by Chemical Dependencies." Some university administrators think of continuing education for the professions as the postgraduate offerings of their professional schools, others as the offerings of their continuing education units. Some association figures are available only for the national offices, while ten to twenty times the national offices' budgets are spent by state-based affiliates. Employers and individual professionals differ when costing continuing education; some include tuition only, and others include the total cost of the experience, adding to the tuition price the cost of the professional's salary or the loss of revenue during the professional's time away from the office and the travel and per diem expenses involved. Fully costed, a continuing professional education experience can be five times the tuition expense, a ratio used by some employers in budgeting professional development activities.

## UNTENDED GROWTH: RESULTANT POLICY AND PLANNING ISSUES

The growth of continuing education for the professions has been exponential within higher education. It is probably the most rapidly growing dimension of higher education according to Kenneth Young, former executive director of the National University Continuing Education Association.[3] University efforts range from individual programs costing from $40,000 and led by part-time staff to continuing professional education units budgeted at $2 to $4 million and staffed by twenty-five to thirty-five persons. A few university-based continuing professional education units are budgeted at $13 to $17 million and staffed by fifty persons or more. Annual registrations range from the hundreds to 40,000 persons.

Because the growth of continuing education has also been a natural extension of the research and teaching interests of faculty members, allied with the mission of higher education and institutionally diffuse, its increase in size and diversity has been relatively untended by institutional planning, policies, and controls. With some notable exceptions, such as the Pennsylvania State University, the University of Wisconsin System, and the universities of Georgia, Chicago, and Southern California, the planning in many institutions has not included:

- identifying continuing professional education activities, universitywide or systemwide, or auditing their financial and academic structure, marketing strategies, constituencies, and evaluation

- analyzing and evaluating the nature and purpose of continuing professional education activities in light of institutional mission and ethos, a process yielding preliminary notions of the characteristics desirable in such activities

- encouraging or questioning current programs on the basis of the desirable characteristics yielded by such a process

- examining the current and probably near-future learning demands of the institution's various professional publics and involving professional leaders in this activity

- classifying identified learning needs for desirable articulation with present strengths and planned academic, financial, and physical resources, for anticipated and beneficial side effects on institutional and subinstitutional development, and for major trends not reflected in current resource planning

- reaching a tentative sense of direction by identifying promising resources and constituencies and needs, testing internal and external support, and building consensus

- reviewing current policies and administrative structures dealing with continuing education for the professions and modifying or abandoning them if they are found to be dysfunctional to the general consensus about the direction continuing professional education should take

- identifying and establishing desired patterns of academic governance, program development, and accountability likely to foster excellence and flexibility

- stimulating disciplinary and interdisciplinary approaches to professional needs that are consistent with the institution's strategic plan for continuing education of the professions

- establishing responsibility for pursuing institutionwide interests (identified in the previously stated processes), in an individual, a new position, or new unit directly reporting to the academic vice-president or to the provost, and adequately empowering this position or unit to execute assigned responsibilities

- reviewing the plan periodically in the form of annual reports to the institution's academic community

A commitment of twelve to eighteen months is required for this type of planning process. Failure to set aside the necessary time will leave the in-baskets of academic vice-presidents and provosts overflowing with vexing problems related to continuing education. Examples of some categories of problems follow.

## TURF AND COORDINATION

There are serious questions of turf and coordination in continuing education for the professions. Public administration, computer science, and the school of management may argue over which is the appropriate provider of continuing education in computer topics for professionals with executive responsibilities. A continuing education unit and the schools of medicine and public health may be offering professionals virtually the same program in the management of stress. Public information staff members at colleges and universities may be unable to inform the media at which continuing professional education program the Internal Revenue Service commissioner or the Justice Department's antitrust section chief might be found without the embarrassment of several telephone calls. Financial officers and continuing education directors may argue the merits of autonomy versus economies of scale. In states with one or more system of higher education, legislators may receive complaints about needless duplication of effort or the failure of one regional campus to replicate a popular program for the professions offered by another regional campus in some other part of the state. Quick-fix approaches to turf/coordination issues have included state mapping of "exclusive source" areas or have involved sign-off procedures within and among institutions.

## ORGANIZATION

At a significantly deeper level, there is the issue of how to organize continuing education for the professions. Should it be centralized or decentralized? Although often presented in terms of turf disputes over specific constituencies or program sequences, much more is at stake. There is continuing discussion about how to organize higher education for both diversity and coherence. It is argued in continuing education for the professions that some values seem well served by centralization, that use of interdisciplinary and sometimes inter-professional school resources is more assured by a centralized approach, for example. The question of what the graduate division(s) as well as the professional schools have to offer is more likely to be considered in a centralized approach. The centralized approach favors economies of scale essential for providing seed money necessary for the development of new programs, and protecting against that level of financial exposure at which the enterprise is likely to be entirely market driven, that is, ensuring that the institution can go beyond responding to widely expressed professional needs in order to address longer-range questions and even unpopular issues. Officials have argued that the complex accreditation of programs and providers by professional associations and the relicensure of some professionals on the basis of continuing education participation calls for centralized registration and tracking for professional learning experiences. It has further been argued that continuing education for professionals is so potentially significant to the institution as a whole that a consensual set of priorities should motivate program development, not the random interests of individual entrepreneurial faculty members who are said inevitably to dominate in decentralized models.

Conversely, important values are also sustained by decentralization. Decentralization reflects organizational patterns already in place. Professional school personnel believe they know their professional publics best. Decentralization reduces the risk of controversy about quality since regular academic faculty members will be directing and monitoring programs. It has been argued that programs arising from departments and schools will more likely reflect what faculty members find intellectually exciting and, as a result, any teaching that results is more likely to be spirited. Deans and department heads are more likely to urge faculty participation when their collegiate unit stands directly to gain from the program. It has also been argued that if deans or chairpersons urge faculty members to participate in continuing professional education, there will be fewer conflicts with regularly assigned duties than occur when they participate in programs outside their professional school.

Most institutions have a partly centralized, partly decentralized approach to continuing education needs.[4] The continuing education unit may be responsible for the development of new programs, particularly interdisciplinary programs or general programs addressing the needs of more than one professional group. Program development, some collaborative and some exclusive, is likely to go on in each professional school. The reality of powerful isolates, such as medical and business schools or the more collaborative tradition of many other professional schools, the graduate school(s), and a continuing education unit, is reflected in this mixed model. Even so, the blend of centralized and decentralized variables is almost never a design resulting from institutional self-examination or a calculated balance of institutional and subinstitutional self-interests.

## INVOLVEMENT OF ACADEMIC FACULTY

Involvement of academic faculty in continuing professional education is increasing; however, in the absence of strategic planning, so are the policy issues, and administrative problems. In a 1984 National University Continuing Education Association occasional paper, the authors stated:

> Obtaining the participation of full-time faculty members is difficult. It is quite common to find institutional policies which restrict faculty participation in university-based continuing education, either in regard to a ceiling on earnings or a limit on contact hours. Because restrictions on teaching or consulting outside the faculty member's institution are less common and probably unenforceable, directors of continuing professional education programs find access to academic faculty at other institutions easier than access to faculty at their own institutions.[5]

These policy formulas also lead faculty members to "avoid the hassle" by teaching for other institutions, for corporate or government agencies, or for profit-seeking seminar providers. Some provosts or academic vice-presidents have had to deal with the issue of groups of faculty members incorporating themselves as consulting firms, a prelude to offering continuing education programs, some of which are inevitably in competition with their own institution's offerings. Other administrators recognize that current policies result in the loss of their own faculty members to their continuing professional education efforts; however, they are reluctant to address the issue since increasing the level of faculty involvement will open a range of difficult compensation issues. Additional compensation for continuing education sometimes has the appearance of "double dipping" in state funds, for example.

The increasing demand for faculty members by providers of continuing professional education has had an inflationary impact on the range of fees expected by faculty members. This can have the effect of raising faculty compensation demands to a level that increases the price of the program to the professional. The constituency that can be served under these conditions may be at variance with the constituency envisioned by the institution's mission.

Faculty members' obligations for community service or continuing education, when a part of their full-time responsibility, are unclear and do not find expression in ongoing programmatic relationships with the professions. The responsibility for maintaining these educational relationships is often a murky affair. It is generally acknowledged that effective teaching in professional schools requires faculty involvement in corresponding fields. However, the view that faculty responsibility ends with the last day of class in professional school continues to persist. There is need for a definition of what constitutes satisfactory discharge of obligations as well as a need for the adoption and implementation of policies to provide appropriate recognition and reward for such activities. Involved in this issue are credit toward promotion and tenure as well as adequate financial compensation. The evaluation of a faculty member's contribution to continuing education, as distinct from research and traditional teaching, will probably remain a problem until continuing professional education experiences become more genuinely and intellectually interactive, that is, until they are stimulating to the faculty member as well as to the professional and create the interchange likely to lead to the identification, funding, conduct, and dissemination of research. In other words, ways must be found to end the existence of continuing education as an academic function parallel to research and teaching. Once this occurs, any promotion and tenure review of faculty research and teaching quality will automatically include the dimension of continuing education. The key to resolving this issue is to make continuing education for the professions a genuine part of the intellectual life of an institution, not a charitable service softened by the prospect of honoraria and play money credit toward promotion and tenure.

## ACADEMIC GOVERNANCE AND ACCOUNTABILITY

Academic governance and accountability have not automatically followed the increasing involvement of faculty members in continuing education. There is a need for institutions to track and evaluate continuing education programs provided to the professions. They need to respond effectively to the new generation of professional association-based accrediting agencies and to record the various types of credit that employers and associations attach to "noncredit" offerings. They need especially to provide academic accountability for programs involving multiple professional schools and/or departments. It is also important to represent the institution's academic concerns in discussion with major associations or employers of professionals. Several accountability models are currently in use. Frequently, the continuing education/extension dean or director assumes this responsibility. In some institutions, it is found appropriate to assign these responsibilities at the level of the associate provost or associate vice-president for academic affairs; in other institutions a coordinating council or committee structure is employed. At several institutions the creation of a position somewhat similar to that of the dean of graduate education, a matrix with the professional schools, is under consideration. The mixed structure remains most common, and each professional school and the continuing education/extension unit develop individual policies and structures relative to academic governance and accountability.

## FINANCIAL ACCOUNTABILITY

In most institutional settings characterized by a mixture of structures, programs, and reporting lines, ineffective financial management can be the price of diversity. Economies of scale are difficult to achieve with each school operating or contracting for printing, mailing, advertising and promotion, registration, on- and off-campus facilitation, audiovisual support systems, and fee billing processes. Management of continuing education in professional schools is typically undertaken by faculty or staff on a part-time basis. Many are also relatively new to the field. A 1979 survey revealed that 38 percent of the staff members had been involved in continuing education management for less than five years.[6] When continuing education offerings in an institution depend on individual faculty initiative, there may be inadequate auditing procedures in use and little likelihood that the full costs of the program are budgeted. This type of continuing education activity is usually not reflected in the budgets of either the professional school or the continuing education unit, and many opportunities to link institutional constituencies (the professional public is often the public most interested in liberal arts and sciences) are missed.

## UNCERTAINTY IN EDUCATIONAL DESIGN

Suboptimal program design may be the most critical educational result of continuing professional education's untended growth. Demand has caused a rapid increase in the number of persons directing programs and engaged in program development. Such persons come from the ranks of corporate training, psychology, and teaching, but especially from the teaching or practice of the corresponding profession. Expansion has been so rapid that many are surprised to learn that adult and continuing education is itself a field of concentration in many schools and graduate departments of education. A rich history of research exists, including motivation to lifelong learning, adult learning styles, needs analysis, group process, patterns of anxiety in adult learning situations, group and intergroup development, and curriculum and methodological approaches. This body of research is reinforced by the literature concerning the practice of the field, including continuing education for professions. Many programs in continuing professional education reflect the field's progress, but many appear to be merely extensions of the professional school classroom or copies of one or two designs in common use. Persons whose primary identification lies with engineering, law, medicine, architecture, or social work are needlessly limited unless they discover they have a common bond with other continuing educators. Valuable assistance is available to them in the research and practice of adult and continuing education. Several national organizations, particularly the National University Continuing Education Association, make an effort to bring such persons together, introduce them to the field, and interact with other continuing educators.

## INSTITUTIONAL VALUES SERVED

The high level of energy required to point out and correct the results of untended growth is rewarded by the many benefits higher education receives from continuing professional education. Institutions that offer continuing professional education programs:

- fulfill their public service or lifelong learning commitment in a highly visible way
- continue to serve the same constituencies with which they already have graduate or collegiate connections
- address the needs of the population most likely to look to higher education for continued learning

- place those who teach in professional schools in regular educational contact with practitioners in corresponding professional fields
- pursue an indirect strategy for strengthing the quality of teaching, that is, practicing professionals are relatively more stimulating and demanding than professional school students and are frequently best served through methodologies with which faculty are unpracticed
- discover individual professionals with potential for making contributions in professional school curricula as guest lecturers, practicum directors, etc.
- conduct programs that implicitly, and sometimes explicitly, validate or raise questions related to professional school or curricula
- expose professional school graduates to academic resources outside their professional schools
- discover opportunities for supported research into significant issues of some immediacy to the professions (e.g., nutrition and behavior, compensation and motivation) or into questions of professional life itself (e.g., patterns of adaptation of innovation, the role of constitutive myths, assessment of performance, and so on)
- enhance the placement opportunities of professional school graduates
- nurture a development network of persons of higher-than-average income, influence, and inclination to be supportive of higher education through endowments and gifts

That these values can be served at no expense to the institutions, even when continuing professional education is fully costed, sustains the growth of continuing education despite the characteristic untidiness of its planning and structure.

## HIGHER EDUCATION PROVIDERS

As providers of continuing professional education, institutions of higher education are diversely represented. Professional schools may have educational relationships with their traditional professional fields of practice (civil engineering refresher courses), or professional schools may address new fields of practice (implications for chemical engineers of recent environment law). Higher education is also represented in more complex ways. A setting of practice for many different professions (the criminal justice system, for example) may be addressed by a number of academic units (law, business, social service, behavioral sciences, and public policy analysis) in a single coherent program (designed by continuing education staff) devoted to executive development in the criminal justice system. Both the simple and more complex approach could include a variety of relationships with the corresponding professional associations and with corporate or government employers. These relationships foster dialogue on professional needs, educational design, and evaluation. Jointly sponsored programs often result, in which the financial risk is shared by the association or the program is entirely funded by the employer.

Generally, available programs include refresher courses or experiences that update professionals in fields related to their preprofessional education. New conceptual ideas may also be offered by programs through which familiar knowledge can be reconfigured in more useful ways. Programs may even be virtually identical with preprofessional course material but offered to professionals changing careers. For the most part, programs of this type are offered in traditional instructional modes, although the instruction may employ innovative audiovisual systems (e.g., closed circuit television, versions of the "magic blackboard," audiotapes, computer terminals). The instructional mode implies that some persons have knowledge or skills that will be imparted to others.

Other continuing professional education programs are in an inquiry mode, which sometimes implies the creation rather than the transfer of knowledge. A program may inquire, for example, about the societal implications of a decade without a military draft. Observers of these programs might notice a relatively more collegial relationship between resource persons and participants than occurs in the instructional mode, where there are the knowing and the unknowing. Programs in the inquiry mode also have a problem-solving orientation. A program might inquire, for example, into the factors motivating parents to reinforce early reading gains of first- and second-grade children. A high degree of participant interaction characterizes the inquiry mode and implies that the provider institution has the educational skills to nurture productive group interaction and to guide the inquiry.[7].

Programs vary in their degree of intentional relatedness to professional performance, and both the modes of inquiry and instruction can be appropriate. Some programs are designed to fill the gap between inadequate and adequate knowledge for competent performance. Other programs address knowledge and skills at levels related to enhancing performance. There are programs that address personal habits of work that, if remediated or enhanced, can trigger substantially higher levels of performance, such as time management, the planning and organizing of work, and so on. Others address the challenges that excellent personal habits of work can bring to professionals in midcareer, such as supervising numbers of other professionals in complex organizational contexts such as banks, hospitals, judicial systems, public aid agencies, and higher education. There are also programs that address personal impairments, such as programs about stress management, the control of chemical dependence, or distracting financial or family problems. There are professionals whose performance is declining through the erosion of values and motivation over years of repetitive patterns of work and diminished energy; some programs aim at helping these professionals regain the romance of their professions and their more ennobling motives for entering professional life. Most programs rely safely on the "zest for learning" characteristic of the majority of professionals.[8] This zest, together with the motivation to succeed, leads most professionals to continue their education in ways that include programs provided by colleges and universities. Highly successful professionals accept responsibilities for civic and philanthropic activities and will search for programs to acquaint themselves with the issues and structures of school systems, hospitals, foundations, churches, and other agencies they advise or support.

## THE ROLE OF LIBERAL ARTS COLLEGES

Continuing education for the professions is viewed by few liberal arts colleges as appropriate to their mission and resources. Few working relationships with university professional schools are developed by liberal arts colleges because of the view that these institutions have little to offer to the professions. However, Cyril Houle protested, "The study of general or liberal education helps lay an indispensable basis for occupational excellence."[9] Liberal education leaders speak of their students as developing the capacity to integrate theoretical perspective with learning from direct experience and to integrate and find bases for choice in complex and contradictory data. They speak of fostering their students' ability to discern and address value conflicts and to make—and take responsibility for—grounded commitments. These are the critical skills of mind crucial to professional life. Houle comments that much of the instruction in every profession introduces learners to the realms of thought distinctive to each discipline.

> The alert practitioner gains insights into the vagaries of human character and behavior and acquires the habit of synthesizing a number of discrete elements into a whole.

Thus professional and general education are interrelated in personal self-enhancement and professionals must be sure that in undertaking the first they do not forget the second.[10]

Studies are emerging that strongly suggest performance and success during the second half of professional careers are more a function of a strong liberal arts background than narrow professional or technical specialization. The critical skills of mind related to judgment and choice, the discernment of themes and connections, the capacity for pluralistic approaches of thought (to say nothing of the tolerance of ambiguity and the sense of the history and culture of organizations) are outcomes of liberal education and hallmarks of professional leadership. Without them, professional life may be a short trip to obsolescence. It is precisely these residuals of the experience of liberal learning that are essential to superior professional contributions.

The demand for continuing professional education is often based on the concept that professionals fall farther behind each year due to expanding knowledge. Yet being at the very frontier of knowlege is not the same thing as excellence of professional performance. The need is, therefore, all the greater for anchoring professional competence in less changeable seas: the generic skills of mind and self-evident truths through which liberal education empowers people.

Liberal education is not diminished because it is found to have immediacy in a complex and highly changeable professional environment. Terms such as "magic but useless" have diminished public understanding of liberal education's benefits. It has yet to be argued that liberal education is limited to developing critical thinking in persons of college age. There is indeed a broad and active role in providing continuing education to professionals, at least for those liberal arts colleges convinced of their value.

## COLLABORATION WITH PROFESSIONAL ASSOCIATIONS

Most universities engaged in continuing education for the professions find it desirable to collaborate in a variety of ways with associations of professionals, even those that are significant continuing education providers in their own right. Collaborative programming is almost universally characteristic among institutions with major programmatic and financial commitment to continuing education for the professions. Professional associations can provide ready access to their membership in a number of useful ways, such as by specialization, by years in practice, by location, and the like. Professional associations are able to articulate issues and problems of various specialties and settings of practice and can reflect strongly felt educational needs of their membership. Endorsement of programs by associations is relied upon by many professionals as a type of consumer guide to effective continuing education programs.

A survey of cooperative relationships in providing continuing education to the professions was made in 1978 and 1979. The survey was sponsored by the National University Continuing Education Association with the cooperation of the American Society of Association Directors and was administered by the University of Chicago.[11] There were 110 professional associations and 136 universities and colleges that participated, with 102 associations and 122 universities and colleges reporting regular educational relationships (other than degree programs) with the professions. A total of 53 associations (48 percent) and 116 universities and colleges (85 percent) reported cooperative relationships in planning or providing continuing professional education, and 49 associations and 107 universities considered the cooperative relationship and/or program(s) successful.

The initiation of the relationships was found to be equally distributed between associations and universities, with faculty or staff members specifically charged with continuing education responsibilities representing universities. The assessment of education need, the formulation of objectives, and the esablishment of curricular content were joint efforts 75 percent of the time. Faculty members were regularly selected from both higher education and the field of practice. A formal evaluation was conducted 87 percent of the time. Testing of professionals' proficiency was conducted in 34 percent of the formal evaluations. Cooperative programs were generally administered by universities, and 50 percent of the relationships risked out-of-pocket expenditures as well as indirect costs in developing and announcing the program. The universities were viewed as benefiting more financially from collaborative efforts than the associations by both the associations and universities.

Of the associations responding, 28 percent identified one or more aspects of the relationship with universities as troublesome. The most often-cited difficulty was the definition and negotiation of distinctive responsibilities in the cooperative venture. It was indicated by several associations and universities that they would not enter into another cooperative venture because of this problem. Other troublesome factors included the view that university hierarchies were too complex for effective decision making. Role delineation was found to be the most difficult part of the collaboration in 40 percent of the responding universities. Less troublesome, but significant for universities, was both the discovery that indirect costs of sustaining the relationship were higher than expected and the perception that associations were insufficiently rigorous in evaluating learning.

Continuing education in association-accredited programs is mandated by some associations for their membership. Programs of higher education which may be directly competitive with association programs are subjected to the accreditation review. The assertion of authority to accredit competitors has at least the appearance of conflict of interest. Universities and colleges considering starting or expanding their own continuing professional education programs will need to become familiar with the climate for collaboration in their states and regions.[12]

## COLLABORATION WITH EMPLOYERS

It is unusual to find professionals who are in practice solely on their own. They are usually in complex, multimember partnerships, in groups that may be based partly on fee for service or partly on capitation from third-party payers or in groups employed by organizations ranging from small business to government agencies and multinational corporations. The needs of their professional partners or employees are understood and represented by these organizations in much the same manner as professional associations. They frequently look to higher education to provide a significant portion of their professional development needs. Substantial amounts of educational funds are devoted each year to support professional development—on-site and off-site—during the work day and during nonwork hours. The general consensus of the National University Continuing Education Association's Division of Continuing Education for the Professions is that 80 percent or more of the tuition charged for credit and noncredit programs is paid by employers.

The characteristics of employer collaboration are quite similar to those of association collaboration. The assumption that higher education can respond rapidly to educational needs frequently characterizes employers' initial approach. Like associations, joint exploration of resources and needs with a view toward identifying desirable multiyear relationships is recommended. Discussions with both the chief operations officer and the vice-president for human resources are likely to lead to a balanced understanding of the employers' organizational objectives, a significant baseline for use in responding to the educational needs of individual professionals.

## EDUCATIONAL ISSUES

To be in the world and yet not of the world is the classic tension essential to higher education's balance. Values for contemporary society, some of which are quite immediate, are held by higher education. Yet for higher education to be entirely captured by contemporary societal perceptions and for its research to be entirely applied and its teaching wedded to projections of occupational need is to sacrifice other values—values that require some distance and detachment from short-range trends and opinion. Mina Shaughnessy Scholar Carol Schneider wrote:

> The objective is to find ways of enabling people to step outside the boundaries of their immediate context and experience, in order to inquire how that context works, what its values are, the gains and costs of participation within that system, and alternative ways of construing the purposes of the systems.[13]

Higher education officials cannot simply argue that what people need rather than what they want should be provided. Nor can higher education allow itself to be market-driven. Few suggest that higher education ever gets the balance just right, but the tension in its role is genuine and very desirable.

Continuing professional education exists in that same tension. Professionals often want recipes and formulas to make things easier, clearer, and more rewarding on Monday morning. Academicians, on the other hand, often encourage questions more often than they provide answers; indeed, learning has much to do with asking the right questions. It is probably only theoretically possible for these differences to be balanced perfectly by each continuing professional education program. Yet, higher education providers owe it to themselves and to the professions to ensure that their educational relationship with the professions will combine the characteristics of responsiveness and questioning.

## PROGRAM DESIGN, EVALUATION, AND QUALITY

Professionals' desires for some relief from the pressure of Monday morning's in-basket or the Friday 5:30 deadline should not be ignored when designing programs. Adults will block viewpoints that are relatively long-range—sometimes openly and bluntly—until attention is given to strongly felt, short-range needs. Beginning with issues of some immediacy is both good pedagogy and sound marketing. By cleverly doing so, providers can move professionals beyond those concerns to overarching conceptual frameworks, decision trees, or historical analyses related to professional performance at deeper levels over longer periods of time. There is acceptance of the notion that the "active half-life" of the information-packed seminar promising short-range relief is modestly brief (but acceptably so) when learning objectives are short-range. Yet, even in programs addressing short-range professional needs, professionals are led to perceive personal and organizational dimensions of relatively greater significance. Those programs that only address the short-range may get good marks from professionals as they leave the meeting site, but different grades are received by sponsoring institutions six to twelve months later when professionals discover that recipes and memory alone no longer fit the circumstances. Excellence, then, has something to do with maintaining in individual learning experiences the tension between responsiveness and questioning that is characteristic of higher education.

If the question of excellence in continuing professional education is key, it is also elusive. Excellence is not ensured by increasing full-time faculty involvement, although it is generally believed there is a relationship. Excellence does not lie precisely in the congruence of what was learned with what was taught, in the congruence of the educational experience with the educational design, or in the congruence of what was learned with the needs originally expressed and understood; however, it has something to do with all three. Some would add that excellence has something to do with the qualities of rigor and seriousness, with the access to libraries, or (at least) with the cultural island effect of intensive residential periods. Others hold that excellence resides in and flows from the careful administration of an ongoing system in identification of other related potential learning activities.[14]

Again, the lively discussion of excellence in continuing education for the professions mirrors the general higher education dialogue about input versus output determinants of quality, an issue sustaining the interest of accrediting agencies for the last decade. Well-planned higher education programs for the professions will certainly be marked by a number of evaluation points of input and output characteristics, both formative and summative.[15]

## WHOSE EVALUATION COUNTS?

The casual observer might believe that only the program registrants' evaluation counts, expressed as it often is on a one-page survey distributed as registrants are checking out of hotel rooms or finding a taxi in the rain. Typically, program registrants' opinions about the relative effectiveness of speakers, relevance of topics, and quality of accommodations are gathered by the use of these instruments. Exit surveys do accurately rate the relative entertainment value of presenters, although a question such as "Would you highly recommend this program to professional colleagues?" might provide a baseline that holds up better over time.

The judgments of program registrants count; however, in an educational field that is overwhelmingly dominated by third-party payers, so does the judgment of the senior partner, department head, or executive vice-president who sent the registrant or agreed to finance the registrant's participation. The opinions of the third-party payers of the effect of the learning experience on the organization as well as the individual raises an important program design question. Should designs go beyond the modes of instruction or inquiry to address the questions of adaptation or implementation? In some cases failure to do so unnecessarily limits the capacity of the program to maintain or improve professional performance in the wider patterns of life into which it must be integrated. In other cases, to do so would place an intolerable burden on all concerned. It cannot and should not be assumed that those skilled in teaching or leading inquiries in law, medicine, or journalism are equally versed in patterns through which law firms, hospitals, or newspapers accept innovation or resist change. The question of integrating what Cyril Houle called the mode of performance[16] with the modes of instruction and inquiry must be faced by program planners. It is possible that adaptation and performance strategy in the wider settings of actual practice could be an elective option appropriately added to any number of programs. It is equally possible for entire programs to be designed around such problems as they are faced by the professions in specific work contexts.

The opinions of registrants and third-party payers are not the only ones that count. The judgments of professional associations about the excellence of programs are also important. Even when their leaders are not collaboratively involved in program design, associations have an extremely crucial stake in the capacity of continuing education to sustain general levels of professional performance. Associations are looked to frequently on the state level for informal references regarding the relative quality of professional learning opportunities.

Evaluation by program leaders and instructors and other academic colleagues is essential if evaluation is to be more than market-driven. Consumer satisfaction is not the last word on excellence. Exposure of program series and course sequences to periodic review by appropriate faculty members can be essential to the intellectual vitality of continuing professional education and can lead to the identification of new learning opportunities.

Excellence is a single concept with pluralistic content, reflecting the values and tensions of higher education. Its pervasive presence as an issue in continuing professional education is taken as a sign of the health, strength, and promise of the field.

## SUMMARY

It requires time and a wide-angle lens for academic leaders to decide what role in continuing education for the professions their colleges and universities are likely to find educationally worthy and institutionally appropriate. Continuing education for the professions is part of a complex societal movement with influences and structures that do not easily lend themselves to a hasty search for conceptual or administrative focus. Powerful tensions, contrasting objectives, and sometimes dazzling improvisation have marked its swift growth.

The manner in which continuing education for the professions can be structured to address policy and educational and administrative concerns, while at the same time preserving its diversity, flexibility, and interdisciplinary characteristics, must be explored by each institution. The most appropriate ways of assuming the lively and essential roles that could maintain and enhance the knowledge, values, and skills of the mind critical to lifelong professional contributions must be implemented by liberal arts colleges.

Teaching the skills in self-directed learning and self-assessment that allow professionals to make discriminating judgments as lifelong learners must be integrated within the regular preprofessional curricula by professional schools. Professional schools should reflect upon whether sufficient attention is given the often complex organizational structures in which professionals' contributions are increasingly organized and which, in turn, enhance or diminish those contributions.

Graduate education leaders should be given the opportunity to consider the professions as a field of research with special opportunities for sociology, anthropology, education, public policy, economics, history, and the behavioral sciences. Centers for the Study of the Professions might include:

- development of the research base without which judgments of professional adequacy or excellence and key variables in performance maintenance and improvement remain in the realm of opinion
- development and validation of competence and performance-related self-inventory instruments for various professions and professional subspecialties
- development of models related to the adaptation of innovation, particularly in complex practice settings
- identification and assessment in interprofessional learning of particular importance to expressions of individual professional competence

Opportunities for forging broad-purpose "learning relationships" with corporations, government agencies, and professional associations, particularly those relationships that offer promising research as well as teaching opportunities, should be considered by college and university officials.

Program administrators, designers, and evaluators of continuing education for the professions, whether they are based in continuing education units or in the professional schools, should regularly convene under the auspices of one or another of the national associations of continuing higher education. Frequently, continuing educators representing major employers and professional associations should be invited to join in conversation with their colleagues in higher education.

An atmosphere of conceptual pluralism and programmatic experimentation should be encouraged even if the short-term cost is administrative ambiguity.

## REFERENCES

1. *Crain's Chicago Business,* June 27, 1983, T #7.

2. Gollin, A. *Programs and Courses for Practicing Professionals,* Council of Graduate Schools/Graduate Record Examination Board Conference, October 11, 1983 (Washington, D.C.: Council of Graduate Schools, 1984).

3. Young, Kenneth *Programs and Courses,* Council of Graduate Schools/ Graduate Record Examination Board Conference (Washington, D.C.: Council of Graduate Schools, 1984).

4. Veri, D., and Craig, D., "Organizational Patterns in Continuing Education" (papers presented at the National University Continuing Education Association Regional Meeting, Bloomington, Ind., 1980–1981).

5. Nowlen, P., and Queeney, D., *The Role of Colleges and Universities in Continuing Professional Education,* National University Continuing Education Association Occasional Paper (Washington, D.C.: National University Continuing Education Association, 1984), p. 6.

6. Nowlen, P., and Hohman, L., *1979 Survey of Continuing Education in the Professions* (Chicago: University of Chicago Press, 1980).

7. Houle, Cyril O., *Continuing Learning in the Professions* (San Francisco: Jossey-Bass, 1980), pp. 31–33.

8. Houle, Cyril O. *Patterns of Learning* (San Francisco: Jossey-Bass, 1984), pp. 227–228.

9. Houle, op. cit., p. 47.

10. Ibid., p. 48.

11. Nowlen and Hohman, loc. cit.

12. Nowlen, P., and Stern, M. R., "Partnerships in Continuing Education for the Professions," *Partnerships with Business and the Professions,* 1981 Current Issues in Higher Education (Washington, D.C.: American Association for Higher Education, 1981).

13. Schneider, C., "Sources of Coherence in Undergraduate Liberal Arts Degree Programs" (Keynote Address presented to the National Collegiate Honors Society, April 1984).

14. Houle, Cyril O., *The Design of Education* (San Francisco: Jossey-Bass, 1972), pp. 31–58.

15. Bloom, B. S.; Hastings, J. T; and Madaus, G. F., eds., *Handbook on Formative and Summative Evaluation of Student Learning* (New York: McGraw-Hill, 1971).

16. Houle, op. cit., pp. 185–186.

# -13-
# A LOOK TO THE FUTURE FOR CONTINUING HIGHER EDUCATION

## Quentin H. Gessner

Adult learners constitute the most rapidly growing segment of American education. If colleges and universities accept the challenge to provide the growing population of adult learners with expanded educational opportunities, continuing education will become the largest and most important component of higher education. It is the intent and purpose of this chapter to focus on the broad outlines in an evolutionary process that will define the future for continuing higher education.

The future, however, does not arrive at once. It generally emerges over time through signals that suggest what can be expected to happen. There are identifiable trends that foreshadow the future for continuing higher education. There are proactive responses to these trends that can offer an exciting future for continuing higher education. Academic planners will want to consider the internal and external shifts that may be necessary to position or reposition their institution to move forward in the years ahead in continuing education. Institutions can take advantage of the new emphasis on continuing learning to reassess, reevaluate, and realign their educational outreach efforts. Patricia Cross states:

> Continuing higher education is the closest thing we have to a bridge between the sheltered environment of the college campus and the emerging world of the Learning Society. Those who work in continuing higher education are in a position to help their institutions and communities come together for a decade of challenge in the 1980s.[1]

Possibilities abound. Considerable change may be necessary at some institutions, repositioning at others, and only minor modifications at still others. To help look at the future, twelve trends that appear to be shaping the future for continuing education are identified below. These trends offer excellent opportunities for institutions to make changes as necessary and appropriate to serve adult learners.

1. *Higher education's role and its relationship to society will continue to evolve with continuing education serving as a major catalyst for change.* The explosion of knowledge, the increasing complexity of life, the advancements in technology, the creation of new jobs and the displacement of others, a longer life expectancy, and instantaneous communication technologies are indicators of a changing world. These external forces will provide institutions with special opportunities to broaden their constituency. To serve this mission, institutions will need to determine how to serve major segments of society rather than concentrating all or most of their resources on a small percentage of students residing on campus for a short period of time. Resources can be focused on continuing education to help graduates avoid obsolescence, particularly in professional areas, and to satisfy the demands of older adults who have educational needs that can only be served through higher education.

Continuing education, long considered by many in the academic community as a marginal activity, instead can serve as a catalyst for a new era in higher education.

2. *Institutions of higher education are shifting their emphasis from serving the traditional-age student to reaching new expanded markets.* There will be more older adults attending school in the future. The numbers of 18- to 25-year-old students are insufficient to sustain enrollments of recent years. Consequently, the number of part-time enrollments is expected to continue to increase. With the increase in part-time students, a more diverse student population can be expected that will include adults who previously have not had access to higher education.

Institutions where a retrenchment strategy is pursued may not survive or will be limited to a relatively small share of the educational market. A proactive posture designed to meet the educational needs of adult learners, both credit and noncredit, is an option that provides an opportunity for growth. Many traditional colleges and universities are already engaging in a growing number of activities not directly related to producing graduates with degrees.

Before deciding how to address this opportunity, however, academic planners at each institution need to review their particular situation through a self-study process. The self-study can be used to identify the unique resources their institution has to offer for the education of adults. Self-studies will be particularly important and useful because of the increasing numbers of educational providers and the need for local and statewide coordination. Data obtained from a self-study can be used to determine an institution's niche in the marketplace through the development of a strategic marketing plan.

3. *Significant internal shifts are taking place within institutions related to the development and delivery of continuing education programs.* Higher education does not serve in a vacuum. As its role and relationship to society continue to evolve with attention placed on reaching new markets, there will be opportunities for internal changes to shift campus priorities and resources to accommodate the needs of adults. The following are some of the areas in which changes can be expected.

- *Organization.* New institutional relationships and efforts to reach new markets provide an opportunity for continuing education to become more fully integrated into the mainstream of the academic community. Instead of the primary responsibility and function resting with the continuing education unit, continuing education is embraced by the entire institution as a significant part of its role and mission; responsibility for its implementation becomes one of an institutional focus and effort.

- *Financing.* To conduct financially successful programs with the necessary support services, continuing education requires a flexible financial plan to support programs that are needed but that do not generate sufficient income to break even. Income to support such programs must generally be obtained from outside sources or from programs that provide a surplus. Mixing income sources can lead to the development of new programs and new patterns of budgeting to assist a college or university to finance its continuing education programs successfully.

- *Support services.* An emphasis on continuing education requires increased attention to the support services offered adult learners. Nontraditional, part-time, older-age students have different needs than traditional-age, full-time students. The adult learner is usually employed full-time and has family commitments. Attendance at school is a secondary responsibility. Employment and family responsibilities create a situation in which adults interested in continuing their education seek classes at times and places convenient to them. Part-time students need access to faculty or staff and facilities for counseling, admission and financial aid information, libraries, health services, registration assistance, and other support services at times outside the eight-to-five daytime schedule.

Academic planners interested in meeting the needs of adult learners have an opportunity to assess how successful their institution is in providing programs and services for adults by using the Institutional Self-Study Assessment and Planning Guide prepared by the Commission on Higher Education and the Adult Learner.[2] A team consisting of two to four persons attends a workshop to receive instructions in ways to use the Self-Study Assessment and Planning Guide effectively. Following the workshop the team returns to its home campus and initiates an action research plan designed to measure how well their institution is serving adults; based on the results of the self-assessment, institutional changes are made as necessary.

- *Faculty reward system.* A college or university that decides to place a high priority on serving adult learners should plan to review its faculty reward system. There are few institutions where the reward system remunerates or promotes faculty for participating in continuing education programs and activities on the same basis as the more traditional teaching and research functions. This issue is of such critical importance to institutions of higher education that the National Association of State Universities and Land-Grant Colleges (NASULGC) has published a monograph that deals with the problematic aspects of awards for faculty engaged in professional service. The monograph indicates there is increasing pressure on faculty to become involved in service programs. While there is a growing reliance on faculty, there is a widening gap between the extent to which faculty are engaged in such academic work and the capabilities of institutional reward structures to accommodate these activities.[3]

Academic planners interested in improving their faculty reward system for participation in continuing education programs need to develop incentives to accommodate to the variety of instructional methods now available to reach adults. If continuing education programs are to be successful, a faculty reward system that is acceptable to all concerned parties is crucial so that faculty members who are competent in the development and instruction of continuing education programs will be rewarded and not penalized for their efforts.

- *Faculty recruitment.* In providing programs for adult learners, it is often necessary to recruit a more diverse faculty. Adjunct faculty, persons usually holding positions outside the university, are used at many institutions to teach both adults and traditional-age students. This is done to supplement regular faculty loads and to obtain specific and practical skills and knowledge that may be required in the instruction of adults. Faculty members with practical experience can be used to supplement faculty members with a heavy theoretical orientation.

- *Residency requirements.* Institutions conducting off-campus continuing education programs will need periodically to review their campus residency requirements to determine if they are reasonable and practical from the student's perspective. Attention will need to be given to the number of contact hours necessary to learn the content of a course within a specific timeframe rather than to the physical location of the learner. Long-distance learning through telecommunications systems will undoubtedly hasten the need for institutions to review residency requirements.

- *Content.* Content developed for noncredit continuing education programs often becomes the substantive base for new courses assimilated into the regular academic curriculum. Many required courses listed in college and university catalogs evolved from continuing education programs. Many noncredit courses and workshops are offered to meet the specific content needs of discrete client groups, such as engineers, realtors, social workers, medical technologists, retirees, corporate executives, and law enforcement officers. Participants enroll to gain knowledge, acquire new skills to cope with work-related or personal issues, and enrich themselves culturally. Institutions active in the development and delivery of noncredit continuing education programs can integrate new information and knowledge gained from these programs into the regular academic curriculum.

- *Motivation/participation.* As discussed in *Adults as Learners,* by Patricia Cross,[4] considerable research has been conducted by Cyril Houle,[5] Alan Tough,[6] and others to determine motivations for participation in adult learning. We know that adults seek education to improve the quality of their lives in some way. Some are interested in degrees or certification, while others search for ways to gain money, health, or self-confidence. They may wish to improve their performance as an employer, parent, or citizen, or they may simply want to learn for the joy of learning. Academic planners will want to become familiar with the basic motivations that underlie adult learners' willingness to participate in continuing education programs and activities.

   4. *The development of new institutional relationships is leading to increased numbers of consortia and other forms of collaboration*

*between colleges/universities and other institutions.* As programs to reach new clientele expand at colleges and universities, new forms of collaboration with other institutions, agencies, associations, and the private sector become possible. The Compact for Lifelong Educational Opportunities program (CLEO) was a consortium of thirty-eight colleges and universities in the Delaware Valley of Pennsylvania. Joint programs by its member institutions were offered by CLEO in cooperation with business, industry, and government. The National Technological University, comprised of a number of leading engineering schools, offers graduate degree programs via videotape and plans to use satellite transmission in the future. The Association for Graduate Education in North Texas is a consortium of colleges and universities in the Dallas–Ft. Worth area that cooperates to provide on-site educational programs over television to business and industry. These types of consortia and collaborative arrangements allow institutions to offer joint programs by sharing resources, information, equipment, and marketing efforts.

Colleges and universities that develop collaborative working relationships with other providers and user groups can implement and deliver programs based primarily on the unique resources of each institution.

While the establishment of consortia and collaborative working arrangements is not a new phenomenon in continuing education, it will continue to be an important way for working with external groups, such as professional associations, business and industry, local, state, regional, and national agencies, and labor unions and voluntary groups.

5. *New forms of telecommunication and new methodologies are being used to reach a broader segment of the population.* The wide variety of delivery formats offers institutions a number of choices. Newspapers, television, computers, and audiotapes and videotapes have been used to offer programs off-campus for years by schools such as Penn State, Purdue, San Diego State, Stanford, Orange Coast and Dallas Community Colleges, and others. By using various methodologies and new forms of technology, educational programs can be delivered to the student, replacing under certain conditions the need to bring the student to the campus. As a result, institutions can meet the needs of large numbers of people through new forms of delivery. These new forms of telecommunication also provide opportunities to design new program formats that will allow for effective and interactive individualized instruction. If the use of technologically based delivery systems is expanded at institutions, the impact on the development and delivery of continuing education programs should be significant.

6. *Outcome measures are being used more for identifying the success or failure of instruction.* In marketing programs, continuing educators have always been concerned with outcome measures since continuing education programs are generally based on user demand. If the value is not evident, people do not enroll. Participants usually expect that information and material received in a program will be of immediate value, or participants measure the outcome by the extent to which they are able to do their job more effectively or differently as a result of the educational experience. While not all outcome measures can be based on immediate use of the content, the concept is important to the consumer making a decision about which course or program to enroll in at which institution. It should also be noted that outcome measures can be more precisely defined in some content areas than in others.

The improving quality of noncredit courses in general and of corporate training programs in particular appears to be one of the interesting by-products of the attention being given to outcome measures. A look to the future suggests that outcome measures will become increasingly more important in the development and marketing of programs.

7. *New data bases to reflect institutional productivity more accurately are being formulated.* With continuing education programs being offered at an increasing number of institutions, the opportunity exists for development of new data bases to report more accurately *all* students served by colleges and universities. On many campuses, continuing education has been left to the discretion of each academic unit, and the development and delivery of program offerings have been within the province of individual faculty members. As a result, there has not been a clear understanding or accurate reporting of the size and scope of the total campus outreach at some institutions. Under these conditions, enrollments and registrations through a continuing education/extension unit may not be included in institutional enrollment reports to legislators and to the general public, even though students are matriculating in courses applicable toward a degree. These omissions can include students taking classes at off-campus locations, by television or radio, or through independent study by correspondence. To avoid this type of omission, the Southern Association of Colleges and Schools, through its Standard Nine,[7] requires its member institutions to include all enrollments and registrations, both credit and noncredit. This mechanism provides for a complete and accurate description of institutional productivity. As a general practice, it would seem useful and appropriate in the future for all students, credit and noncredit, to be included in college and

university enrollment reports. This procedure would seem particularly advantageous considering the need to inform legislators and the general public of the contributions made by institutions of higher education to society.

8. *Endowments and public funds are being used to support continuing higher education.* Funds for programs in music and art in Nebraska and a conference center in North Carolina illustrate how endowment funds can be used to support continuing education programs and activities. Penn State University's PENNTAP program is an example of how public funds are used to support continuing education. Many other examples could be given of public institutions utilizing public funds to support continuing education programs. As continuing education becomes more fully integrated into the academic mainstream, fund-raising efforts and endowments can be targeted to provide funds for programs and to reach segments of the population that might not otherwise be served. This possibility appears particularly promising in situations where there is a collaborative programming arrangement between an institution and an association, agency, or private organization. In some cases, state or local appropriations can be obtained or increased to support continuing learning opportunities for government employees or other specific client groups.

9. *More attention is being given to the relationship between education and the effective use of human capital.* The development and use of the nation's human resources are critical to the social, political, and economic well-being of the country. Economic consultant Anthony Carnevale points out that "a disquieting series of studies suggests that America's failing competitive advantage in foreign markets owes, in part, to the nation's underinvestment in human capital."[8] Ernest A. Lynton, Commonwealth Professor, University of Massachusetts, states: "Human resources are of critical importance to the vitality of a post-industrial society. The development of human capital through extensive education is an important and valuable investment."[9]

The relationship between education and the effective use of human capital is obvious in the private sector. Evidence points to significant growth in corporate education to the extent that it rivals institutional programs. At least eighteen corporations award academic degrees. Many corporations offer in-house educational programs and have educational and training facilities that resemble college campuses. Nearly $60 billion is spent on corporate education each year.[10] Although the private sector continues to increase its investment in educational programming, postsecondary institutions have a significant role to play in the development of human resources through continuing education programs.

10. *Public interest in continuing education is increasing.* Herman Niebuhr, president of Learning Systems Associates, in his book, *Revitalizing the American Learning System,*[11] suggests that the nation is between old and new learning processes. He provides three propositions to support his position: (1) society is moving through a period of fundamental change and discontinuity, (2) the national learning process within which schools and colleges provide only a small part of the necessary life learnings is in disarray and is inadequate to guide persons through the change, and (3) a new, stronger learning process is being born. If, as Niebuhr states, we are becoming more self-directed and lifelong learners, and institutions are starting to coalesce to guide the new learning system, it can be expected that society will focus more attention on education to assist people to become more productive citizens and increase its investment in human capital. Since the competencies required for citizens to function in the next quarter of a century will be partially the responsibility of colleges and universities, there will be opportunity for continuing education programs and activities to be more closely linked to the education, training, and retraining of the nation's workforce with the potential for an increase in public support for continuing learning.

11. *Increased attention is being given to public policy as it relates to continuing education.* As mentioned previously, greater utilization of human resources is one of the nation's most urgent needs. There appears to be growing interest in the development of public policies that provide adults with improved access to further education and training, particularly in the technology and service industries. The Commission on Higher Education and the Adult Learner has called for

> a new policy in the federal government, in the 50 states, and in the corporations and educational institutions, that adults be enabled to continue learning regardless of their financial resources, ethnic and socio-economic status, age, and sex—long enough and effectively enough to be competent in adult roles and to contribute productively to American life.[12]

The State Higher Education Executive Officers, a national organization (SHEEO) has appointed a task force to explore the need for public policies related to the need of adult learners. State coordinating boards and commissions responsible for the coordination of higher education and legislative bodies responsible for the allocation and use of tax funds for education have increased their interest in public policy as it relates to continuing education. The increased attention to public policy has been partially the result of competition and turf problems created when institutions expand their efforts, particularly off-campus, to meet the educational needs of adults and to increase enrollments.

As a result of the increased attention being given to continuing education and its implications for public policy, institutions have an opportunity to become more involved in the formation and implementation of public policies that may have a direct impact on their continuing education programs and activities.

12. *Continuing professional education is becoming increasingly more important in college and university outreach.* Legislators and consumers, along with various professional associations, have long recognized the need to emphasize continuing professional education by mandating its practice in selected disciplinary areas. While the effectiveness of mandatory continuing education is a debatable issue, particularly where there is an absence of outcome measures, it does reflect the rising concern of citizens.

Academic planners have the opportunity to stress the importance of continuing education to undergraduate and graduate students. Professional schools that provide continuing education programs have the potential to generate new sources of income, increase research opportunities, secure endowments, and develop a support network for faculty and staff.

## SUMMARY

Twelve trends that are shaping the future in continuing higher education have been identified. Proactive responses have been described that suggest possibilities for colleges and universities to improve, expand, or enhance the extension of their faculty and staff resources to serve adult learners and address some of the complex problems of society.

Will continuing education at colleges and universities emerge as a major component of the academic enterprise in the years ahead? The answer to this question will depend on how each institution perceives its role and mission in relation to the social, political, and economic climate in which it operates.

Many institutions can be expected to move forward in continuing higher education. The demand for continuous learning by people of all ages, races, and ethnic heritage can be expected to increase and will be made available through self-directed learning materials by a variety of educational providers. The demand and need for continuous learning provide colleges and universities with both an opportunity and a responsibility to play a leadership role in the development of a future learning society.

If this is to occur, conceptual changes in the manner in which colleges and universities approach continuing higher education are needed. The traditional notion that an individual acquires sufficient information and knowledge during the early stages of life to forever cope with life's complexities needs to give way to the concept that adults must continue to learn.

The tenets of adult and continuing education need to be included in the academic framework of higher education to produce graduates with positive attitudes toward continuous learning.

The increasing demand for continuous learning by the graduates of our present education system suggests a need for a revitalization of that system. Colleges and universities have the resources to provide continuing education programs to meet the educational needs of their graduates as well as other adult learners. However, higher education must realign its vision, goals and objectives, and organizational structure to assist in the formation of a society in which continued learning is not a marginal activity but is an important component of the overall educational system.

With these fundamental shifts on the horizon, continuing higher education can be expected to grow in stature, in the numbers of programs offered and people served, and in the quality of programming. With increasing numbers of professionally prepared continuing educators providing leadership, continuing higher education can look forward to a dynamic and exciting future.

## REFERENCES

1. Cross, K. Patricia, "CHE in the 1980's," *The Journal of CHE*, 31 (1) (Winter 1982), p. 6.

2. Commission on Higher Education and the Adult Learner, *Postsecondary Education Institutions and the Adult Learner: A Self-Study Assessment and Planning Guide*, 1984.

3. Elman, Sandra E., and Smack, Sue Marx, *Professional Service and Faculty Rewards* (Washington, D.C.: National Association of State Universities and Land Grant Colleges, 1985).

4. Cross, K. Patricia, *Adults as Learners* (San Francisco: Jossey-Bass, 1982), p. 81.

5. Houle, Cyril O. *The Inquiring Mind* (Madison: University of Wisconsin Press, 1961).

6. Tough, Alan A., *Why Adults Learn: A Study of the Major Reasons for Beginning and Continuing a Learning Project*, Monographs in Adult Education, No. 3 (Toronto: Ontario Institute for Studies in Education, 1968).

7. Southern Association of Colleges and Schools, Commission on Colleges, *Standards of the College Delegate Assembly, Standard IX, Special Activities*, December 14, 1977, pp. 30–38.

8. Carnevale, Anthony Patrick, "Higher Education's Role in the American Economy," *Educational Record* (Fall 1983), p. 12.

9. Lynton, Ernest A. "Higher Education's Role in Fostering Employee Education," *Educational Record* (Fall 1983), p. 18.

10. Eurich, Nell, *Corporate Classrooms: The Learning Business* (Princeton: Princeton University Press, 1985).

11. Niebuhr, Jr., Herman, *Revitalizing American Learning* (Belmont, Calif.: Wadsworth, 1984).

12. Commission on Higher Education and the Adult Learner, *Adult Learners: Key to the Nation's Future* (Columbia, Md.: The Commission, 1984), p. 5.

# SUGGESTED READINGS

## CHAPTER ONE

Anderson, Lester G. *Land-Grant Universities and Their Continuing Challenge* (Lansing: Michigan State University Press, 1976).

Boyer, Ernst L, and Hechinger, Fred M., *Higher Learning in the National Service,* (Washington, DC: The Carnegie Foundation For the Advancement of Teaching, 1981).

Chickering, Arthur W. and Associates, *The Modern American College* (San Francisco: Jossey-Bass, 1981).

Cowen, R. B. "Higher Education Has Obligations to a New Majority," *The Chronicle of Higher Education, 23 June 1986, p. 48.*

Epstein, Howard V. *"The Older College Student: A Changing American Tradition," International Journal of Lifelong Education* 5(1), January–March 1986, pp. 33–43.

Knapper, Christopher K. and Cropley, Arthur J., *Lifelong Learning and Higher Education* (Dover: Croom Helm, 1985).

Peterson, Richard E, and Associates, *Lifelong Learning in America* (San Francisco: Jossey-Bass, 1979).

Striner, Herbert E. *Continuing Education as a National Capital Investment* (Kalamazoo, MI: The W. E. Upjohn Institute for Unemployment Research, 1972).

Vermilye, Dychman W., ed. "Lifelong Learners—A New Clientele for Higher Education," in *Current Issues in Higher Education,* (San Francisco: Jossey Bass, 1974).

## CHAPTER TWO

Eddy, Edward D., Jr. *Colleges for Our Land and Time* (New York: Harper, 1956).

"Fact-File: The 100 Oldest Colleges and Universities in the U. S.," *The Chronicle of Higher Education,* 6 April 1981, p. 8.

Franklin, Benjamin. *Autobiography* (Philadelphia, 1818).

Long, Huey B. *Continuing Education of Adults in Colonial America* (Syracuse, NY: Syracuse University Publications in Continuing Education, 1976).

Moreland, Willis D., and Goldenstein, Erwin H. *Pioneers in Adult Education* (Chicago: Nelson-Hall Publishers, 1985).

Thompson, C. O. *University Extension in Adult Education* (Chicago: University of Chicago Press, 1943).

## CHAPTER THREE

Centron, Marvin, and O'Toole, Thomas. *Encounters With the Future: A Forecast of Life Into the 21st Century* (New York: McGraw-Hill, 1982).

Etzioni, Amitai. *An Immodest Agenda* (New York: McGraw-Hill, 1983).

Drucker, Peter F. *Managing In Turbulent Times* (New York: Harper and Row, 1980).

Loye, David. *The Knowable Future* (New York: Wiley-Inter Science Publications, 1978).

Toffler, Alan, ed. *Learning for Tommorow: Role of the Future in Education* (New York: Random House, 1974).

## CHAPTER FOUR

Astin, Alexander W. *Achieving Educational Excellence* (San Francisco: Jossey-Bass, 1985).

Baldridge, Victor J., et al. *Policy Making and Effective Leadership* (San Francisco: Jossey-Bass, 1978).

Botkin, James; Dimancescu, Dan; and Stata, Ray. *The Innovators: Rediscovering America's Creative Energy* (New York: Harper and Row, 1984).

College Entrance Examination Board. *The Admissions Strategist*, No. 3, 1985.

Eurich, Neil P. *Corporate Classrooms: The Learning Business* (NJ: The Carnegie Foundation for the Advancement of Learning, 1985).

Kreitlow, Burton W., et al. *Examining Controversies in Adult Education* (San Francisco: Jossey-Bass, 1981).

McCorkle, Chester O., Jr., and Archibald, Sandra Orr. *Management and Leadership in Higher Education* (San Francisco: Jossey-Bass, 1982).

Peters, John M., et al. *Building an Effective Adult Education Enterprise* (San Francisco: Jossey-Bass, 1980).

Peters, Tom, and Austin, Nancy. *A Passion for Excellence* (New York: Random House, 1985).

## CHAPTER FIVE

Baldridge, J. Victor, and Tierney, Michael L. *New Approach to Management* (San Francisco: Jossey-Bass, 1979).

Blanchard, Kenneth, and Johnson, Spencer. *The One Minute Manager* (New York: Berkley Books, 1982).

Comfort, Robert W. "Integration: The Fusing of Tradition with Uniqueness," *Continuum* 46(1), 1981.

Cross, K. Patricia. "The Changing Role of Continuing Education," *Fortune,* 30 May 1983.

Keller, George, *Academic Strategy* (Baltimore: Johns Hopkins University Press, 1983).

Scammahorn, Jack; Wendel, Frederick; and Henry, Thomas. "Leadership in Continuing Education: Major Challenges of the Future," *Continuum* 45(2), 1981, pp. 11–17.

Strother, George B., and Klaus, John P. *Administration of Continuing Education* (Belmont, CA: Wadsworth, 1982).

Williams, Frederick, and Dordick, Herbert. *The Executive's Guide to Information Technology* (New York: Wiley, 1983).

## CHAPTER SIX

Buskey, John H., ed. "Attracting External Funds For Continuing Education," *New Directions for Continuing Education,* No. 12, 1981 (San Francisco: Jossey-Bass).

Matkin, Gary W. *Effective Budgeting in Continuing Education* (San Francisco: Jossey-Bass, 1985).

Shipp, Travis., ed. "Creative Financing and Budgeting," *New Directions For Continuing Education,* No. 16, 1982 (San Francisco: Jossey-Bass).

Strother, George B., and Klaus, John P. *Administration of Continuing Education* (Belmont, CA: Wadsworth, 1982).

Tinnon, Gene. "Conference Budget Preparation and Management (Part I and Part II)" *The Forum For Continuing Education,* Fall 1980, Winter 1981.

## CHAPTER SEVEN

Boone, Edgar J. *Developing Programs in Adult Education* (Englewood Cliffs, NJ: Prentice-Hall, 1985).

Sample, John A., and Kaufman, Roger. "A Holistic Program Development Model for Adult Educators," *Lifelong Learning* 9 (4), 1986, pp. 18–23.

Spikes, W. Franklin, and Spikes, Janice M. "An Educator's Guide to Strategic Planning," *Lifelong Learning* 9 (7), 1986, pp. 6–11.

Willard, Joyce, and Warren, Lee. "Using Strategic Planning for Effective Program Development: Beginning the Planning Process," *Journal of Continuing Higher Education* 33 (3), 1985, pp. 5–9.

## CHAPTER EIGHT

Benseman, John R. "The Assessment and Meeting of Needs in Continuing Education," *Report on Education and Psychology,* No. 1, 1980 (Department of Educational Research, Stockholm Institute of Education, Eric Document ED 193 466).

Kaufman, Roger, and English, Fenwick W. *Needs Assessment: Concept and Application* (Englewood Cliffs, NJ: Educational Technology Publications, 1979).

Monette, Maurice L. "Needs Assessment: A Critique of Philosophical Assumptions," *Adult Education,* Vol. 23, 1979, pp. 83–95.

## CHAPTER NINE

Alford, Harold, Jr. *Continuing Education in Action,* W. K. Kellogg Foundation, (New York: Wiley, 1968).

Buskey, John H. "Residential Conference Centers: The First, the Present, and the Future," *Continuum* 48(1), January 1984, p. 1.

Cell, E. *Learning to Learn From Experience* (Albany, NY: State University of New York Press, 1984).

Chamberlain, Martin N., ed. "Providing Continuing Education by Media and Technology," *New Directions for Continuing Education,* No. 5, 1980 (San Francisco: Jossey-Bass).

Childs, Gayle B. "Correspondence Study: Concepts and Comments" (Paper presented at the meeting of the National University Continuing Education Association, Omaha, Nebraska, 1973).

Goldstein, Sheldon, "Communication Technology and Continuing Education," *Continuum* 48(3), September 1984, p. 169.

Henderson, E., and Nathenson, M., eds. *Independent Learning in Higher Education* (Englewood Cliffs, NJ: Educational Technology Publications, 1984).

Kaswarm, Carol E., ed. "Educational Outreach to Select Adult Populations," *New Directions in Continuing Education,* No. 20 (San Francisco: Jossey Bass, December, 1983).

Olgren, Christine H., and Parker, Lorne A. *Teleconferencing Technology and Applications.* (Dedham, MA: Artech House Inc., 1983).

Solinger, Janet, "The Smithsonian Resident Associate Program: A Different Species of Continuing Education," *Continuum* 46(1), October 1981, p. 13.

Strange, John H. "Adapting to the Computer Revolution," in *Current Issues in Higher Education: New Technologies for Higher Education* (Washington, DC: American Association of Higher Education, 1981).

Watkins, Barbara L. "Independent Study: Meeting the Challenges of the Future," *Continuum* 48(1), January 1984, p. 35.

Zigerell, James. *Distance Education: An Information Age Approach to Adult Education* (Information Analysis Series, ERIC Clearinghouse on Adult, Career, and Vocational Education Publications, 1984).

## CHAPTER TEN

Draves, William A., ed. *The Marketing Manual for Noncredit Programs* (Manhattan, KS: Learning Resources Network, 1983).

Farlow, Helen. *Publicizing and Promoting Programs* (New York: McGraw-Hill, 1979).

Fisk, Margaret. *Encyclopedia of Associations* (Detroit: Gale Research Company, 1982).

Kotler, Philip, and Fox, Karen, F. A. *Strategic Marketing for Educational Institutions* (Englewood Cliffs, NJ: Prentice-Hall, 1985).

Leffel, Linda G. *Designing Brochures for Results* (Manhattan, KS: Learning Resources Network, 1983).

Lenz, Elinor. *Creating and Marketing Programs in Continuing Education* (New York: McGraw Hill, 1980).

Lovelock, Christopher H., and Weinberg, Charles B. *Marketing For Public and Non-Profit Managers* (New York: John Wiley, 1984).

Standard Rate and Data Service, Inc. *Business Publication Rates and Data.* Skokie, IL, Annual).

Standard Rate and Data Service, Inc. *Direct Mail List Rates and Data.* (Skokie, IL, Annual).

Stone, Bob. *Successful Direct Marketing Methods* (Chicago: IL: Crain Books, 1975).

Vicere, Albert A. "Marketing Communications for Continuing Education: A Planning Model," *Continuum* 46, January 1982.

## MAILING LIST SOURCES

Direct Mail List Rates and Data Book Standard
Rate and Data Service, Inc.
5201 Old Orchard Road
Skokie, Illinois 60076

Encyclopedia of Associations
Gale Research Company
Book Tower
Detroit, Michigan 48226

## CHAPTER ELEVEN

Bakken, David, and Bernstein, Allen L. "A Systematic Approach to Evaluation," *Training and Development Journal,* August 1982.

Baugher, Dan, ed. *Measuring Effectiveness* (San Francisco: Jossey-Bass, 1981).

Boyd, Robert H., and Rice, Daniel. "An Overview of Research Activity in Adult and Continuing Education," *Continuum* 50(1), Winter 1986.

Guba, Egon G., and Lincoln, Yvonna S. *Effective Evaluation* (San Francisco: Jossey-Bass, 1981).

Knox, Alan. *Developing, Administering and Evaluating Adult Education* (San Francisco: Jossey-Bass, 1980).

Long, Huey B., Hiemstra, Roger and Associates. *Changing Approaches To Studying Continuing Education* (San Francisco: Jossey-Bass, 1980).

Morris, Lynn Lyons, and Fitz-Gibbon, Carol Taylor. *How to Measure Program Implementation* (Beverly Hills: Sage, 1978).

Pattan, John E. "Return on Investment: Transferring the Results of Management Training to On-the-Job Performance," *Personnel,* July–August 1983, pp. 33–47.

Rossi, Peter H., and Freeman. *Evaluation: A Systematic Approach* (Beverly Hills: Sage, 1982).

Tedrick, William E. *Workbook for Planning and Conducting an In-depth Educational Program Evaluation,* D737 (College Station, TX: Texas Agricultural Extension Service).

Thompson, Mark S. *Benefit-Cost Analysis for Program Evaluation* (Beverly Hills: Sage, 1982).

Weiss, Carol H. *Evaluating Action Programs* (Boston: Allyn and Bacon, 1975).

## CHAPTER TWELVE

Green, Joseph S. et al., eds. *Continuing Education for the Health Professions* (San Francisco: Jossey-Bass, 1984).

Linnell, R. H. *Dollars and Scholars* (Los Angeles: University of Southern California Press, 1982).

Lowenthal, W. "Continuing Education for Professionals: Voluntary or Mandatory?," *Journal of Higher Education* 52, 1982, pp. 519–538.

Rockhill, K. "Mandatory Continuing Education for Professionals: Trends and Issues," *Adult Education* 33, 1983, pp. 107–115.

Winter, D. G.; McClelland, D. C.; and Stewart, A. J. *A New Case for the Liberal Arts* (San Francisco: Jossey-Bass, 1982).

## CHAPTER THIRTEEN

Ackell, Edmund F. "Adapting the University to Adult Students: A Developmental Perspective," *Continuum* 46(2), January 1982, pp. 30–45.

Carnegie Council on Policy Studies in Higher Education. *Three Thousand Futures: The Next Twenty Years in Higher Education* (San Francisco: Jossey-Bass, 1980).

Comfort, Robert W., "Integration: The Fusing of Tradition With Uniqueness," *Continuum,* 46(1), October, 1981.

Cross, Patricia K., "The Changing Role of Higher Education in the Learning Society," *Continuum,* 49(2), Spring 1985.

Downes, Frank A., and Ford, Roger. "The Journey Toward a Learning Society," *Continuum,* 46(3), April 1982.

Frandson, Phillip E., ed. *Power and Conflict in Continuing Education* (Belmont, CA: Wadsworth, 1980).

Gros-Louis, Kenneth R. R. "Making a Beginning: Adult Learners and the 21st. Century University," *Continuum*, 49(2), Spring, 1985.

Harrington, Fred Harvey. *The Future of Adult Education* (San Francisco: Jossey Bass, 1977).

Keller, George. *Academic Strategy* (Baltimore: Johns Hopkins University Press, 1983).

Koepplin, Leslie W., and Wilson, David A., eds. *The Future of State Universities: Issues in Teaching, Research, and Public Service* (New Brunswick, NJ Rutgers University Press, 1985).

Naisbitt, John. *Megatrends: Ten New Directions Transforming Our Lives* (New York: Warner Books, 1982).

Toffler, Alan. *The Third Wave* (New York: William Morrow, 1980).

*Previews and Premises* (New York: William Morrow, 1983).

Yankelovich, Daniel. *New Rules* (New York: Random House, 1981).

# INDEX